The Educated Brain

D0913770

The emerging field of neuroeducation, concerned with the interaction between mind, brain, and education, has proved revolutionary in educational research, introducing concepts, methods, and technologies into many advanced institutions around the world. *The Educated Brain* presents a broad overview of the major topics in this new discipline: part I examines the historical and epistemological issues related to the mind/brain problem and the scope of neuroeducation; part II provides a view of basic brain research in education and use of imaging techniques, and the study of brain and cognitive development; and part III is dedicated to the neural foundations of language and reading in different cultures, and the acquisition of basic mathematical concepts. With contributions from leading researchers in the field, this book features the most recent and advanced research in cognitive neurosciences.

ANTONIO M. BATTRO is a member of the National Academy of Education, Argentina, and the Pontifical Academy of Sciences.

KURT W. FISCHER is Charles Warland Bigelow Professor of Education & Human Development, and Director of the Mind, Brain, & Education Program at the Harvard Graduate School of Education.

PIERRE J. LÉNA is Emeritus Professor of Astrophysics at the Université Paris VII, member and delegate for education of the French Académie des Sciences, and a member of the Pontifical Academy of Sciences.

The Educated Brain

Essays in Neuroeducation

Antonio M. Battro,

Kurt W. Fischer,

&

Pierre J. Léna

Editors

CAMBRIDGE
UNIVERSITY PRESS

CAMBRIDGE UNIVERSITY PRESS

Cambridge, New York, Melbourne, Madrid, Cape Town, Singapore,
São Paulo, Delhi, Dubai, Tokyo, Mexico City

Cambridge University Press
The Edinburgh Building, Cambridge CB2 8RU, UK

Published in the United States of America by Cambridge University Press, New York

www.cambridge.org
Information on this title: www.cambridge.org/9780521181891

© Pontifical Academy of Sciences and Cambridge University Press 2008

This publication is in copyright. Subject to statutory exception
and to the provisions of relevant collective licensing agreements,
no reproduction of any part may take place without the written
permission of Cambridge University Press.

First published 2008
First paperback edition published 2011

Printed in the United Kingdom at the University Press, Cambridge

A catalogue record for this publication is available from the British Library

ISBN 978-0-521-87673-5 Hardback
ISBN 978-0-521-18189-1 Paperback

Cambridge University Press has no responsibility for the persistence or
accuracy of URLs for external or third-party internet websites referred to in
this publication, and does not guarantee that any content on such websites is,
or will remain, accurate or appropriate.

This volume is dedicated to the beloved memory of His Holiness, Pope John Paul II.

The opinions expressed with absolute freedom during the presentations of the papers of the meeting on *Mind, Brain and Education* at the Pontifical Academy of Science represent only the points of view of the participants and not those of the Academy.

Contents

Figures

Tables

Contributors

ANTONIO M. BATTRO, Pontifical Academy of Sciences and National Academy of Education, Buenos Aires.

JOHN T. BRUER, The James McDonnell Foundation, St. Louis

DANIEL P. CARDINALI, Department of Physiology, School of Medicine, University of Buenos Aires.

STANISLAS DEHAENE, Collège de France, Paris.

KURT W. FISCHER, Graduate School of Education, Harvard University.

USHA GOSWAMI, Faculty of Education, University of Cambridge.

HIDEAKI KOIZUMI, Advanced Research Laboratory, Hitachi Ltd, Japan.

PIERRE J. LÉNA, Pontifical Academy of Sciences, Observatoire de Paris, University of Paris VII.

RITA LEVI-MONTALCINI, Pontifical Academy of Sciences, Institute of Neurobiology, Rome.

JÜRGEN MITTELSTRASS, Pontifical Academy of Sciences, Center of Philosophy and Science Theory, University of Konstanz.

LAURA-ANN PETITTO, Department of Psychology, University of Toronto, Scarborough.

MICHAEL I. POSNER, Department of Psychology, University of Oregon.

MARY K. ROTHBART, Department of Psychology, University of Oregon.

M. ROSARIO RUEDA, Department of Psychology, University of Oregon.

WOLF SINGER, Pontifical Academy of Sciences, Max Planck Institute for Brain Research, Frankfurt.

HENDERIEN STEENBEEK, Faculty of Behavioral and Social Sciences, Department of Psychology, University of Groningen.

PAUL VAN GEERT, Faculty of Behavioral and Social Sciences, Department of Psychology, University of Groningen.

FERNANDO VIDAL, Max Plank Institute for the History of Science, Berlin.

MARYANNE WOLF, Center for Reading and Language Research, Tufts University.

Preface

In his address of November 10, 2003 to the members of the Pontifical Academy of Sciences gathered in Rome to celebrate the 400th Anniversary of the Foundation of the Accademia dei Lincei, origin of the Academy, and in reference to our meeting on *Mind, Brain, and Education*, which is the source of this book, His Holiness Pope John Paul II, said:

Scientists themselves perceive in the study of the human mind the mystery of a spiritual dimension which transcends cerebral physiology and appears to direct all our activities as free and autonomous beings, capable of responsibility and love, and marked with dignity. This is seen by the fact that you have decided to expand your research to include aspects of learning and education, which are specifically human activities.

We will always remember the support of His Holiness for the challenging work of the neurocognitive scientists engaged in the field of education, a most humane and humanitarian endeavor.

The editors of this book are pleased and honored to present the work of the distinguished scientists who were invited to discuss their research at the workshop on *Mind, Brain, and Education* held at the Vatican (November 7–8, 2003). This volume has been edited from the papers presented by the authors and organized in a book that will be of interest not only to experts but also to a larger audience of educators and teachers. We are thankful for the effort the authors have made to fulfil this extended purpose well beyond the strict proceedings of a scientific meeting. Indeed it was a great honor to all of us to have shared this important anniversary meeting of the Pontifical Academy of Sciences with a second advanced workshop dedicated to *Stem Cell Technology and other Innovative Therapies*. This is a good match for our *Mind, Brain, and Education* topic, which represents also a new scientific frontier for the new century.

This workshop was attended by the presidents of the academies of sciences of many nations, special guests from all around the world, and a full audience of Pontifical Academy members, who participated in the lively discussions at the Casina Pio IV, a Renaissance jewel in the beautiful Vatican gardens. We thank all of them and in particular we are grateful to Professor Nicola Cabibbo, president of the Pontifical Academy of Sciences, to the Chancellor of the Academy, Monsignor Marcelo Sánchez Sorondo, and to the Honorary President of our meeting, Professor Rita Levi-Montalcini, for their generous and continuous support towards our work.

The opinions expressed with absolute freedom in our meeting represent only the points of views of the participants. The Academy endorsed the following final statement:

The rapid development of neurosciences, the advances in psychology and education research, and interdisciplinary cooperation between these fields of investigation lead to a better understanding of learning, cognition, emotions, consciousness. Education of children, and in some respects of adults, often practiced with traditional methods, should not ignore this progress, even though it is in an early stage. Education is an art which needs to integrate scientific knowledge on brain and mind as well as other social, political and ethical aspects, in order to deal with its highly complex goal: namely, raising the child to full adult stature as a conscientious and educated person. Considering the deep societal changes throughout a globalized world and the impact of information technologies on human life, appropriate changes in education can enrich the lives of millions. The workshop on *Mind, Brain, and Education* addressed many facets of the immense challenges for education related to brain development, neural plasticity, developmental psychology, learning language and reading, dynamic modelling of learning and of development. The discussions in the Workshop converged on the following conclusions:

1. The promises of neuro- and cognitive sciences for a better understanding of the underlying basis of learning are developing rapidly. Cross-disciplinary research should involve educators and deal with real educational practices.
2. Given the complexity of the matter, care should be exercised to avoid hasty conclusions on education, driven by superficial implications of recent findings, such as uncritical statements about "Brain-based schools."
3. There are nevertheless areas where knowledge appears sufficiently solid to support conclusions impacting learning (e.g. sleep needs, arithmetic, reading abilities and bilingualism) and should be seriously considered. Relationships between brain, mind, consciousness and the self must be explored respectfully on an ethical basis in order to preserve human dignity and to promote equity. This can offer a rich opportunity to broaden the representation that men and women have today of themselves, of their states of individual development and of their achievement potential.

We are grateful also for the great help of many colleagues and friends in the editing of this book: To the vision and generosity of Sarah Caro, responsible for the several books published by Cambridge University Press dedicated to the new field of mind, brain, and education, including

The Educated Brain. To her successor in this difficult job Andrew Peart and his staff. To our collaborators Mary Kiesling in Cambridge, Massachusetts, and Percival J. Denham in Buenos Aires, Argentina who made easier the heavy traffic of emails and documents between America and Europe and provided much needed editing and computer skills to produce a satisfactory final version of this book. To the *Mind, Brain, and Education* initiative at the Harvard Graduate School of Education, to our Harvard students in the course *The Educated Brain* (Battro & Fischer, 2002–2003), who gave the title to this book and helped us to prepare the workshop at the Pontifical Academy of Sciences. Funds to support preparation of this book were provided by the Pontifical Academy of Sciences and the Harvard Graduate School of Education.

Finally we thank also IMBES, *The International, Mind, Brain, and Education Society*, launched at the Vatican meeting, the *Ettore Majorana Centre for Scientific Culture* at Erice (Sicily) and its president Antonino Zichichi, where we had the pleasure to invite several of the authors of this book to give a course also called *The Educated Brain* (July, 2005). The promising young scholars who attended the conference at Erice point the way to the exciting future that is growing from connecting biology and cognitive science with education to further knowledge and improve educational practice.

A. M. Battro, K. W. Fischer, and P. J. Léna

Foreword: Towards a new pedagogical and didactic approach

Rita Levi-Montalcini

The remarkable scientific developments of these last centuries, and particularly those from the Renaissance until our day, did not always contribute to a substantial change in the educational system, which constantly needs to be updated. In past centuries the total lack of knowledge about the cerebral structures and functions underlying cognitive capacities in the post-natal period has influenced in a negative way the adoption of more pertinent educational practices. In the twentieth century two events of fundamental importance have occurred: the understanding, however incomplete, of the activity of the cerebral organ and most recently the formidable development of computer systems that have imposed a total transformation of individual life in contemporary society.

At the beginning of the third millennium the changes in life styles at a global level require a revision of pedagogical and didactic systems. This radical revision is imperative in education from infancy through puberty and adolescence in order for students to be adequately included in computer science. The individual of tomorrow is the result of the formative attitude of today's child.

Current educational systems are still greatly influenced by the Victorian attitude based upon the principle that the child can be an object of reward or punishment, as is the case with a puppy. In what way does the brain of a child differ from that of a puppy? In both cases the brain has developed the paleo-cortical component known as the limbic system in ways that are not substantially different; this system underlies the emotional, affective, and aggressive functions of behavioral processes that have remained invariant for millions of years, from the appearance of mammals to *Homo sapiens*.

Human children differ from those of other mammals in the slowness of their brain development. This is why they become more dependent on parents or educators during the long maturational period extending from birth to puberty and beyond. Even if the slow maturation of brain faculties favors the development of such a stupendous and complex device as the brain of *Homo sapiens*, the protracted dependency on parents, or on those who act as parents, leaves a permanent mark on the nervous structures that guide the individual's behavior when growing out of childhood to become part of human society.

It is important to give a child, in the first years, information that can so heavily influence his or her relations towards the world. It is in this stage that adults exercise a fundamental influence upon the young child through the religious/political belief system of the tribe or social group to which he or she belongs. Hate for the "different" instilled at a tender age, whatever the definition of this term might be, produces the tragic consequences of genocides and wars, which today still bloody the whole globe. Education imposed by these beliefs in the first years of life strongly influences the character and behavior of the adult of tomorrow. Totally different is the cognitive development of the child that has its origin in the neocortical component of the brain. The neocortex, in contrast with the paleo-cortex or limbic system, reaches a remarkable elaboration with the folding of the cortical lamina, which in turn makes possible an increase and reorganization of neural networks.

During childhood in primary school, children learn the first rules of social relations, and in a few months they travel the paths traveled for tens of thousand of years by their ancestors, from the time these remote predecessors discovered those formidable symbolic communication tools that make up spoken and written language. With this discovery, the possibility of exchanging messages between individuals, between the individual and the masses, between those who belong to generations past and those living today, between those today and the generations to come, has multiplied a hundredfold in our species.

It has recently been discovered that cognitive capacities are already at work in the child's brain and that they are far greater than recognized in the past. What is the basis of this statement? For one thing, those who belong to the new generation show a totally unexpected and natural tendency towards the use of information systems such as computers from the early years, using a formal-logical approach.

The evolution of information technologies has revealed the enormous and unbelievable capacity of the child and the pre-adolescent not only to receive information, which was considered in the past to be the privilege of the mature brain, but also to use it immediately and thus even to surpass adults, surprisingly. The skill and enthusiasm shown by children when using the computer is amazing. The average age of the first contact with these technologies is tending to decrease continuously.

Today the necessary task in educational and didactic systems is not to indoctrinate the child and the pre-adolescent by transmission of knowledge through traditional textbooks but to make them aware of their own capabilities and to help them use these capabilities to progress from the passive condition of "loading" information into memory to the active condition of learning by direct experience. This last property of active learning comes from the neocortical circuits which develop luxuriantly from birth and are stimulated by messages from the external environment.

Seymour Papert, a renowned supporter of novel pedagogic-didactic theory, affirms that the child needs to be recognized in his or her role as "active producer" and not as "passive consumer" of learning (Papert, 1992). How is it possible to reach a revolution that implies such a total revision of the pedagogic-didactic systems?

I argue that the use of the computer in the first stages of the individual's development stimulates the creative capacity of the young user. The learning of mathematics, generally considered as a distasteful discipline in the first years of schooling, becomes a tool of active thinking via the computer. Mathematics as taught by traditional methods is in my judgment not only difficult to learn but completely useless because of the lack of direct application to the events young people are observing.

Participating with the child in the creation of computer programs, such as videogames or computer control programs, and not vice versa, Papert has created a program called LOGO that allows the child using the computer to develop creative activities in music, the arts, games, and other areas (Papert, 1980). It has been shown that with this kind of practice children learn better and faster in comparison with traditional school methods.

A typical example of learning precocity is confirmed by the results obtained at the *Diana* elementary school in Reggio Emilia in Italy, which is not only widely recognized in Europe but is described as a model program by Harvard University's Project Zero in the essay *Making learning visible*, which describes the methodology and techniques involved and the resulting autonomous learning by the children, in conjunction with care from the teachers (Project Zero, 2001). It is the teacher's duty to support the child and to help him/her to develop as an individual. She guides him/her, and at the same time they learn new things together.

Thanks to the computer and this kind of new pedagogy it is possible to have this experience, as expressed by various authors. While learning acquired from the reading of textbooks decays with time as the knowledge is forgotten and only retrieved from time to time, the knowledge acquired from the use of computers and active learning can be remembered better.

The new didactic system should not be based on a triangle – teacher-textbook-student – but instead should be built on the professional ability to generate creative learning based on an educational project developed in an open environment, as is proposed by Paolo Manzelli, president of CreaNET (see *Laboratory for Educational Research, Florence University*).

We need to think about a new school, a different school. We need not only replace current study programs but also change teaching methods. This change is already at work in the United States and is producing relevant results. The "interactivity" of a new educational and didactic system connecting school, research centers, and society is the keystone to reaching community objectives corresponding to European social demands.

This cultural revolution will evoke reactions of support and opposition. It is interesting to observe, as has the mathematician and teacher Papert, that the use of information technologies in arenas such as education has been accepted and applied more easily in the so-called developing countries than in many of those of a more advanced level, which have been characterized by conservative trends (Papert, 1996). Moreover, the developing process of new technologies is irreversible, and change is urgent: The goal is to see members of the new generation become actors and not spectators in the world arena of life.

References

Papert, S. (1979). *Mindstorms: Children, Computers and Powerful Ideas.* New York: Basic Books.

(1992). *The Children's Machine: Rethinking School in the Age of the Computer.* New York: Basic Books.

(1996). *The Connected Family: Bridging the Digital Generation Gap.* New York: Basic Books. www.ConnectedFamily.com/

Project Zero and Reggio Children (2001). *Making Learning Visible: Children as Individual and Group Learners.* Contributors: Claudia Giudici; Carla Rinaldi; Mara Krechevsky; Paola Barchi; Howard Gardner; Tiziana Filippini; Paola Strozzi; Laura Rubizzi; Amelia Gambetti; Paola Cagliari; Vea Vecchi; Giovanni Piazza; Angela Barozzi; Ben Mardell; Steve Seidel. Cambridge, MA: Reggio Emilia, Italy: Reggio Children, International Center for the Defense and Promotion of the Rights and Potential of all Children www.pz.harvard.edu/Research/MLV.htm

creaNet *Laboratory for Educational Research. Florence University EGO-CreaNet Association, Telematic Network.* www.thinkquest.it/egocreanet/stating.html

Part I

The mind, brain, and education triad

1 Introduction: Mind, brain, and education in theory and practice

Antonio M. Battro, Kurt W. Fischer, and Pierre J. Léna

> *As the entomologist chasing butterflies of bright colors, my attention was seeking in the garden of gray matter, those cells of delicate and elegant forms, the mysterious butterflies of the soul, whose fluttering wings would someday – who knows? – enlighten the secret of mental life.*
>
> Santiago Ramón y Cajal (*Recuerdos de mi vida*, 1981)

Many scientists and educators feel that we are advancing toward new ways of connecting mind, brain, and education (MBE). This feeling arises, in part, because the disciplines related to the cognitive sciences, neurobiology, and education have made considerable advances during the last two decades, and scholars in the disciplines are beginning to seek interactions with each other (Fischer, Bernstein, & Immordino-Yang, 2006). Moreover, the increased connectivity among these disciplines has been enhanced by the growth of communication and information in the globalized world. The "digital environment" of our planet is a new phenomenon in evolution and in history (Battro, 2004), as Rita Levi-Montalcini describes in the preface to this book. We are lucky to live in a time when changes in education can rapidly reach and enrich the lives of millions. This opportunity invites us to foster the coordinated work of scientists, teachers, and students of many nations, races, and religions in the new transdisciplinary field of mind, brain, and education (Léna, 2002, and Koizumi, this volume).

One name for this effort is neuroeducation (Bruer, this volume), which emphasizes the educational focus of the transdisciplinary connection. Another is educational neuroscience, where the focus is on neuroscience, to which education connects. We use the name "mind, brain, and education" to encompass both of these focuses and others that bring together cognitive science, biology, and education. On one side, this emerging field touches on all levels of modern neuroscience: from molecules to genes, from synapses to artificial neural networks, from reflexes to behaviors, from animal studies to human brain imaging (Dawson & Fischer, 1994). On the other side, the term "education" is as vast as human culture itself. Because of the process of globalization, which intermingles

3

so many different cultures, languages, and beliefs, the field of mind, brain, and education is becoming increasingly complex and necessarily diverse.

There is no doubt that education is much more than its neural aspects, but the brain and biological sciences can illuminate many of its processes and methods. New brain imaging and DNA-analysis techniques make increasingly visible hidden brain and genetic processes. In a few cases, scientists and educators seem to be on the verge of being able to observe the effects of educational interventions on brain processing and genetic expression. These important advances have stimulated great excitement and increasing expectations from society, which is enamored of biology because it has made so many impressive advances in recent decades. These great expectations, although sometimes unrealistic, reflect a genuine need for advances to improve education and deal with the complex new world of the twenty-first century, with its explosion of information and population and the shrinkage of the world through communication and globalization.

The need for major advances in education is urgent. In an earlier workshop entitled *The Challenges for Science – Education for the Twenty-First Century*, held at the Pontifical Academy of Sciences in Rome in November 2001, the issue of science in basic education was addressed: How can the world deal with the increasing gap, in almost every country, between the level of scientific knowledge and technology on the one hand and the scientific literacy of the population on the other, no matter what the stage of economic development? The remarkable success of the scientific and technological revolution in the twentieth century has created a major new problem for education. This earlier workshop and the questions it raised set the stage for the workshop on *Mind, Brain, and Education* in November 2003 that led to this book.

The issue of science education and the gap in knowledge is fundamentally important for justice and democracy and requires a revolution in educational practice. There is no magic recipe for success in such a venture, and a number of on-going, successful experiments are on their way in various countries, from the United States to Brazil, from Chile and Argentina to France, often introduced by the academies of sciences. All these programs try to restore the questioning role of the child, to open ways to his or her curiosity through active attitudes, language dialogue, and direct contact with nature through observation and experiments. These experiments have much to learn from a better knowledge of brain development, the role of stimulus and motivation, and the relation of learning and memory. Of special interest is early childhood, from ages two to six, where recent work in cognitive psychology shows the learning child acting as a "scientist" exploring and experimenting with the world at this early age (see Léna, 2002).

Progress in mind, brain, and education requires a genuine collaboration between researchers and practitioners, with both groups working together to contribute to investigation and knowledge. Research evidence can illuminate educational practice, and educational observations can provide important questions and insights for research. Our first book with Cambridge University Press, *Mind, Brain, and Education in Reading Disorders*, focuses on the connection of research with practice in children with learning problems. The current, second book emphasizes primarily the best scientific research that is relevant to connecting biology and cognitive science with education. We are preparing a third book, *Usable Knowledge in Mind, Brain, and Education*, which aims to promote an effective dialogue between scientists and educators that will create knowledge that can directly illuminate educational practice. That is the long-term challenge of this new field.

What we envision happening is not an all-encompassing new paradigm or a patchwork of unrelated research. Instead, we see the dynamic unfolding of many different scientific trends toward the formation of new networks of knowledge. One component will not swallow the other. Instead, we will expect a healthy growing organism of knowledge that will thrive with all kind of links and functions between the subcomponents in the system and outside the system. It will be the result of the efforts of many coordinated teams with clear aims and objectives, a realistic schedule, a great sense of adventure and a commitment to moral responsibility. This book is an attempt to express this growing international and transdisciplinary trend.

Plan of the book

The book is comprised of three sections. The first provides a historical, epistemological, and methodological framework for the new transdisciplinary field of mind, brain, and education. The second focuses on research that connects neuroscience research to learning and education, including dynamic, biologically based approaches to brain and cognitive development and especially the impact of brain imaging techniques on research and practice. The third section reviews research on brain processing of language and mathematics, areas where scientific advances have been substantial, with the promise of connections to educational practice in the not too distant future.

We are honored by a preface written by Rita Levi-Montalcini, honorary president of our conference on *Mind, Brain, and Education* at the

Pontifical Academy of Sciences, Nobel Prize winner for her discovery of the Nerve Growth Factor and a leading personality in the neurosciences of our time. She stresses the slow maturation of the human brain as well as the luxuriant development of the human neocortex, which relate to the protracted dependency of children on parents and teachers. This slow, lengthy period of development and learning leaves a permanent mark on the developing nervous structures of the child. Moreover, researchers have discovered that the cognitive capacities already functioning in infants' brains are greater than we thought in the past. From these findings, the importance of early education becomes ever more evident. In recent history information technologies became available to young children, and they started to use these technologies actively and productively, adapting to them easily. The amazing cognitive capacities of human beings and the relentless proliferation of new information together require a revolution in education. We certainly need, as Levi-Montalcini says, new generations "dressed as actors and not as spectators in the world arena of life."

Part I The mind, brain, and education triad

In this section the authors analyze important issues, assets, and obstacles in forming convergent paths toward the transdisciplinary field of mind, brain, and education. These involve historical frameworks for understanding human nature, epistemological analyses of knowledge of human brain and behavior, and methodological approaches to framing research and practice on development of mind, brain, and behavior.

In the chapter "Historical considerations on brain and self," Fernando Vidal, a distinguished historian of psychology at the Max Planck Institute in Berlin, describes the historical transition from considering the brain the "seat of the soul" to viewing it as the "organ of the self," a concept for which he coins the term "brainhood." The modern history of this significant conceptual change started in the eighteenth century when the brain began to be understood as the only organ essential to the self. Indeed, the recent development of biology and medicine, in particular of the neurosciences, has reinforced the idea of a "cerebral subject," a brain-based person. Many classical puzzles related to this conception (thought-experiments or philosophical brain-fictions like brain transplants, extra-bodily conservation, etc.) are still used in current debates about human identity, and the conception has pervasive practical and ethical implications, such as the notion of "brain-death" in medical practice. Vidal coined the new term "brainhood" to name the condition of being a brain – the "human being *as* brain" – which gives a wide anthropological and social picture and will certainly influence education in the future, in ways we cannot predict today. This idea of brainhood also inspires the work of some artists, as in the remarkable picture in this chapter of a "self-portrait" by Helen Chadwick – two caring hands holding a brain. Most important, the ethical impact of this conception in education is fundamental, requiring careful consideration of possible controversial observations, experiments, and even "non-invasive" interventions and assessments on students' brains. Groups such as the recent Committee on Neuroethics of the Ministry of Education of Japan will help human society to illuminate the implications of this conception of humanity (see Koizumi).

John Bruer, a philosopher by training and president of the James S. McDonnell Foundation, has been a key person in shaping early research in cognitive neuroscience and education in the United States and abroad. In "Building bridges in neuroeducation," he sharply criticizes how results of cognitive neuroscience are often used in educational practice and policy. One of the typical misuses is related to a very popular claim among educators that the critical periods shown in the visual system are the best model to explain cognitive development and life-long learning – a claim that Bruer demonstrates is fundamentally wrong. Moreover, the common idea that we need an elevated brain metabolism and synaptic density in order to learn new concepts and skills is not consistent with controlled experiments. As Bruer says, "over-reliance on developmental neurobiology generates pseudo-implications for teaching and learning." We should follow instead a broader approach to learning, where previous experience in a specific domain is more important than a presumed biological "window of opportunity" or critical period.

Bruer's analysis is that neurobiology can connect to education through its illumination of cognitive science research on learning and teaching. He argues that neurobiological research cannot connect directly to a better understanding of education. He uses the example of mathematics, in which programs like *RightStart* showed impressive results in teaching mathematics, especially to children at risk (Griffin, Case, & Siegler, 1994), and those cognitive results and concepts in turn relate to the neuroscientific work of Stanislas Dehaene and colleagues (Dehaene, this volume) on the multiple cortical representation of number concepts (number words, Arabic numerals, and analogue magnitudes). Together, the neuroscientific research and the cognitive research illuminate the educational pathways toward mathematical skill, but separately, he argues, the neuroscientific research does not connect to education. Similar connections from neuroscience to cognitive science to education seem to be happening in research on acquisition of language and reading (Dehaene, Goswami,

Petitto, & Wolf, this volume). Bruer concludes that we need to refine our neuroeducation research strategy to connect neuroscience to cognitive science, and he asks for increasing "recursive interactions" between the fields involved in basic neurocognitive research and educational practice.

Self-consciousness and the brain are of central concern for contemporary philosophy, neuroscience, and education. Jürgen Mittelstrass, professor of philosophy and director of the Center of Philosophy and Theory of Science at the University of Konstanz, a recognized expert in the mind/brain problem, critically analyzes the different conceptual frameworks of monism and dualism. He proposes a constructivist mediation between "the overwhelmingly dualist research program of philosophy, and the overwhelmingly monistic research program of natural science (which includes scientifically oriented psychology)." He introduces the model of a "pragmatical dualism" in what he calls the "career of the mind-body problem." He defends independent psychological (cognitive) concepts on the grounds of their *explanatory value* and rejects the restricted view of neuro-reductionism. Perhaps this pragmatic model can help us to introduce to the practice of education the most advanced theoretical terms of modern neurocognitive science without making an ontological statement about what they refer to. We will always need the help of philosophical criticism in order to build a new field such as mind, brain, and education. Many blunders and simplifications can be avoided through strict and rigorous philosophical analysis and synthesis. However, many concepts being introduced in neuroscience, cognitive science, and education are new to the history of philosophy and will need careful examination.

New concepts and new technologies imply the use of new research methodologies. The joining of mind, brain, and education into a coherent field requires a profound transformation of many habits of thinking, of many traditional standards in order to enrich the scope of psychological and educational research in the era of biology. The brain itself is a very complex organ that cannot be studied with only conventional intellectual tools. First, traditional linear analysis (which has dominated behavioral and cognitive research) cannot alone capture the brain's complexity, where the whole is so much more than the sum of its parts. The number of connections in the brain is astronomical, the number of interactions between parts in different time scales is overwhelming. Of all the tools in the scientific toolkit, only dynamic systems theory has the potential to capture how these parts form this remarkable organ. Second, mind/brain, body, and world are each complex systems in permanent interaction.

In this volume Paul van Geert, professor of psychology at Groningen University, and his colleague Henderien Steenbeek provide an overview of the complexity and dynamic system approach to neuropsychological development and how it can begin to be applied to analyzing educational processes. They define four features of complex systems: (1) non-linearity and self-organization, (2) superposition, (3) substance vs. process, and (4) the multi-layered and multi-scaled nature of causality. The first describes the increase of order and structure during development, including the emergence of new organization. The second means that a phenomenon can be characterized by two (apparently) incompatible properties at the same time, such as genes and environment in learning. System dynamics routinely include contradictory or "incompatible" processes. The third refers to how different levels of analysis for a phenomenon relate to its apparent nature as a stable substance or a variable process. For example, an individual skill such as kicking a ball can be treated as substance to the degree that it is stable over long time periods, and simultaneously it involves process because it varies intrinsically over shorter time periods as a function of factors such as practice, fatigue, the nature of the ball, the context of the frame, etc. Fourth, the layers that go from the individual to the species in the human being are organized in different strata such as person, group, society, and culture. The layering also occurs in time scales such as microdevelopmental, ontogenetic (macrodevelopmental), historical, and evolutionary. They all interact in "mutual or reciprocal causality," as the authors say.

One practical implication of this conceptualization of complex systems is that measurements need to capture the intrinsic richness of a system as it changes over time. Inadequate measurements misrepresent the system and make it seem static. For instance, if we can identify a brain region for a certain mental activity, such as reading, we still cannot say that we know what reading is. In the author's words "knowledge of the brain adds another piece to the complexity puzzle and will thus contribute to solving the puzzle, [but] it does not replace the puzzle by the real picture."

Van Geert and Steenbeek provide a good example of the predictive power of these models in a research study of the way children of different leadership status interact. There are many other examples where complexity analysis can predict diverse phenomena, including sudden emergence of new concepts such as conservation of quantity (in the sense of Piaget), stable stages, fluctuating skills, inverted U curves of learning or development, regressions, etc. These methodological considerations are of great importance for education and should be stressed by the educators of the twenty-first century.

Part II Brain development, cognition, and education

One of the great challenges in science is to make links between fundamental or basic research and everyday life. The success of modern societies is related to this enterprise, and the success of education too. Such great changes have been introduced at all levels of learning and teaching by the computer and the communication technologies, and of course the changes include the brain (Battro, 2002). We expect the next frontier in education to come from technologies deriving from the cognitive and brain sciences.

Along with the societal changes created by technology come epistemological changes created by "opening" and making known the brain mechanisms involved in the process of knowing. Wolf Singer states this point from the viewpoint of a brain scientist: "Search for the sources of knowledge is equivalent with the search for processes that specify and modify the functional architecture of the brain." The scientific enterprises of explaining the neurobiology and genetics of learning and thinking are building radical conceptual change, something that only a few educators could imagine several decades ago. Scientists today are tracking the sources of knowledge with the multiple and powerful tools of neurobiology and analyzing the relations between genetics and epigenetics, between phylogeny and ontogeny, and among the different levels of learning and memory across the whole of the human life span.

This is basic research, performed by thousands of talented scientists around the world, and right now its relevance to the field of education is not yet clear. For instance, one of the most important handbooks in the new cognitive neurosciences (Gazzaniga, 2003) does not even mention the term "education" in its index, while the term "learning" has multiple entries. This omission probably does not indicate a lack of personal interest in education by the many prominent authors, but it tells us that there is a scientific gap to be filled, a new field to explore. The space for working to fill this gap is *beyond* the laboratory and its strict, traditional models of learning. The new "learning space" for the neuroscientist is the classroom! In the rich learning and teaching environment of the school the cognitive neurosciences can grow to ask deeper, more useful, more meaningful questions.

In the first chapter in this section, Wolf Singer, leader of the Max Planck Institute for Brain Research at Frankfurt, proposes two specific topics where scholars and practitioners can bridge the gap from basic neuroscience to educational practice: critical periods in vision, and sleep time in day-care centers for babies. (The latter is relevant also to the chapter on chronoeducation by Daniel Cardinali in this volume.) He discusses research with animals and babies which shows the complex sequences of sleep and wakefulness and their importance in developmental processes, memory consolidation, and learning improvement. Regarding critical periods Singer relies on his vast experience with animal models, in particular in the visual system, where he has analyzed the principle that "neurons wire together if they fire together." In this model of neuronal synchrony, circuits undergo a test of functionality, in which connections are either consolidated or removed for the rest of life. When the window of development closes, it seems that neurons stop producing new synapses and existing connections can no longer be removed. The extreme case is "sensory deprivation" of visual input: Babies who have suffered from infections of their eyes and have not developed proper visual circuitry at the cortical level in early development can remain functionally blind even if their retinas come to function normally later.

At the same time, there is often enough plasticity in the brain to undo apparent irreversibility, as Bruer discusses in his chapter and elsewhere (Neville & Bruer, 2001). Even adult brains can produce new neurons and connections in the hippocampus and the olfactory bulb, and perhaps in other areas of the cortex as well (Gage, 2003), a promising phenomenon mentioned by Singer. Of course these facts do not translate directly into educational programs, but relations to education are likely to be discovered as the number of scientists engaged in basic research with a focus in education increases. What we still need are teachers and neuroscientists engaging together to grapple with crucial features of education that have not yet been explored in laboratories. We hope the next generation will build a dynamic cycle of connection from neuroscience to education and from education to neuroscience, which will dramatically affect views and findings relating to education.

A topic for which such a positive cycle already exists is chronoeducation. Daniel Cardinali, director of the Department of Physiology of the Medical School of the University of Buenos Aires, is a world leader in this field and explains in his chapter how the biological clock influences the learning process and affects education. First he describes the circadian rhythms of about 24 hours in all the cells of the body, which respond to signals generated by a pacemaker, a biological clock that is written in the gene-protein-gene feedback loops. In mammals a major circadian oscillator is located in the suprachiasmatic nuclei (SCN) of the hypothalamus and acts as a timer. An entraining agent (Zeitgeber) can reset or phase-shift (advance or delay) the internal clock. For instance, light exposure during the first part of the night delays the phase, but in the second part it advances the phase. In the opposite direction, melatonin, the "endogenous code of the night" (a hormone produced by the pineal gland), produces a phase advance in the first part of the night and a delay in the second part. The most conspicuous circadian cycle is the sleep-wakefulness rhythm. It changes dramatically from childhood to adulthood from a period of 14–16 hours of sleep per day in babies to 8 hours in young adults.

Sleep, which is essential for life, is divided into two states – rapid eye movement sleep (REM) and non-REM sleep (NREM) – which alternate in cycles of 90–100 minutes. A person 75 years of age has spent 19 years in NREM and 6 years in REM sleep. The NREM state is protective of cells, promotes their synthesis, and produces a significant reduction in brain metabolism. The REM state, on the contrary, is antihomeostatic – cannot regulate temperature, for instance – but can activate the brain even more than during wakefulness, and vivid dreams are produced in this state.

From the educational point of view it is important to assimilate these and related findings in order to provide the best correspondence of the internal clock with the state of alertness, motivation, mood, disposition to learn, and capacity to learn. Our world has changed to a 24-hour society, and adolescents in high school often shift sleep times and go to bed very late, yet they must awake early for classes, when they are sleep deprived. This shift affects significantly their learning performance in many ways. Cardinali suggests that fitting with the adolescent circadian cycle, students should receive lessons toward evening when their cognitive functions are at their peak. Many other considerations of educational importance can be developed from the point of view of chronobiology.

The great challenge of the neurocognitive sciences is to deal with many different scales of space and time, starting from the molecular and moving toward behavior, including both cognition and emotion. Several levels of analysis need to be analyzed to build a real integration of the brain sciences and education. One great puzzle is how neural networks form and how they are reorganized with learning and cognitive development. It takes years to develop a skill such as reading or writing, but only microseconds to switch on and off a receptor. Neurons grow and develop synapses to build networks based essentially on inhibition and excitation. This growth and change in neural networks is one of the great puzzles to be solved in the coming years.

The growth of neural networks in the cortex and their connection to learning and education is the topic of the chapter by Kurt W. Fischer, founder and director of the Mind, Brain, and Education program at the Graduate School of Education of Harvard University. He leads the first academic training program that systematically and broadly connects biology, cognitive science, and education. With Antonio M. Battro, Juliana Paré-Blagoev, and other colleagues he launched *the International*

Mind, Brain and Education Society, IMBES, at the working session of the Pontifical Academy of Sciences and is the President of IMBES. Building the new kind of relation connecting mind, brain, and education requires researchers and practitioners who are knowledgeable about all three areas, and so can join research and educational practice in active collaboration.

An example of both the possibilities and the pitfalls is the discovery of striking correspondences between growth patterns of cognition and brain (Fischer & Rose, 1994). Children and adolescents demonstrate clear spurts in optimal cognitive performances at specific age intervals from birth to the mid 20s, and scaling properties show jumps or gaps in performance at the same points. In parallel and at similar ages, cortical activity moves through strong spurts and other discontinuities in various properties, including energy and connectivity in the electroencepha-logram (EEG), and even cortical anatomy shows parallel changes. This converging evidence has led to a developmental scale that is being used to assess students' learning, curriculum materials, and teachers' teaching, all on a common scale (Dawson & Stein, in press).

Unfortunately, the findings about brain growth spurts have at times led to bogus recommendations for educational practice based on over-simplifications and unsupported conceptual leaps. For example, arguments were made that students could not learn anything new when their brains were not showing a spurt – a leap that is not at all supported by the evidence about learning. The key to creating usable knowledge in mind, brain, and education is not simply to apply neuroscientific evidence but to proactively study the relations of brain to learning and behavior. People should not jump from brain findings to new models of education without research that directly examines the ways that children learn in school and in everyday life, including how their learning relates to their brain functions.

Another approach to neural networks is in the chapter by Michael I. Posner, professor at the University of Oregon, written in collaboration with Mary K. Rothbart and M. Rosario Rueda: We can now "glimpse inside the human brain as people think" by using imaging tools to view brain activity. Posner is one of the pioneers in the field of neuroimaging and cognition, and he and his colleagues make an important argument about the role of genes and experience in the development of attention networks in the brains of preschool children. These neural networks have a major node in the anterior cingulate gyrus and are important for the acquisition of new cognitive, affective and social skills during school life and beyond. Extensive research has identified three functions in this attention network: alerting, orienting, and executive control.

Of course, attention is fundamental to learning in school, since students must maintain attention during a task; but the ability to concentrate varies greatly among individuals and tasks. One question is how much of attention is inherited, which was addressed through a specific test of attention in a study of monozygotic and dizygotic twins. The data supported a role for genes in the executive attention network. In other experiments the alleles of two genes related to dopamine produced different activation within the anterior cingulate. Another question is how much people can enhance the functioning of attention networks in their brains. Teachers know well that the ability to concentrate for long periods of time, deal with conflict or ambiguity, and refrain from seeking immediate reward are valuable in the classroom (and in life). It takes years to develop these abilities, but Posner and colleagues have found encouraging results for specific attention training even in 4-year-old children, as evidenced in both cortical activity and school performance. Similar results were obtained for children with attention deficit disorder and autism. The authors hope that this technique of attention training will be useful for preschools, providing a kind of "brain support" for mastering the curriculum. This kind of reliable scientific evidence is crucial for building effective practices to improve neuroeducation.

Brain imaging techniques are key aids in this process, but from the educational viewpoint the best technologies are impractical, complex, and expensive for addressing most questions about learning in educational settings. They require advanced and sophisticated tools, and a whole team of experts, and contrived situations in which children typically must sit or lie very still. These limits of the imaging tools mean that most brain imaging sessions are done not in schools but in laboratory settings or hospitals. Research will more readily influence education when it can happen in a natural setting such as a classroom. New technologies are needed that can be used in schools and analyzed with the help of the teachers.

Hideaki Koizumi, chief scientist of Hitachi and director of the Brain Sciences and Education Program of the Ministry of Education, Culture, Sports, Science, and Technology (MEXT) in Japan, describes the impressive feats accomplished by a promising new technology. He and his team have invented Optical Topography (OT) (also called Near Infrared Spectroscopy, NIRS), which uses near-infrared light to assess changes in blood in the cortex during various activities. The OT apparatus is compact and portable, with the person wearing a relatively comfortable array of optical fibers on the scalp and sitting in a chair that allows greater mobility than the widely used techniques of functional magnetic resonance imaging (fMRI), magnetoencephalograpy (MEG), or EEG. This relative freedom of movement and position has great advantages for studying children as well as brain processes during talking or motor activity, and OT is also non-invasive, low cost, and low maintenance, and relatively simple to handle in comparison to the other tools. OT seems likely to be introduced into research in schools soon. Koizumi gives several examples of questions that OT can address about the brain while a student performs tasks like reading, calculating, thinking, and imaging. OT has already provided insights into the process of neurological rehabilitation in brain lesions and dementia, and Koizumi sees applications to learning and educational sciences, which is a focus of his chapter. He proposes also to discuss moral and ethical issues that may arise from the possible misuse of these brain-imaging technologies that might "deprive people of privacy because of its potential for revealing the personal mind." He advocates strongly the creation of neuroethic committees to address these questions, as has been done in Japan.

Part III Brain, language, and mathematics

Maryanne Wolf, director of the Center for Reading and Language Research at Tufts University and an expert in the field of dyslexia, states that "the essence of intellectual change in recent human evolution lies not in the birth of new structures in our brain, but rather in the brain's extraordinary potential for the rearrangement of its existing neuronal pathways." Reading is exemplary of this human capacity for mental rearrangement, and the more that is known about the brain processes of reading, the better educators and students can cope with reading breakdown such as dyslexia, a common "cultural pathology" of our times. Of course, dyslexia was not a problem before written text became prominent in human culture – a process that took several thousand years. Wolf analyzes the remarkable cognitive feat accomplished by the first scripts, the cuneiform and hieroglyphic systems, and the pedagogy involved with them. Remarkably, one of the advanced technologies in dyslexic intervention (Wolf's RAVE- O curriculum) recalls the multi-dimensional nature of words in old Sumerian. When the alphabet was first conceived, it started only with the vowel sounds, as in the Ugarit language. The Greeks, much later, added the consonants and thus could depict all the phonemes of their language in a remarkable way, rearranging the Phoenician script. But it was not so simple to read in these ancient times, because words were not separated by spaces or points and the direction in which words were written switched from one line to the next.

In modern alphabetic scripts reading is easier than in Sumerian, but the cognitive feat implied by reading is still considerable. First, the child must learn the rules for grapheme-phoneme correspondence. Any deficit in this phonological step can lead to a particular form of dyslexia that has come to be understood scientifically in recent years, with treatment methods that are successful for most dyslexic students. But there are other types of dyslexia that cannot be explained by this phonological cause alone. Reading also requires a fast automatic process that influences naming speed, which is independent of phonology. A deficit in this process requires different treatment methods. Wolf's Double Deficit Hypothesis allows the identification of three categories of dyslexia, those children with a phonological impairment, those with a lack of fast automatic processes, and those with both deficits. The third group has profound impairment of reading fluency and comprehension and requires extensive interventions to compensate.

In fact, the RAVE-O program (Retrieval, Automaticity, Vocabulary, Engagement with Language, and Orthography) developed by Wolf and colleagues is built around the importance of reading speed, which is a powerful predictor of reading failure among children with fluency problems. Reading fluency requires a strong interaction between orthographic, phonological, semantic, and syntactic components of language. The end goal of the program "is not about how rapidly children read, but about how well they understand and enjoy what they read." This intervention is a good example of how knowledge of the cognitive and brain mechanisms of reading can help to improve education for the important topic of literacy.

Usha Goswami, professor in the Faculty of Education of Cambridge University, is the leader of one of the few university initiatives in the world concerning mind, brain, and education. An expert in language acquisition she describes her original research comparing reading across languages. People use their mind/brains to process particular languages in so many diverse cultural and linguistic settings. Goswami describes how illiterate adults are not aware of phonemes in words, but children learn phonemes via letters while learning how to read. Phoneme awareness, a key component in reading in an alphabetic language, can be tracked as a language universal. First, before being taught to read, children become sensitive to syllables and what are called "onset" and "rime" in words. For instance in the words "seat," "sweet," and "street" the onset corresponds to the initial consonant sound of the syllable (s, sw and str), the rime to the next vowel and following sounds (s-*eat*, sw-*eet*, str-*eet*). But onset and rime are relatively large features of sound, while the letters are smaller units that represent abstract units in the speech stream called phonemes. In Goswami's view awareness of these small sound units or phonemes is a consequence of learning to read and write. This is why pre-readers show poor performance in phoneme awareness in all the languages that were studied, while in contrast they easily identify syllables.

One major finding is that the rate of learning and skill level in phoneme awareness depends on the orthography of the language being learned. Children need to map phonology to orthography in reading and writing, but languages differ widely in the kind of mapping they support. It is easier for children to read in languages with consistent orthographies such as Spanish, where one letter consistently maps to a unique phoneme, and onset-rime segmentation corresponds directly with phonemic segmentation. Languages with complex, inconsistent orthograpy, such as English, slow down and interfere with learning phoneme awareness. This difference seems to explain the finding of fewer dyslexic children in Spanish-speaking schools than in English-speaking schools.

Goswami argues that the difficulties that dyslexics have in representing the sound patterns of words in their own language are explained by a deficit in rhythmic timing. Goswami has compared the detection of beats that determine speech rhythms by dyslexic children and comparable children without dyslexia, examining both their language skills and the evoked electrical potentials from their cortex. The results suggest that "the auditory system of dyslexic children are immature rather than deviant."

Laura-Ann Petitto, professor at the Department of Psychology, University of Toronto, is a pioneering scientist in the new field of educational neuroscience, which involves neuroscience research that relates to educational issues. She presents her findings in young children regarding the use of the new technique called either near-infrared spectroscopy (NIRS) or optical topography (OT), which is described by Koizumi in this volume. She shows how infants – well before they can speak – activate neural linguistic tissue when perceiving linguistic stimuli, suggesting that infants use brain structures specific to language from an early age, well before they can produce or understand language sounds. Understanding the role of these cortical areas in the acquisition of language may improve the understanding of language development as well as the early prediction of language disabilities such as dyslexia. The integration of brain imaging tools such as NIRS with behavioral and cognitive studies represents an incredible opportunity for educators to gain new insights into learning successes and problems for important skills such as language.

We have been asked many times, "Why should brain research be relevant to education?" In closing this volume, Stanislas Dehaene, a leader of the renowned Cognitive Neuroimaging group at Orsay, France, gives a detailed and compelling answer to this question. He formulates a biologically based understanding of language and arithmetic that brings new insights to the interpretation of the cultural tools of literacy and mathematics and their use in education. Mathematician by training as well as experimental psychologist and expert in the field of neuroimaging,

Dehaene discusses findings on the acquisition of arithmetic and reading to define education as a neuronal recycling process. He proposes an alternative to the popular view that the brain is a universal learning machine and the mind a blank slate to be filled by learning cultural objects such as numbers and words. Recasting the argument that written words and numbers are recent cultural constructs not to be found in nature, he argues that these cultural objects connect to the evolutionary and developmental history of the human brain to help explain why people can learn to read and do mathematics.

People have constructed the cultural systems for reading and mathematics based upon the specific capacities of the human brain. Research demonstrates that there are small areas of the cortex in primates and humans that are pre-tuned to detect numerosity as well as other features related to the shape of written symbols. Also, many species show a sense of numerosity, and even human babies demonstrate a proto-concept of quantity, which involves fundamental processing in the parietal lobe (left and right intra-parietal sulci). In humans this functional location is stable and can be disrupted by brain lesions in this area, which produce acalculia (inability to do arithmetic). Also particular groups of neurons in monkeys are tuned to a preferred numerosity of one to five visual objects (linked to the numbers 1 to 5) and these are located in the analogous part of the parietal lobe.

For letters and words, reading activates a very stable area of the left ventral visual region (occipito-temporal sulcus). This pattern occurs for readers of all the languages that have been studied, whether they are using alphabetic reading systems or not. A lesion in this area produces alexia (inability to read). Moreover, in monkeys minimal shape features that resemble alphabetic letters activate specific occipito-temporal neurons. From this converging evidence Dehaene concludes that "new cultural acquisitions are possible only inasmuch as they are able to fit within the pre-existing constraints of our brain architecture (which) delimits a space of learnable objects."

In a similar way, the joining of biology and cognitive science with education will transform people's understanding of ourselves, our tools, and our cultures. These new understandings will not only provide deeper and more accurate knowledge about mind, brain, and education but also lead to better tools for learning and teaching. The intensive work of the scientists and educators in this book presage the broad work of a large network of scientists and educators around the world, testimony to a new era in the search for knowledge based in the new field connecting biology, cognitive science, and education. We predict that this emerging field will contribute profound changes in the way we teach and learn in the twenty-first century.

References

Battro, A. (2002). The computer: a tool for the brain. In *The Challenges of Science: Education for the 21st Century*. Pontifical Academy of Sciences. Scripta varia. Vatican.

(2004). Digital skills, globalization and education. In M. Suárez-Orozco and D. Baolian Qin-Hilliard (eds.), *Education, Culture, and Globalization in the New Millennium*. Berkeley, CA: University of California Press.

Dawson, G. and Fischer, K. W. (1994) (eds.) *Human Behavior and the Developing Brain*. New York, NY: Guilford Press.

Dawson-Tunik, T. L. and Stein, Z. (In press). Cycles of research and application in science education. In K. W. Fischer and T. Katzir (eds.), *Building Usable Knowledge in Mind, Brain, and Education*. Cambridge, UK: Cambridge University Press.

Fischer, K. W., Bernstein, J. H., and Immordino, M. H. (2006). *Mind, Brain, and Education in Reading Disorders*. Cambridge, UK: Cambridge University Press.

Fischer, K. W. and Rose, S. P. (1994). Dynamic development of coordination of components in brain and behavior: A framework for theory and research. In G. Dawson and K. W. Fischer (eds.), *Human Behavior and the Developing Brain* (pp. 3–66). New York: Guilford Press.

Gage, F. H. (2003). Brain, repair yourself. *Scientific American*, 289(3), 47–53.

Gazzaniga, M. S. (ed.) (2003). *The New Cognitive Neurosciences*. Cambridge, MA: MIT Press.

Griffin, S. A., Case, R., and Siegler, R. S. (1994). Rightstart: Providing the central conceptual prerequisites for first formal learning of arithmetic to students at risk for school failure. In K. McGilly (ed.). *Classroom Lessons*, (pp. 25–50). Cambridge, MA: MIT Press.

Léna, P. J. (2002). Science education in France: La main à la pâte. In *The Challenges of Science: Education for the 21st Century*. Pontifical Academy of Sciences. Scripta varia, Vatican.

Neville, H. J. and Bruer, J. T. (2001). Language processing: How experience affects brain organization. In D. B. Bailey, Jr., J. T. Bruer, F. J. Symons, and J. W. Lichtman (eds.), *Critical Thinking about Critical Periods* (pp. 151–172). Baltimore, MD: Paul H. Brookes Publishing.

Ramón y Cajal, S. (1981). *Recuerdos de mi vida: Historia de mi labor científica*. Madrid: Alianza Editorial; (1937) *Recollections of My Life*. Philadelphia: American Philosophical Society.

Fernando Vidal

Overview

This chapter explores some historical developments concerning ideas about the connection between brain and self, and suggests that they constitute the background – and, indeed, the historical and intellectual conditions of possibility – for projects, such as the one that inspires this volume on the "educated brain," aimed at integrating the neurosciences with (or into) traditional areas of the human sciences. Such integration can be conceived of in reductionistic terms (the area in question, e.g. education or psychoanalysis, is to be entirely reformed on the basis of neuroscientific knowledge, and to be made dependent on advancements in the neurosciences), or in more collaborative terms (the human sciences maintain their epistemic and methodological independence, but are to be enriched and partially modified by available neuroscientific information). If the neurosciences seem so crucial, it is ultimately because – beyond what is relevant for each area of application or cooperation – they show the extent to which the brain is a fundamental organ for the constitution of human personhood. The author suggests, however, that the significance which the neurosciences have gained is, at least in part, dependent on the belief that one's own brain is the only organ each of us needs in order to be himself or herself. Such a belief is obviously supported by neuroscientific findings, but did not originate in them; on the contrary, it precedes modern knowledge of the brain. This might sound counterintuitive, but if it is indeed the case, then history should help us understand the roots, as well as the implicit values and beliefs of contemporary enthusiasm about the consequences of the neurosciences for other disciplines.

The Editors

The cerebral subject and the *neuro* sciences

In order to speak about brain and self in a historical perspective, I have found it useful to coin two terms, "brainhood" and "cerebral subject." The neologism brainhood is patterned by analogy with personhood. Since personhood is the quality or condition of being an individual person, brainhood can be used to name the quality or condition of being a brain. I would like to suggest that, starting around the second half of the twentieth century, brainhood was thematized as the defining property of human beings. Human beings explicitly became what we might call a "cerebral subject." From science fiction in writing and film to neurophilosophy and the practices of intensive care and organ transplantation, humans came to be thought of not merely as having a brain, but as being a brain. Of course, many other properties of human persons were recognized. Nevertheless, whole or in part, the brain emerged as the only organ truly indispensable for the existence of a human self and for defining individuality. Indeed, contrary to what occurs in all other cases of organ transplantation or body modification, it is assumed that if the brain of A is transplanted into the body of B, then it is not B who receives a new brain (as would be the case for every other organ of the body) but A who gains a new body.

At least in the industrialized western nations since the second half of the twentieth century, the cerebral subject has been a hugely influential anthropological figure, one that has had and will have extremely far-reaching consequences for all sorts of decisions in private lives and public policy (see, for example, Blank, 1999). The cerebral subject presupposes what historian of the brain sciences Michael Hagner has called *homo cerebralis* (Hagner, 1999; see also Breidbach, 1997a). This expression captures the transformation that the brain underwent during the nineteenth century: from seat of the soul, it became the organ of the self. The notion of cerebral subject also implies something like Jean-Pierre Changeux's "neuronal man," a notion that underlines the material foundations of personal identity (Changeux, 1983/1997). Yet the idea of a cerebral subject defined by the ontological property of brainhood is broader than both *homo cerebralis* and *l'homme neuronal*. It designates an anthropological figure – the human being as brain – with a great diversity of social inscriptions, embodiments and crystallizations, both inside and outside the philosophical, psychological, and neuroscientific fields. As such, it constitutes one of the conditions of possibility for projects that aim at bringing together the neurosciences and certain areas of the human sciences, and to reform the latter on the basis of knowledge about the brain. New such projects are constantly developing.

Indeed, the emergence of *neuro* domains of inquiry constitutes a salient feature of the current cultural landscape. Although the prefix neuro is in usage since the seventeenth century, for our topic the pioneer term is "neuroscience," invented in the early 1960s. Others followed, and today (to mention only some) we speak not only of neuropediatrics, neurogerontology, and neurogeriatrics, but also of neuroesthetics, neuroeconomics, neuropsychoanalysis, neuroethics, neurotheology and, of course, neuroeducation. Whether these domains will grow into full-blown disciplines, or remain zones of intersection or interaction between fields, their names are in themselves significant. While neurons are not only in the brain, neuro neologisms tend to refer only to that organ. The prefix certainly makes for more euphonic terms than words derived from brain or cerebrum; but it also immediately ties the recent neuro domains to the well-established and prestigious neurosciences. Therein resides the promotional efficacy of the neologisms. Yet publicity is clearly not every-thing: the *neuro* prefix declares that the advancement of the neurosciences both poses crucial challenges and offers exciting opportunities for the disciplines concerned.

Neuro areas are about material foundations – the brain in its early and late developmental stages in the case of neuropediatrics and neuro-gerontology, for example. Neurotheology aims at investigating the neuro-logical bases of spiritual and mystical experience (see for example Newberg, D'Aquili, & Rouse, 2001). Similarly, according to one defini-tion, neuroesthetics "seeks to establish the biological and neurobiological foundations of aesthetic experience;" the field already has an institute at University College London, and holds annual conferences in Berkeley (see www.neuroesthetics.org). (The somewhat different "neuronal esthetics" is rather an attempt at constructing a naturalistic esthetics; see Breidbach, 1997, and the analysis by Kleeberg, 2004, § III). As for neuropsychoanalysis, it focuses on the neurological underpinnings of the processes described by psychoanalytic theory (see for example Kaplan-Solms & Solms, 2000, as well as the journal *Neuro-psychoanalysis*). Neuroeconomics, perhaps the most developed of the new areas (and the only one to make it into the recent *Encyclopedia of Cognitive Science*), is "the study of how the embodied brain interacts with its external environment to produce economic behavior," with an emphasis on indi-vidual decision-making (McCabe, 2003; Glimcher, 2003; Camerer, Loewenstein, & Prelec, 2003); Claremont Graduate University houses a Center for Neuroeconomics Studies (http://fac.cgu.edu/~zakp/CNS/).

Neuroethics, an area that promises to be of crucial importance for the neuro future, is somewhat different. Certainly there is the quest for the neurological basis of moral behavior, but most of its efforts are directed at the ethical, social, and legal consequences of neuroscientific knowledge and its applications (Marcus, 2004; for the law, see Garland, 2004). All these areas emphasize not reductionism, but dialogue, interdisciplinarity, and two-way interactions between the neurosciences and the other fields. While they are not homogenous and are open to debate, they all manifest a certain corticocentric inclination, and place – even with caveats such as those that formulate this volume's editors – enormous hope on the contributions of neuroimaging techniques.

Neuroeducation is no exception. As the editors of this volume put it, although education is much more than its neural aspects, the neurosciences "can illuminate many of its needs" (Battro, Fischer, & Léna, this volume). The quest for methodologies and bodies of knowledge capable of transforming the art of education dates from at least the Renaissance, and has figured prominently in pedagogy since the early-twentieth-century progressive education movements. The neuroeducational project is no exception. Like its predecessors, it implies that the progress of science is the essential condition for its success: it believes that the advancement of the neurocognitive sciences will eventually give education a firmer empirical basis, and lead to appropriate pedagogical reforms.

It is worth noting that the views about the nature and the history of science that underlie such a belief have so far been formulated in terms that are inconsistent with those that prevail among historians of science, according to which objectivity, evidence, and facts are themselves historically constructed, rooted in particular contexts, and subject to intellectual and institutional negotiation. John T. Bruer, who has curbed neuroeducational enthusiasts, and criticized rash attempts at bridging the gap between neuroscience and education on the basis of simplistic or unfounded notions about laterality or critical periods, writes for example, "We simply do not know enough about how the brain works to draw educational implications from changes in synaptic morphology," and he concludes that "[n]euroscience has discovered a great deal about neurons and synapses, but not nearly enough to guide educational practice" (Bruer, 1997, 10 and 15; see also Bruer, 1999).

Thinking of these matters in quantitative terms, and with the image of a progressively cumulative science in mind can hardly do justice to the complexity of the issues involved. To begin with, more significant than quantity in itself are the kinds of knowledge and the technologies that turn out to be relevant: in the case of education, developmental neurobiology and brain imaging techniques have emerged as the decisive areas for opening the way to neuronal and neurocognitive intervention. Neuroeducation shares with the other neuro fields a strong faith that the advancement of science will provide solutions (or is the essential condition for finding such solutions). Yet, perhaps more than others, neuroeducation emphasizes two-way relationships: neuroscientists must move into the classroom, and teachers should bring their questions into the laboratory. This is a first step towards counterbalancing its scientistic discourse by raising central questions about the aims of education, the ethics of research and intervention, the political and policy dimensions and impact of future reforms. Ultimately, as the other *neuro* fields, neuroeducators will have to think about their anthropological assumptions, about their beliefs about what human beings and societies are and should be.

The neurologizing trend

The neurologizing trend manifest in the emergence of the neuro sciences rests on assumptions about the relationship between "being human" and "having a brain" – namely the belief that the brain (or eventually a functional equivalent) is the only and truly irreplaceable part of our bodies that we need in order to be ourselves. In one of Roald Dahl's most famous stories, a man called William is willing to survive the death of his body as a detached brain. Before the operation takes place, he asks his doctor to maintain the optic nerve and one eye attached to "him" so that he can still read the newspaper, one of his favorite occupations. William thus keeps on living as a brain floating in a solution, with an eyeball attached to it. Yet, for neither William nor the surgeon was the eye necessary for William's persistance as exactly the same person he was before being, so to speak, survived by his own brain (Dahl, 1960/1979). This fantasy corresponds to some people's real aspirations: the latest fashion in the quest of immortality through "cryonics," partly driven by its lower cost, is "neuropreservation," i.e. to keep the brains and get rid of the rest of the body (see Alcor Life Extension Foundation, www.alcor.org?FAQs/faq02.html#neuropreservation).

It is likely that even some neuropreservation clients, and *a fortiori* many of those who promote the neurologizing of the human sciences, would not recognize themselves in the ontology of brainhood, and would reject the idea that we can be reduced to our brains. In a historical perspective, however, the conditions for the emergence of the trend in question include, as a crucial element, the anthropological figure of the cerebral subject. As noted by Hagner and Borck (2001, 507–508), the neurosciences differ from other branches of the life sciences such as molecular biology in that its success "has not originated from a technological or conceptual breakthrough, nor has it been followed, accompanied, or enhanced by a similarly rich and constant flow of technological developments." Reciprocally, the cerebralization (or, more precisely, the corticalization) of personhood is not an inherently necessary result of neuroscientific progress (as suggested in the otherwise lucid article by Zimmer, 2004). Rather, it is a historically contingent assumption of the modern neurosciences. In the course of the eighteenth century, the brain became not only the seat of personal identity, but, more radically, the only bodily part essential to the self – the only organ that we need to have, and that has to be intrinsically our own, in order for us to be ourselves. The development of neurology and the neurosciences in the nineteenth and twentieth centuries crucially reinforced this early view. Then, in the 1960s, philosophers of the Anglo-American analytic tradition discussed personal identity by means of thought experiments that took the brain as its object, and turned cerebral surgical fictions into an indispensable conceptual tool for thinking about personal identity (Ferret, 1993; Noonan, 1991; Perry, 1975).

The rise of philosophical brain-fictions coincided chronologically with the increasing symbolic, institutional, and financial weight of brain research in the comparative growth of academic areas, the distribution of funding, and the public perception of which research fields are most decisive for the future of humankind. The International Brain Research Organization, a non-governmental organization recognized by UNESCO, was established in 1960 with the goal of promoting the neurosciences and facilitating training and communication among scientists; in 1973 it was admitted with associate status in the International Council of Scientific Unions, became a full member in 1993, and has held annual Neuroscience Schools since 1999 (see www.ibro.org). This early sign of the international growth of the brain sciences was in the late twentieth century followed by vigorous outreach and philanthropic endeavors: the government of the United States declared the 1990s the Decade of the Brain (lcweb.loc.gov/loc/brain/), and two major American foundations have made brain research and public education about it the focus of their programs. In 1992, the Charles A. Dana Foundation established an Alliance for Brain Initiatives, and later launched a yearly Brain Awareness Week aimed at advancing public knowledge about the progress, promise, and benefits of brain research (www.dana.org); since the year 2000, "Bridging Brain, Mind, and Behavior" is one of the three program areas supported by the Twenty-First Century Science Initiative of the John S. McDonnell Foundation (www.jsmf.org). Jean-Pierre Changeux (2000) announced that the twenty-first century will be the century of the brain; and for memory specialist and Nobel laureate Eric R. Kandel, "cognitive neuroscience – with its concern about perception, action, memory, language and selective attention – will increasingly come to represent the central focus of all neurosciences" (quoted in www.cogneurosociety.org/content/welcome).

These are only some visible signs of the place the neurosciences occupy in the universe of contemporary scientific research, at least in western industrialized nations. They speak not only about the history and sociology of science and medicine since the mid-twentieth century, but also about the core of personhood. In 1989, James D. Watson, co-discoverer of the structure DNA and first director of the Human Genome Project, declared, "We used to think our fate was in the stars. Now we know, in large measure, our fate is in our genes" (quoted in Jaroff, 1989, p. 67). If all goes as prophesied, in the twenty-first century we will not cease to be our genes – but we shall become our brains. A historical perspective on brain-hood might help anticipate and face up to the ethical and psychological challenges the coming neuroworld will inevitably pose.

Brain, body, and self

The question of brainhood is different from the problem of the relations between soul and body. To simplify, we can say that there are in western Christianity up to the Enlightenment two major moments, and basically one tradition in the history of ideas about the relations between soul and body. The moments are the Aristotelian and the post-Aristotelian; the tradition is that of Galenic medicine and physiology. In the Christian Aristotelian frameworks that dominate scholastic thinking until the late sixteenth century, the soul is defined, in Aristotle's words, as the "form" or "first actuality of a natural body which potentially has life" (De Anima, 412a20). This means not only that the soul (psuchè, anima) is a principle of life, or that which animates certain types of matter, but also that soul is not really separable from body. Aristotle's own analogies on this point are eloquent: "if the eye was an animal," he wrote, "then sight would be its soul, ... so that when sight leaves it, it is no longer an eye except ... in the way of a stone or painted eye" (De Anima, 412a–413a).

The soul conceived in this way is responsible for all the essential functions of living beings. These were defined as faculties or powers, with the names of nutritive or vegetative; perceptive or sensible; appetitive or desiderative; motor or locomotive; and rational or intellective (see Kessler, 1990; Michael, 2000; Park, 1990). The faculties were sometimes also described as different souls, but the debate around this point does not concern us here. What is important is that the human soul had all these faculties; other living beings were said to lack a rational soul; and plants were attributed only a vegetative soul. All these organisms were considered animals or ensouled bodies; and that is why, until the end of the seventeenth century, the term psychology (in use by 1590) or its synonymous expression "science of the soul" (scientia de anima) designated a generic science of living beings, including plants, animals, and humans (Vidal, 2006). The intellect or rational soul posed particular problems. Aristotle spoke of an "active intellect" which he described as separate, immortal, and eternal. This rather un-Aristotelian notion gave rise to centuries of debate; in the thirteenth century, however, the idea that the soul was a unitary substance, and that the rational soul was "by itself and essentially" (*per se et essentialier*) the "form" of the body (in Aristotle's sense) became the official doctrine of the Christian Church.

As the Aristotelian frameworks disintegrated, the soul ceased to be responsible for the nutritive, vegetative, and sensitive functions, and, as in the philosophy of René Descartes, became equal to the mind or rational soul. This was a radical transformation of the soul concept, and necessitated rethinking the union of the soul and the body. In the seventeenth and eighteenth centuries, three positions framed discussions about soul-body union (Vidal, 2003). According to the system of physical influence, the two substances affect each other materially. In Nicolas Malebranche's occasionalism, God is the causal agent of their union. For example, when the soul desires to move the body, God makes it move. Finally, Gottfried Wilhelm Leibniz saw the relationship between soul and body as regulated, like two perfectly synchronized clocks, by a pre-established harmony. A difference was made between the postulate of soul-body union, and soul-body interaction as a topic of empirical enquiry. While their union was accepted as a fact confirmed by faith, reason, and inner sense, yet in itself mysterious, their interaction (*commercium*) could be elucidated by examining the phenomena of human beings that seemed to manifest the mutual dependency of soul and body. This interaction constituted a major focus of the field of "empirical psychology" as it developed in the eighteenth century (Vidal, 2000; Vidal, 2006).

In spite of the major difference between the Aristotelian and post-Aristotelian periods, the manner of seeing the interaction of soul and body remained for many centuries very much the same, based on physiological theories derived from Galen, a second-century Greek philosopher and physician (Temkin, 1973). On the basis of older ideas attributed to Hippocrates, Greek physician born about 460 BCE, Galen proposed to consider health as a balance of the four main fluids or "humors" of the body. These humors – the blood, yellow bile, black bile, and phlegm – are made up of mixtures of the four elements (fire, air, water, and earth), and share in their basic qualities (hot, cold, humid, and dry). Therapeutic, dietetic, and hygienic prescriptions for a healthy life are based on considerations aimed at maintaining the balance of the humors. In each individual, these are present in various proportions and mixtures that determined the so-called "temperament." Temperaments, in turn, were said to dictate what we would now call an individual's personality and capacities – an idea expressed in the title of Galen's influential treatise

Quod animi mores corporis temperamenta sequantur ('That Capacities of the Soul Follow the Blends of the Body'). The essential point for our present purpose is that the human being was defined as a composite of two substances, body and soul, intimately connected and in constant interaction with one another.

The interaction itself was explained in a purely physiological manner. According to Galen, the body includes three systems: the brain and the nerves; the heart and the arteries; the liver and the veins. Blood, which is formed in the liver, is transported by the veins to the rest of the body, is consumed by the organs, and transformed into various "spirits" or increasingly subtle and thin fluids. It first becomes a "natural spirit," responsible for nutrition and growth. In the lungs, the blood combines with air; it then passes into the heart, and a portion of it becomes the "vital spirit," on which motor and vital functions were supposed to depend. The final transformation of blood takes place in the brain, where it becomes the "animal spirit" necessary for sensitive and intellectual functions. The qualities of these spirits, such as their temperature or density, are closely linked to those of the humors. For example, if a person's blood is too cold, his or her animal spirits will also be cold, and the mental acts that depend on them will be weak and slow. The animal spirits were believed to reside in and move among the brain ventricles which (as illustrated from front to back in Figure 2.1) operated as the seat of the "common sense" where sensory information was collected, the imagination and fantasy, judgment and the intellect, and memory (Clarke & Dewhurst, 1973; Harvey, 1975; Kemp, 1990).

The brain functions here as the factory of the animal spirits, but it is these spirits themselves, together with the rest of the humors, that determine a person's character and capacities. For example, in his renowned *Examen de ingenios para las ciencias* of 1575 (which a late seventeenth-century translator entitled 'The Tryal of Wits. Discovering the Great Difference of Wits Among Men, and What Sort of Learning Suits Best With Each Genius'), the Spanish physician Juan Huarte de San Juan followed Galen's *Quod animi mores*, and explained there is a correspondence between humidity and memory, dryness and the understanding, heat and the imagination. Individual differences in these faculties therefore depended on the physical qualities of the brain, namely its temperature and degree of humidity and dryness.

In the seventeenth and eighteenth centuries, the humoral theory lost some ground against mechanistic and solidistic alternatives, but remained extremely influential. As far as the interaction between soul and body was concerned, and especially the cognitive functions, the nerves gained new significance. They were conceived either as solid and elastic fibers, or as

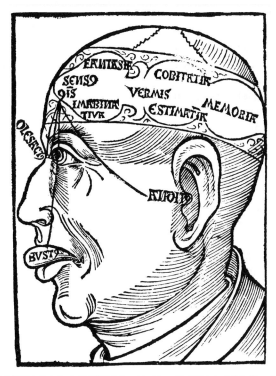

Figure 2.1 A depiction of the "cell theory" of mental function. The tongue, the nose, and the ear are connected to the "common sense" in the anterior ventricle, which also encloses fantasy and the imagination. From Hieronymus Brunschwig, *The Noble Experyence of the Vertuous Handy Warke of Surgeri* (London, 1525), first published in German in 1497.

hollow tubes. In both cases, they constituted the intermediate between the body and the soul; their role is highlighted by the fact that some authors (such as the Genevan naturalist and philosopher Charles Bonnet) placed the seat of the soul at a conjectural point inside the brain where the nerves would converge. Even more substantially than in the Galenic framework, where the humors and temperament played a crucial role, the brain became the organ of the self, and crucial to the developing science of empirical psychology. Two of the most important psychological thinkers of the Enlightenment, the Scot physician David Hartley in his 1749 *Observations on Man, His Frame, His Duty, and His Expectations,* and Bonnet in his *Essai de psychologie* ('Essay on Psychology,' 1754) and *Essai analytique sur les facultés de l'âme* ('Analytical Essay on the Faculties of the Soul', 1760), elaborated psychologies that emphasized the role of the nerves and the brain in habit-formation, association mechanisms, and the development of concepts out of sense impressions.

Chiefly for technical reasons, however, the brain remained for many centuries the most difficult organ of the body to examine scientifically (Brazier, 1988; Clarke & O'Malley, 1968; Clarke & Jacyna, 1987; Corsi, 1990; Finger, 1994; Neuburger, 1897/1981). Thus, the cerebralization or neurologization of psychology was not really due to what one might genuinely qualify as advances in the knowledge of brain structure and function. A crucial factor was precisely the anthropological revolution I tried to capture with the term *brainhood*. And it is to this revolution that we must now turn.

The brainhood revolution

In spite of the importance of the brain in Galenic physiology and, later, in Enlightenment neuropsychology, the emergence of the ontology of brainhood depends on other scientific and philosophical factors. In order to understand these factors, we must first recall something essential about Christianity as a religious tradition: the fact that it is based on the mystery of the Incarnation, that is to say that the Christ was God made flesh. There were of course early debates about the nature of Christ's body and about the exact relationship between his human and his divine natures. But the position that became official was that Christ had an entirely human body, and was both God and man. From this followed the basic principle of Christian anthropology, which is that a human person can only exist as a body.

It has often been said that Christianity sees the individual as a duality, torn between an immortal soul to be elevated and redeemed, and a perishable body to be mortified and despised. Nevertheless, from an anthropological point of view, it holds the opposite of Descartes's fiction of a bodyless self in the first of his *Meditations on First Philosophy* (1641). The idea that, for the Christian tradition, "being human meant being an embodied mind" (Porter, 1991, 212) is inaccurate. The common expression "embodied self" involves the idea of a (potentially) disembodied self. Christianity, however, rejects the possibility of a person existing otherwise than as a composite of body and soul. As the theologian Antoine Vergote put it, a person "is not someone who has a body but [someone] whose existence is corporeal;" "the body is the whole man" (Vergote, 1979, 96 and 97; see also Bynum, 1995; Keenan, 1994).

This anthropology has radical consequences, the most mysterious of which is perhaps the doctrine of the resurrection of the body. Again, there were debates in the early centuries of Christianity, but the official position became that both the bodily and the psychological identity of resurrected individuals will be the same as that of the persons they were while alive. "Identity," in the sense of the Latin reflexive pronoun *ipse*, therefore necessitates "sameness," in the sense of *idem* (used when two predicates are referred to the same subject or in the comparison "the same as . . ."). There are some complicated problems involved in this view. Some were raised at the beginning of Christianity, and kept thinkers worried until the eighteenth century (Vidal, 2002). They involved such questions as, If all our flesh has to be restored to our resurrected bodies, what happens with all the matter we lose and replace throughout our lives? Or, more dramatically: If you are eaten by a cannibal who assimilates your flesh to his own, where is the assimilated flesh going to end up, in the cannibal's resurrected body, or in yours?

These questions expressed an ontological problem. The doctrine of the resurrection states that our resurrected bodies will be "spiritual" and will be endowed with some special qualities. At the same time, it asserts that resurrected bodies will remain "numerically" identical to the bodies of flesh we possessed during our life on earth, i.e. identical not only qualitatively, but in their physical matter. Among Christians, the issue never was whether the resurrection will take place, or whether, as resurrected persons, we will indeed be our own selves. The conceptual difficulty was to envision bodily self-sameness and its relation to what it means to be ourselves. Will resurrected bodies be numerically identical to the corresponding terrestrial bodies? If yes, how? And if not, what will their qualitative identity depend on? The problem of the resurrection thus highlights the principle of Christian anthropology, namely that the body is the whole person, that there is no such thing as a disembodied human existence, and that for each of us to be ourselves, we need to have bodies – not just any body, but our own. In the late seventeenth century, however, this view was reconsidered and challenged.

As far as our topic is concerned, three interrelated processes began in the context of the Scientific Revolution: a relative disincarnation of personhood, the psychologization of personal identity, and the increasing focalization of the body on the brain. Two components of what was then called the "new philosophy" combined to bring about a first form of brainhood: the corpuscular theory of matter, and John Locke's theory of personal identity. The corpuscular philosophy (which was the one espoused for example by Isaac Newton) explains the phenomena of nature by the motion, figure, rest, and position of interchangeable particles of matter. Differences among physical bodies did not derive from the nature of their substance, but from the mechanical properties of their composing particles. This had an immediate and explicit consequence for the doctrine of the resurrection, namely that resurrected bodies no longer had to be made up of exactly the same matter as the corresponding terrestrial bodies. Material continuity lost its importance as a constitutive element of personal identity; and this, as philosopher John Locke would soon make clear, applied not only to resurrected persons, but to person-hood in general.

In the second edition of his *Essay Concerning Human Understanding* (1694/1988, Book 2, ch. 27), Locke proposed to separate substance and personal identity. His theory starts with the distinction between man and person. The identity of the man, Locke writes, consists in "a participation of the same continued life, in succession vitally united to the same organized body;" thus, if the soul of Heliogabalus were trans-ported into one of his hogs, nobody would say "that hog were a man or Heliogabalus" (§ 6). In contrast, Locke defined the person as "a thinking being, that has reason and reflection, and can consider itself as itself, the same thinking thing, in different times and places" (§ 9). Personal iden-tity, therefore, resides in a continuity of memory and consciousness, in what Locke called "the sameness of a rational being: and [he added] as far as this consciousness can be extended backwards to any past action or thought, so far reaches the identity of that person" (§ 9). Personal iden-tity, he explained, depends exclusively on the "same consciousness that makes a man be himself to himself" – and that, regardless of the sub-stances to which consciousness might be "annexed" (§ 10). It follows that self (which is for Locke that which the word "person" names, § 26) also depends on consciousness and not substance. Thus, the philosopher imagines that if my little finger is cut off my hand, and my consciousness happens to stay with it, then "it is evident the little finger would be the person, the same person; and self then would have nothing to do with the rest of the body" (§ 17). In this perspective of possessive individualism, we do not say that we "are" bodies, but that we "have" bodies; objectified and distanced from our "selves," our bodies become for us things we own, not entities we are (Taylor, 1989). Personal identity thus becomes psy-chological, and distinct from bodily identity.

In comparison with the earlier emphasis on the essential corporality of the self, the Lockean approach implies an obvious loss of body. But this sort of disincarnation could not be total. In Locke's fictions, the memory and consciousness necessary for identity were still attached to a little finger. In the empirical psychology of the Enlightenment, they were localized in the brain. It therefore remained the case that a separate disembodied soul could not, by itself, constitute what Locke called a man. The question was, what part of our bodies do we need in order to be ourselves? And the answer was that, in order to be a person, all an individual needs is his or her own brain – the one that encloses his or her memory and consciousness. The rest of the body is disposable, and when present, it no longer has to be the person's own. It will come as no surprise that the brain sciences did not engage directly with such questions. Three internal debates have dominated them since the end of the eighteenth century. One is the mind-brain, monism-dualism debate. The question here is whether cognition and behavior in general on the one hand, and on the other hand, the brain as their material foundation, can somehow be considered as separate entities, or whether the mind and its functions can be reduced to the brain. The second debate opposed localism and holism, the question here being whether neurons and different areas of the brain have specific functions, or whether the brain works as an integrated totality. The third concerns the nature of consciousness, and how it might be brought about by the brain. In this connection, the recurrence of the term "soul" in contemporary neurosciences and neurophilosophy is likely not a simple figure of speech or an ironic statment (as in Crick, 1994), but the sign of a major problem to be resolved.

The nineteenth century offers many signs of the emergence of the cerebral subject. Phrenology is the most familiar example (Clarke & Jacyna, 1987; Renneville, 2000; http://pages.britishlibrary.net/phrenology). Based on the theories of the Viennese physician Franz Joseph Gall (1758–1828), phrenology was at the same time a faculty psychology, a theory of the brain, and a method to assess people's characters and abilities. It was based on several premises: that the brain is the organ of the mind; that the mind is composed of innate faculties; that each faculty has its own seat or "organ" in the brain; that the size of an organ is proportional to the strength of the corresponding faculty; that the brain is shaped by the differential growth of these organs; and, finally, that since the skull owes its form to the underlying brain, its surface, or "bumps," reveal the psychological aptitudes and tendencies of an individual.

Although the alleged brain-organs turned out to be imaginary, phrenology was the first system to attribute psychological qualities and behavior to localized regions of the cerebral cortex, and some of its premises were confirmed in the second half of the nineteenth century, when foundational advances were made, especially concerning cerebral localizations and cytoarchitectonics (or the cellular architecture of the brain, including the discovery of the neuron). These discoveries were encouraged by (and obviously confirmed) the idea that the brain is the organ of the self. This belief materialized in research on the brains of geniuses, criminals, and the mentally ill, whose extraordinary positive or negative qualities were supposed to be inscribed in their brains (see for example Hagner, 2004). Since that time, the neurophilosophical assumption of a correlation between brain states and psychological states has not lost any of its fascination – on the contrary, its attraction has increased thanks to the spread of neuroimaging techniques that generate pictures whose dynamic beauty and apparent immediacy, seeming legibility and intuitive appeal confer to them the status of compelling facts about who we are (Dumit, 2003, 2004).

An ontology of brainhood

The developments sketched above conspired to bring about *homo cerebralis* and *l'homme neuronal*, as well as the implicit belief that a human being, in order to be a person, needs nothing other than his or her brain. An ontology of brainhood, however, crystallized only in the 1960s, in certain philosophical discussions about personal identity. These discussions were characterized by the use of imaginary experiments analogous to the ones John Locke employed in his *Essay* – only that the experiments now concerned the brain. As far as I can tell, the first instance can be found in *Self-knowledge and Self-identity*, a book published in 1963 by Cornell University philosopher Sidney Shoemaker.

In the context of discussing bodily and psychological criteria of personal identity, Shoemaker presented one of Locke's arguments, which he called the "change-of-body argument." Locke had remarked that if the soul of a prince, "carrying with it the consciousness of the prince's past life," were transferred to the body of a cobbler, and the cobbler's body abandoned by his own soul, then it would be obvious that what still looks like the cobbler "would be the same person with the prince, accountable only for the prince's actions" (Locke, 1694/1988, 2.27.15). As Shoemaker (1963, 22) observes, Locke's idea is that "a person might cease to have the body that had been 'his' in the past and come to have a different body."

The philosopher then proceeds to imagine that medicine has developed a technique of "brain extraction," so that a brain can be entirely removed from a person's skull to be examined or operated on, and then put back in the skull. One day, a surgeon discovers that an assistant, while replacing the brains of Mr. Brown and Mr. Robinson after extraction, interchanged them. One of the two men dies immediately, but the other survives. He has Robinson's body and Brown's brain – so, Shoemaker proposes, let us call him "Brownson." When Brownson regains consciousness and looks at himself, he is totally astonished at the appearance of his body, and claims that his body is the corpse of Mr. Robinson lying on a nearby bed. When asked his name, he replies "Brown," recognizes Brown's wife and family, and can describe events in Brown's life. In fact, he displays all the personality traits and other psychological features that had characterized Brown.

Shoemaker rightly notes that many of us would be strongly inclined "to say that while Brownson has Robinson's body he is actually Brown." His comment on this situation, however, is that "it would be absurd to suggest that brain identity is our criterion of personal identity." Indeed, "if upon regaining consciousness Brownson were to act and talk just as Robinson had always done in the past, surely no one would say that this man, who looks, acts, and talks just like Robinson, and has what has always been Robinson's body, must really be Brown rather than Robinson because he has Brown's brain." Shoemaker thus concludes that the relationship between the state of the brain and one's psychological features is "causal and contingent," but "not logically necessary." Browson's having Brown's brain "makes his psychological affinity to the old Brown ... causally intelligible ..... But it cannot itself be our ground for saying ... that Brownson is Brown." Or if we say so, then we are allowing psychological criteria of personal identity to override "the fact of bodily non-identity" (all quotations from Shoemaker, 1963, 24–25). Critics have observed that by speaking of "bodily nonidentity" and calling this argument the "change-of-body argument," Shoemaker treats a decerebrated body as if it were the body *tout court* – totally neglecting the fact that the brain is part of the body (Ferret, 1993, 77). And yet, few figures of thought are in this domain more common than the dichotomy body-brain – as in "Brain not body makes athletes feel tired" (Randerson, 2004).

In the wake of Shoemaker, it became inescapable to resort to surgical brain fictions in order to discuss personal identity. The brain emerged as the somatic limit of the self, such that I cease to be (myself) if I my brain is amputated. The psychological and the bodily criteria can be combined in the following formula: a person A is identical with a person B if and only if A and B have one and the same functional brain (Ferret, 1993, 79). This definition, which reduces the relevant body to the brain, can be taken as the axiom of brainhood.

Understood in this way, brainhood has innumerable cultural materializations outside philosophy and the human and the life sciences: in medical ethics (which deals with such issues as brain death, brain intervention techniques and neural grafting); in theology and religion (encompassing not only "neurotheology," or the quest for the neuroscientific basis of spirituality and religious experience, but also such questions as whether the resurrection of the body should not be reconceived as the resurrection of brains); and, finally, in the expanding galaxy of neurobeliefs and neuropractices that go from learning how to draw or feel with one side of the brain, to various forms of neurohealthism and neuroesotericism. The work of socio-anthropologist of science Joseph Dumit shows how neuroimaging techniques bring about a "digital image of the category of the person," and alter people's lives and self-perception through what he calls "objective self-fashioning" (Dumit, 1997, 2004). Finally, recent studies on body-modification practices suggests that while the extra-cerebral body is seen as a fundamental site of personal identity, and thus as the vehicle for transforming oneself, the practices in question also imply an attitude to the body that makes it something we own, not that which we are (Andrieu, 2002; Featherstone, 2000; Le Breton, 2000). Even if the mind-brain question were effectively suspended or resolved thanks to a unitary notion (e.g. "mindbrain," brainhood is likely to remain an unspoken assumption. It is very significant, for example, that, in an argument against skepticism, Harvard philosopher Hilary Putnam (1981, ch. 1) imagined the following situation: While you were sleeping, a scientist removed your brain, put it in a vat, and hooked it to a computer that send to your nerve endings the kinds of signals that usually informed your brain. When you wake up, everything looks the same as usual, only that you are in fact no more than a brain in a vat. Never mind here how Putnam draws anti-skeptical conclusions from this thought-experiment (he claimed that if you were indeed a brain in a vat, you could not think you were a brain in a vat). What counts is how obvious seems the choice of the brain, as if investigating problems of self-knowledge naturally and necessarily implied brainhood.

So far, there have been several ways of nuancing or resisting the ontology of brainhood; and it is crucial to emphasize that none of them require denying the obviously fundamental role of the brain. One approach is illustrated in Kathleen Wilkes's book *Real People* (1988), whose critique of thought-experiments does not prevent her from devoting many pages to the brain, with emphasis on the need not to over-simplify scientific information, and not to cut back the brain to the cerebral cortex. Another approach has been that of Paul Ricoeur. In his view, cerebral fictions neutralize the body and restrict it to the brain at the expense of the self as flesh (*soi comme chair*). The brain, he observes, is different from the rest of the body in that it lacks "phenomenological status." Indeed, while we have a "lived relation" to other organs of our bodies, be they related to movement (the hand), to perception (the eye), to emotion (the heart) or to expression (the voice), no experience of the same sort applies to the brain (Ricoeur, 1990, 159; 378 for "self as flesh"). A third approach has been that of the late neuroscientist Francisco Varela. Starting with a critique of the equation brain-body and of eliminative neuro-reductionism (according to which there are no mental states, only neuronal states), he developed a "neurophenomeno-logy" aimed at reintegrating into the neurosciences embodiment and the first-person experience (Varela, 1996; Varela, Thompson, & Rosch, 1991; Petitot *et al.*, 2000).

I believe these reactions to brainhood are on the right track. Brainhood studies, however, have barely begun, and the full history and implications of the cerebral subject remain to be explored. The task is not easy, since we certainly cannot be without at least a portion of our brains, and since brainhood functions as an existential condition in which we are all immersed; it already dictates the moment of our deaths – though not unproblematically (Schlich & Wiesemann, 2001) – and will increasingly shape, with benefits and risks, the course of much of our lives. At the same time, insofar as brainhood constitutes a view about what humans are, it is a human creation devoid of inherent necessity, just another instance of the immemorial drive to attribute moral authority to nature (Daston & Vidal, 2004). Understanding and coming to terms with the ontology of brainhood is a long-term future task. Here, I can do no more than indirectly indicate my preferences, and offer an emblem of the challenges I think we have to face.

In 1991, the late Helen Chadwick created a stunning work of art (Figure 2.2).

It is a photograph, printed on a glass plate and illuminated from behind. *Self-portrait* is its disconcerting title. With "delightedly contrary fancy" (Warner, 1996, [1]), Chadwick substituted a brain for the face of traditional self-portraits; she thus seems to be saying, "I am my brain." The depicted brain, however, could not be the artist's own; in contrast, the hands, another traditional element of self-portraits, are indeed hers, with their unique shape, and their characteristic marks and ornaments. They hold the brain in a careful gesture that presents it as if in an act of offering or devotion, almost an imposition of hands, sacralizing its significance and announcing its fragility in what is a portrait of the self. But the very presence of the hands, the convoluted, brain-like flesh-colored background tissue refer us to the entire body of the artist, to her craft, her individuality, her history, her contextual and personal bonds. Helen Chadwick declared, "I want the body to be as much a site of victory as the brain" (quoted in Warner, 1989, 58). Her self-portrait, then, clearly does not say, "I am my brain." Rather, it shows that, indeed, the brain is at the center of the work of art – but also that the person who created the work is not reducible to her brain.

This is consistent with the spirit in which this volume explores neuro-education. The brief historical considerations on brain and self presented here, however, show that such a position is not the only one, and that it itself results from a historical development and from a reflective attitude towards the challenges of the neurosciences. Such considerations sketch

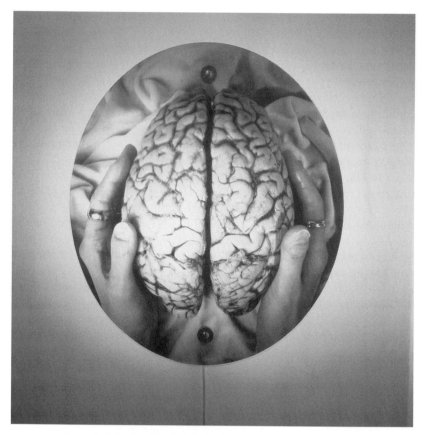

Figure 2.2 Helen Chadwick, "Self-portrait" (1991). © Helen Chadwick Estate. Courtesy Zelda Cheatle Gallery.

the kind of environment in which the neuroeducational project is growing, and might help its actors remain sensitive to its anthropological context and dimensions. Educators in the field might feel that the part of "art" in education will always surpass the part of "science." Yet the problem might be how to bring both in harmony, and how to think the contribution of neuroscience to education in terms other than quantities of available data about brain structure and function. For, as the history of brainhood and the cerebral subject seems to suggest, how the neurosciences will affect education will depend less on technical information, than on knowledgeable, and hopefully wise, moral, philosophical, and political decisions about what it is to be human, and how human society should be organized.

References

Andrieu, B. (2002). *La nouvelle philosophie du corps* (The New Philosophy of the Body). Ramonville: Éditions érès.

Blank, R. H. (1999). *Brain Policy: How the New Neuroscience Will Change Our Lives and Our Politics.* Washington, DC: Georgetown University Press.

Brazier, M. A. B. (1988). *A History of Neurophysiology in the Nineteenth Century.* New York: Raven Press.

Breidbach, O. (1997a). *Die Materialisierung des Ichs. Zur Geschichte der Hirnforschung im 19. und 20. Jahrhundert* (The Materialization of the Self. On the History of Brain Research in the Nineteenth and Twentieth Century). Frankfurt, Suhrkamp.

(1997b). Einleitung: Neuronale Ästhetik – Skizze eines Programms (Introduction: Neuronal Esthetics. Sketch of A Program). In O. Breidbach (ed.), *Natur des Ästhetik – Ästhetik der Natur* (Nature of Esthetics – Esthetics of Nature) (Vienna / New York, Springer).

Bruer, J. T. (1997). Education and the brain: a bridge too far. *Educational Researcher,* 26, 4–16.

(1999). In search of . . . brain-based education. *Phi Delta Kappan,* www.pdkintl.org/kappan/kbru9905.htm.

Bynum, C. W. (1995). Why all the fuss about the body? A Medievalist's perspective. *Critical Inquiry,* 22, 1–33.

Camerer, C., Loewenstein, G., and Prelec, D. (2003). Neuroeconomics: How neuroscience can inform economics, http://sds.hss.cmu.edu/faculty/Loewenstein/downloads/neurojep.pdf.

Changeux, J. P. (1983/1997). *Neuronal Man. The Biology of Mind,* trans Laurence Garey. Princeton: Princeton University Press, 1997.

Changeux, J.-P. (2000). La révolution des neurosciences (The Neurosciences Revolution) [an interview]. *Label France,* n° 38, www.france.diplomatie.fr/label_france/FRANCE/DOSSIER/2000/09neuro.html.

Clarke, E. and Dewhurst, K. (1972). *An Illustrated History of Brain Function.* Berkeley, CA: University of California Press.

Clarke, E. and O'Malley C. D. (1968). *The Human Brain and Spinal Cord.* Berkeley, CA: University of California Press.

Clarke, E. and Jacyna, L. S. (1987). *Nineteenth-Century Origins of Neuroscientific Concepts.* Berkeley, CA: University of California Press.

Corsi, P. (ed.) (1990). *La fabrique de la pensée. La découverte du cerveau de l'art de la mémoire aux neurosciences* (The Fabric of Thought. The Discovery of the Brain from the Art of Memory to the Neurosciences). Milan, Electa.

Crick, F. (1994). *The Astonishing Hypothesis. The Scientific Search for the Soul.* New York: Scribner.

Dahl, R. (1960/1979). William and Mary. In Roald Dahl, *Tales of the Unexpected.* Harmondsworth, Penguin Books.

Daston, L. and Vidal, F. (eds.) (2004). *The Moral Authority of Nature.* Chicago: University of Chicago Press.

Dumit, J. (1997). A digital image of the category of the person. PET scanning and objective self-fashioning. In G. L. Downey and J. Dumit (eds.), *Cyborgs &*

Citadels. Anthropological Interventions in Emerging Sciences and Technologies. Santa Fe, New Mexico: School of American Research Press.

(2003). Is It Me or My Brain? Depression and Neuroscientific Facts. *Journal of Medical Humanities*, 24(1/2), 35–47.

(2004). *Picturing Personhood. Brain Scans and Biomedical Identity.* Princeton: Princeton University Press.

Eickmeier, J. (1004). Make your brain feel younger. www.prevention.com/article/0,5778,s1-5-91-276-2889-1,00.html

Featherstone, M. (ed.) (2000). *Body Modification.* London: Sage.

Ferret, S. (1993). *Le philosophe et son scalpel. Le problème de l'identité personnelle* (The Philosopher and His Scalpel. The Problem of Personal Identity). Paris: Editions de Minuit.

Finger, S. (1994). *Origins of Neuroscience. A History of Explorations into Brain Function.* New York: Oxford University Press.

Garland, B., (ed.) (2004). *Neuroscience and the Law. Brain, Mind, and the Scales of Justice*, New York: Dana Press.

Glimcher, P. (2003). *Decisions, Uncertainty, and the Brain. The Science of Neuroeconomics.* Cambridge, MA: MIT Press.

Hagner, M. (1997). *Homo cerebralis. Der Wandel vom Seelenorgan zum Gehirn* (Homo Cerebralis. The Transformation of the Organ of the Soul into the Brain). Berlin: Berlin Verlag.

Hagner, M. and Borck, C. (2001). Mindful practices: on the neurosciences in the twentieth centuy. *Science in Context*, 14(4), 507–510.

Hagner, M. (2004). *Geniale Gehirne. Zur Geschichte der Elitenhirnforschung.* Berlin: Wallstein.

Harvey, R. (1975). *The Inward Wits. Psychological Theory in the Middle Ages and the Renaissance.* London: Warburg Institute.

Jaroff, L. (1989). The gene hunt. *Time Magazine*, 20 March, 62–67.

Kaplan-Solms, K. and Solms, M. (2002). *Clinical Studies in Neuro-Psychoanalysis: Introduction to a Depth Neuropsychology.* New York: Karnac Books (2nd edn.).

Kemp, S. (1990). *Medieval Psychology.* New York: Greenwood Press.

Keenan, J. F. (1994). Christian perspectives on the human body. *Theological Studies*, 55, 330–346.

Kessler, E. (1990). The intellective soul. In Schmitt *et al.* (1990).

Kleeberg, B. (2004). Vor der Sprache. Naturalistischer Konzepte objektiver Wahrnehmung (Before Speech. Naturalistic Concepts of Objective Perception). In F. Crivellari, K. Kirchmann, M. Sandl, and R. Schlögl (eds.), *Die Medien der Geschichte. Historizität und Medialität in interdisziplinärer Perspektive* (The Media of History. Historicity and Mediality in Interdisciplinary Perspectives). Konstanz: UVK Verlagsgesellschaft.

Le Breton, D. (2002). *Signes d'identité. Tatouages, piercings et autres marques corporelles* (Signs of Identity. Tatoos, Piercings, and Other Body Markings). Paris: Métailié.

Locke, J. (1694/1988). *An Essay Concerning Human Understanding*, ed. Peter H. Nidditch. Oxford: Clarendon Press.

Marcus, S. J. (ed.) (2004). *Neuroethics. Mapping the Field.* New York: Dana Press.

McCabe, K. (2003). Neuroeconomics. In L. Nadel, ed., *Encyclopedia of Cognitive Science*. London: Nature Publishing Group, vol. 3.

Michael, E. (2000). Renaissance theories of body, soul, and mind. In J. P. Wright and P. Potter (eds.), *Psyche and Soma. Physicians and Metaphysicians on the Mind-Body Problem from Antiquity to Enlightenment*. Oxford: Clarendon Press.

Neuburger, M. (1897/1981). *The Historical Development of Experimental Brain and Spinal Cord Physiology Before Flourens*, annotated and translated by Edwin Clarke. Baltimore: Johns Hopkins University Press.

Newberg, A., D'Aquili, E., and Rause, V. (2001). *Why God Won't Go Away. Brain Science and the Biology of Belief*. New York: Ballantine Books.

Noonan, H. (1991). *Personal Identity*. London: Routledge.

Park, K. (1990). The organic soul. In Schmitt *et al.* (1990).

Perry, J. (ed.) (1975). *Personal Identity*. Berkeley, CA: University of California Press.

Porter, R. (1991). History of the body. In Peter Burke (ed.), *New Perspectives on Historical Writing*. Pennsylvania: Pennsylvania State University Press.

Petitot, J., Varela, F., Pachoud, B., and Roy, J. M. (eds.). (2000). *Naturalizing Phenomenology. Issues in Contemporary Phenomenology and Cognitive Science*. Stanford: Stanford University Press.

Putnam, H. (1981). *Reason, Truth, and History*. New York: Cambridge University Press.

Randerson, J. (2004) Brain not body makes athletes feel tired. *New Scientist*, 29 July. www.newscientist.com/article.ns?id=dn6208

Renneville, M. (2000). *Le langage des crânes. Une histoire de la phrénologie* (The Language of Skulls. A History of Phrenology). Paris: Les Empêcheurs de tourner en rond.

Ricoeur, P. (1990). *Soi-même comme un autre* (Oneself as Another). Paris: Seuil.

Schlich, T. and Wiesemann, C. (eds.) (2001). *Hirntod. Zur Kulturgeschichte der Todesfeststellung* (Brain Death. On the Cultural History of the Definition of Death). Frankfurt: Suhrkamp.

Schmitt, C. B., Quentin, Kessler, E., and Kraye, J. (eds.). (1990). *The Cambridge History of Renaissance Philosophy*. New York: Cambridge University Press.

Shoemaker, S. (1963). *Self-Knowledge and Self-Identity*. Ithaca: Cornell University Press.

Taylor, C. (1989). *Sources of the Self. The Making of the Modern Identity*. Cambridge, MA: Harvard University Press.

Temkin, O. (1973). *Galenism. Rise and Decline of a Medical Philosophy*. Ithaca: Cornell University Press.

Varela, F. (1996). Neurophenomenology: a methodological remedy to the hard problem. *Journal of Consciousness Studies* 3, 330–350.

Varela, F., Thompson, E., and Rosch, E. (1991). *The Embodied Mind. Cognitive Science and Human Experience*. Cambridge, MA: MIT Press.

Vergote, A. (1979). The body as understood in contemporary thought and biblical categories. *Philosophy Today*, 35, 93–105.

Vidal, F. (2000). The eighteenth century as 'century of psychology'. *Annual Review of Law and Ethics*, 8, 407–434.

(2002). Brains, bodies, selves, and science. Anthropologies of identity and the resurrection of the body. *Critical Inquiry*, 28(4), 930–974.

(2003). Soul. In Kors, A. C. (ed.). *Encyclopedia of the Enlightenment*. New York: Oxford University Press.

(2006). *Les sciences de l'âme, XVIe–XVIIIe siècle* (The Sciences of the Soul, 16th–18th Century). Paris: Champion.

Warner, M. (1989). In the garden of delights. In H. Chadwick, *Enfleshings*. New York: Aperture.

(1996). In extremis: Helen Chadwick & the wound of difference. In H. Chadwick, *Stilled Lives*. Edinburgh: Portfolio Gallery / Odense: Kunsthallen Brandts Klædefabrik.

Wilkes, K. V. (1988). *Real People. Personal Identity Without Thought Experiments*. Oxford: Clarendon Press.

Zimmer, C. (2004). A distant mirror for the brain. *Science*, 303, n° 5654 (2 January), 43–44.

3 Building bridges in neuroeducation

John T. Bruer

Overview

Mind, brain, and education initiatives should build bridges between educators and behavioral, cognitive, and neurobiological scientists. Some bridges are robust, and others are problematic. Links of cognitive development to education can be straightforward and useful. For example, children with low socioeconomic status typically show delays in the normal acquisition of arithmetic skills and concepts. When these children have access to intensive training, such as the program "Right Start," they overcome the obstacles and improve their level of performance. Some other bridges are not so well founded. In particular, the over-emphasis on sensitive periods for learning connected with brain maturation has led to a restrictive concept of "windows of opportunity" for learning, which is not supported by research on learning. In fact, some research invalidates the common view that high synaptic density is needed for learning. The link from neuroscience to education needs to include assessment of the target behaviors, such as learning arithmetic and reading, and not assume that brain findings link in obvious ways. Other chapters in this book highlight areas where links between brain research and educationally relevant behaviors are being made fruitfully and with appropriate scientific caution, especially for language and arithmetic.

The Editors

In *Education and the Brain: A Bridge Too Far* (Bruer, 1997) I expressed concerns about supposed implications of developmental neuroscience for teaching and learning. I also argued positively that currently cognitive psychology is a better source for educationally relevant basic research than is developmental neuroscience. As for the future, I claimed that cognitive neuroscience was the most promising candidate for a basic science of learning and that it too relied on the methods of cognitive psychology. Educators' best strategy, therefore, was to embrace cognitive psychology and build "applied" bridges from cognitive psychology to educational practice and basic bridges between cognitive science and systems neuroscience.

43

The 1997 article was addressed primarily to the education and policy communities, not to the cognitive or neuroscientific research communities. It addressed the question of where to seek scientific underpinnings for improved educational practice. It did not address, as such, the merits and problems of a research program that would attempt to link brain science and mind science with educational practice – a research program in neuroeducation, the focus of this volume. Here I will attempt to address some of those merits and problems.

I will: (1) Question the dominant role that visual neuroscience has had on thinking about the neural bases of learning; (2) Illustrate the importance of cognitive models for educational research and practice; and (3) Address how cognitive neuroscience can assist in refining educationally relevant cognitive models.

Learning and visual neuroscience

Neuroscientists have known since the late 1970s that in monkeys and humans there is a period in early post-natal development, during which the rate of synapse formation exceeds the rate of synapse elimination, i.e., there are periods of developmental synaptogenesis. (See, for example, Lund *et al.*, 1977, Huttenlocher *et al.*, 1979, Rakic *et al.*, 1985). Behavioral scientists and ethologists had also observed that there are critical periods in animal and human development. (Bailey *et al.*, 2001) Although the definition of "critical period" tends to vary from author to author, the core idea is that there are limited periods in biological development when an organism is susceptible, prepared for, or open to certain types of experience. If that experience does not occur during this period, development permanently diverges from its normal trajectory. Much of what we know about the neural mechanisms underlying critical periods derives from research on how visual deprivation affects the formation, or maintenance, of optical dominance columns in visual cortex (Singer, this volume). There is also a history of research on how rearing rats in complex environments (simulated wild or natural environments) affects the synaptic structure in rat visual cortex (see, for example, Greenough, 1987).

Based on such findings, some educators and neuroscientists attempt to draw far-reaching educational implications. They claim: Developmental synaptogenesis occurs during the first 10–12 years of life. It is a period of elevated synaptic density and brain metabolism. This is the critical period in brain development. During this critical period, children learn more quickly and efficiently than at any time in life.

This claim comes in several varieties, some more extreme than others. It maintains its credibility in education and policy circles, however, only because some neuroscientists explicitly maintain, suggest, or hypothesize that their work has such implications (Bruer, 2002).

For example, Kandell and Schwartz (1991) conclude a discussion of critical periods in the formation/maintenance of ocular dominance columns by suggesting that such periods are likely to be general features of brain development. This would explain "why certain capabilities – such as those for language, music, or mathematics – usually must be developed well before puberty if they are to develop at all . . . ."(p. 957). In arguing for the hypothesis that the period of high synaptic density is a privileged one for learning, Peter Huttenlocher wrote: "Data show good correlations between age of synaptic pruning and decline in brain plasticity, especially in more simple systems, such as visual cortex"(Huttenlocher, 2003). A National Institute of Mental Health press release on the Giedd *et al.* (1999) imaging study showing changes in white matter in the developing teenage brain implied that this too might be a critical period for learning: "Although scientists don't know yet what accounts for the observed changes, they may parallel a pruning process that occurs early in life that appears to follow the principle of "use-it-or-lose-it": neural connections, or synapses, that get exercised are retained, while those that don't are lost. At least, this is what studies of animals' developing visual systems suggest." (NIH Publication) Max Cynader has stated: "The visual cortex represents the best model system that we have for understanding how sensory stimulation of the early brain influences brain circuitry and function throughout life" (Cynader, 2000).

The first questions an integrated mind-brain-education research program should ask are: Is the visual system the best model? Does it have implications for learning over the life span? The short answer is "No."

Harry Chugani's interpretation of Chugani *et al.* (1987) is the most well known example of where over-reliance on developmental neurobiology generates pseudo-implications for teaching and learning. Chugani believes that the developmental periods' high synaptic density and elevated brain metabolism is "the biological 'window of opportunity' when learning is efficient and easily retained . . . ." (Chugani, 1998).

The 1988 Chugani *et al.* study used PET to measure changes in resting-brain glucose metabolism for various brain regions in subjects who ranged in age from infancy to young adulthood. The solid curve in Figure 3.1 shows observed changes in glucose uptake over development for frontal cortex, one of the latest brain areas to undergo developmental synaptogenesis and pruning.

The elevated period of glucose uptake in this brain region occurs between 2 and 11 years of age. Increase in glucose uptake occurs, the authors claim, to support increased synaptic density during developmental synaptogenesis. This should be, then, the critical period, or biological

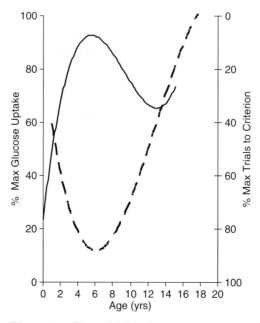

Frontal cortex glucose uptake and
oddity task learning curve

Figure 3.1 The solid line shows the percent maximum glucose uptake over the life span as published in Chugani (1987). The broken line shows percent maximum trials to criterion for learning the one-part oddity task as published by Overman (1996b). Reprinted from *Journal of Experimental Child Psychology*, 62 (2), Overman, W. H., Bachevalier, J., Miller, M., and Moore, K., "Children's performance on 'animal tests' of oddity: Implications for cognitive processes required for tests of oddity and delayed nonmatch to sample," 233–42, Copyright (1996) with permission.

window of opportunity, for learning tasks associated with frontal cortex. During this period, then, children should show some advantage in learning such tasks.

A review of available behavioral evidence does not support this claim. For example, Overman *et al.* (1996b) trained subjects from age 15 months to 20 years on the one-part oddity task – a task commonly assumed to depend on frontal cortex. He tested subjects 5 days a week, 15 trials per day, until they reached a learning criterion of 13/15 correct choices on two consecutive test days or had undergone a maximum of 1500 training trials.

How quickly and efficiently did subjects learn this task at different ages? The dashed curve in Figure 3.1 answers this question. The dashed curve shows change by age in the number of training trials subjects required to reach criterion on the task. The more trials required, the less easy and efficient learning is. The Y-axis on the right of Figure 3.1 for the learning curve is inverted. As the learning curve heads down, learning worsens; as it heads up, learning improves. For the oddity task, ease of learning is *negatively* correlated with frontal glucose uptake. As brain metabolism rises, learning worsens. As brain metabolism falls, learning improves. Furthermore, learning continues to improve after frontal glucose uptake settles at mature levels.

This is not an isolated result. Adult monkeys and humans learn the delayed non-match to sample task more quickly than do immature subjects. (Bachevalier & Mishkin, 1984; Overman, 1990). Adults learn spatial navigation tasks more quickly than young children. (Overman *et al.*, 1996c) Adult humans and monkeys learn discrimination tasks more quickly than do immature subjects. (Overman, Bachevalier, Schumann, & Ryan, 1996a). Simplistic claims based on or extrapolated from the developmental neurobiology of the visual system are simply not consistent with what behavioral research already tells us about ease and efficiency of learning over the life span.

Such simplistic claims are also inconsistent with what cognitive psychologists have established about studied learning and memory over the past 40 years. Cognitive psychological research has established that prior knowledge within a subject domain is the strongest determinant of how quickly and effectively individuals learn. (See Pressley & McCormick, 1995, Ch. 4, pp. 84–109) Ease and efficiency of learning depends on prior experience, not on age or (within limits) brain maturation.

Means and Voss (1985) studied how prior learning and experience influences people's understanding of a story. The story used in the study was Star Wars film trilogy. In their study, novices were defined as subjects who had seen the movies at least once, but not more than three times. Experts had seen the movies four or more times. Subjects ranged in age from age 7 years (2nd grade) through 19 + (college). Thus, subjects in this study included individuals both within and outside the supposed biological window for learning given the neurobiological story at around age 11–12 years of age. The Means and Voss results study are shown in Figure 3.2.

Experts learned more than novices at every age on each of the three learning tasks employed in the study. More to the point, both expert and novice learning *increased with age*. Ease and efficacy of learning did not peak between ages 4 to 10 years. Rather, subjects appeared to reach

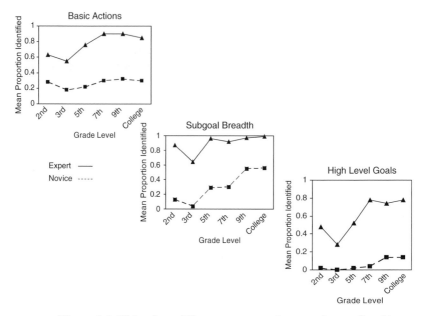

Development of expert/novice knowledge
(Means & Voss, 1985)

Figure 3.2 Using three different measures of story understanding Means and Voss (1985) showed that experts learned more than novices at every age and that for both novices and experts learning and understanding increased with age. Reprinted from *Journal of Memory and Language*, 24, Means, M. and Voss, J., "Star Wars: A developmental study of expert and novice knowledge structure," 746–57, Copyright (1985), with permission from Elsevier.

mature learning levels at around age 11–12 years and retained or exceeded those learning levels in adulthood, that is, after the "biological window of opportunity" closed.

Psychological research has established that experience at any age matters. Any simple connection between the brain's maturational timetable and ease and efficiency of learning is inconsistent with what we know about how prior experience, at any age, influences learning. Developmental neurobiology might eventually help explain what psychological science has already discovered about learning over the life span (see Koizumi, this volume). However, if brain science cannot currently explain these fundamental psychological findings, then neuroscientists' claims and speculations about implications of their research for education should at least be consistent with what behavioral science already tells us.

Any mind-brain-education research initiative should take a critical, interdisciplinary look at claims emanating from developmental neuroscience that the visual system with its critical periods is the best model for explaining life-long learning. The problem may merely be that neuroscientists are unaware of what cognitive and educational psychology have already achieved. One benefit of an integrated research program would be to encourage dialogue between mind and brain scientists so that research, hypotheses, and speculations could be tempered, constrained by, and consistent with what basic research already tells us about learning and instruction.

Cognitive models and education

Educational researchers and classroom teachers are interested in solving instructional problems that arise in teaching reading, mathematics, science, and social studies. Cognitive psychology has offered answers to these educational problems and many others (Bruer, 1994). Cognitive psychology attempts to understand the mental representations and processes that underlie expertise within learning domains. Cognitive models of expert performance allow psychologists to explain domain expertise and allow educators to identify what knowledge and which processes might be lacking in children who struggle to learn in a subject domain. Identifying specific deficits contributes to curricula and teaching materials targeted to ameliorate those deficits.

Learning first formal arithmetic provides an excellent example of how cognitive models can inform and improve learning. Why is it that some children fail to acquire mastery of first formal arithmetic in the elementary grades?

Starting in the mid-1960s, cognitive psychologists discovered that children develop strategies to solve simple arithmetic problems, like $4 + 2$, using their prior understanding of counting and comparing number for size. (For a review see Bruer, 1994, Ch. 4, pp. 81–126). For $4 + 2$, the typical 5- or 6-year-old would determine that 4 is greater than 2 and then count up two number names from 4 to find the answer: "4, . . .5, 6." The Mental Number Line (MNL, Figure 3.3) provides a cognitive model of the knowledge and processes that enable such strategy invention.

To invent such a strategy, children must know that counting requires a one-one correspondence between objects counted and ordered number names, that as one goes through the counting sequence each number name refers to a magnitude one greater than the previous number name,

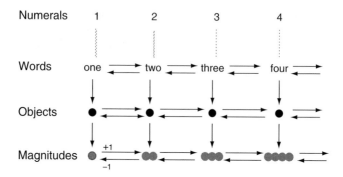

Figure 3.3 The Mental Number Line provides a cognitive model of the conceptual understanding that is required to learn first formal arithmetic. Children must know the number words, how to tag objects with number words to count correctly, understand that the number words name magnitudes that increase from left to right, and the Arabic numerals are written symbols that refer to magnitudes.

that as one goes left to right on the MNL, the magnitudes get larger, and that Arabic numerals also refer to magnitudes.

Case, Siegler, and Griffin developed a Number Knowledge test based on this cognitive model to assess which arithmetic processes and numerical understandings children acquire at specific ages. (Griffin, Case, & Siegler 1994). To norm their test, they tested various student populations in the United States and Canada. They discovered, to their surprise, that acquisition of these basic numerical skills depended not only on developmental timetables, but also on social and cultural factors. Children from low socio-economic status (SES) homes tended to acquire these abilities more slowly than children from middle-class homes. For example, at school entry a low-SES 6-year-old might perform like a middle class 4-year-old on the Number Knowledge test. The most pronounced differences in abilities occurred in making numerical magnitude comparisons and in solving simple mental arithmetic problems, like $4 + 2$. For example, middle class children entering kindergarten could solve such simple problems 72% of the time, compared to 14% for low-SES children.

The good news is that a curriculum based on the prevailing cognitive model – the Right Start curriculum – that includes explicit instruction on counting, comparing, and the associated MNL conceptual structure can redress these learning problems. After one year of Right Start instruction, children identified as at risk for failing first formal arithmetic based on the Number Knowledge test, reached levels of achievement in arithmetic indistinguishable from that found in a middle-class control group. This is but one example of why educators might best look to cognitive psychology as a basic science for an applied science of learning. Other examples can be found across the curriculum and at all grade levels (Bruer, 1994).

Cognitive neuroscience and cognitive models

In the past cognitive models have been based on behavioral studies conducted by cognitive and developmental psychologists. In the last ten years, given the impact of unified mind-brain research, other brain-based sources of evidence have been brought to bear on cognitive models. Dehaene (1992 and Chapter 14) provides a superb review of how these new sources of evidence can be integrated with behavioral evidence to enhance our understanding of numerical cognition. To cognitive psychological studies based on expert-novice and developmental research, Dehaene adds evidence from animal studies on numerosity, neurological lesion studies that provide insights about localization of representations and processes in the brain, and imaging studies that seek neural correlates for basic cognitive processes. The goal of an integrated mind-brain-education research program should be to explore how these converging sources of evidence can generate more refined cognitive models upon which we can build better instruction.

Dehaene's work on the cognitive neuroscience of numerical cognition provides an excellent example of what such a research program might contribute. The MNL model (Figure 3.3) makes an implicit assumption. It assumes that there is a single, abstract representation of magnitude and that number words and Arabic numerals refer to this magnitude representation. There was (is) debate among cognitive psychologists about whether such a common abstract magnitude representation exists. Might it not be the case that number names and Arabic numerals are associated with different internal representations of quantity?

Dehaene and colleagues used the numerical comparison task in both ERP and fMRI (Pinel *et al.*, 2001) studies to answer this question (Dehaene, 1996; Pinel *et al.*, 2001). Subjects were shown either a number word ('EIGHT') or an Arabic numeral ('8') and asked to judge whether the magnitude named by the input symbol was larger or smaller than five. They found that specific brain areas are activated in the numerical comparison task and that these areas are the same for both number words and Arabic numerals. The brain imaging and recording data are consistent with a claim that there is a common abstract representation of

The triple code model and learning problems

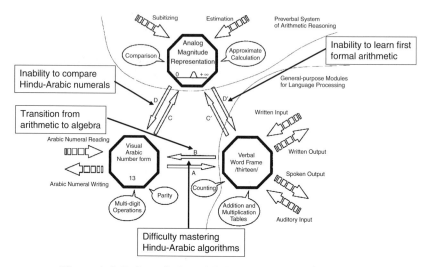

Figure 3.4 Dehaene's (1992) Triple Code model of numeral cognition showing how specific mathematics learning problems can be viewed as difficulties or failures to integrate numerical representations. Reprinted from *Cognition*, 44(1–2), Dehaene, S., "Varieties of numerical abilities," 1–42, Copyright (1992), with permission from Elsevier.

magnitudes as assumed in the MNL model. The imaging study provides converging evidence, independent of behavioral evidence, about which representations and processes should be included in an adequate cognitive model of numerical cognition.

Converging evidence like this has lent support to Dehaene's triple-code model of numerical cognition (see Figure 3.4).

The model posits that we have three distinct representations of number: a word-form representation (the number words), a visual number form representation (Arabic numerals), and a preverbal analogue magnitude representation. The model claims that we can translate between these mental codes and that specific numerical operations, or processes, are associated with one or another of the number representations. Multidigit operations and parity judgments invoke the Arabic representation. Counting and recalling addition/subtraction facts invoke the number word representation. Comparing and approximate calculation invoke the magnitude representation.

A cognitive model like this level provides a unifying structure that can help explain what would otherwise appear to be "isolated" learning problems or "general" failures to acquire number skills. It can help us see how previous cognitive research on learning within the number domain relates to the three basic numerical representations. Case and Griffin's work indicated that children can have difficulty linking number words with magnitudes. Resnick's (1982) research found that children often find it difficult to link written algorithms for Arabic numeral computations with counting procedures using number words. Nathan *et al.* (2000) revealed the instructionally counter-intuitive result that children's prior understanding of verbal numerical representations facilitates acquisition of symbolic representations. Students' prior understanding of verbally represented problems can facilitate the transition to using symbolic representations. Just such a transition is required in moving from arithmetic to algebraic problems solving. Appropriate cognitive models of numerical cognition can help think of instructional problems as failures to link children's pre-instruction representations of number to the representation that is the target of instruction.

As another example, cognitive neuroscience can contribute to more refined cognitive models of the skilled reading. The fundamental reading skill is the ability to process the print representations of words (orthography) into their spoken representations (phonology). Cognitive psychologists have proposed two fundamentally different cognitive models to explain this skill (see Figure 3.5).

The Dual Route model posits that printed words could be recognized in at least two ways. First, for familiar words the reader could convert printed strings into a visual code, where the visual code is then mapped to an entry in a mental lexicon of words familiar to the reader. Or, second, for unfamiliar printed words the reader could phonologically recode the letter string ("sound it out") and match this code to his or her knowledge of words familiar from speech that appear in the mental lexicon. In the Connectionist model there is no lexicon. Rather, when a reader looks at a letter string, units are activated in a connectionist network and this activation spreads to other units that represent phonological or semantic information that ultimately enable the reader to identify the word.

To study this skill and test their cognitive models, psychologists compare subjects' reaction times for recognizing printed words that vary in their lexicality (word vs. non-word), frequency (common vs. uncommon word), and spelling-to-sound consistency (e.g., *lint* vs. *pint*). Subjects recognize words more rapidly than non-words, common words more rapidly than uncommon words, and, when asked to read words aloud, consistent words more rapidly than inconsistent words. There is also an interaction between frequency and consistency. Subjects are considerably slower in reading low-frequency inconsistent words (e.g. *pint*) than in

Phonological processing models

Dual Route   Connectionist

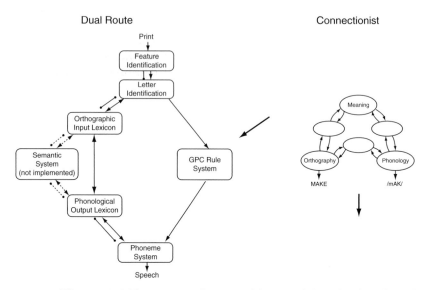

Figure 3.5 Two competing cognitive models of phonological processing underlying skilled reading. The arrows indicate the component of the model that would be correlated with the left frontal activation in Fiez *et al.* (1999). Reprinted from *Neuron*, 25, Fiez, J. A., Balota, D. A., Raichle, M. E., and Petersen, S. E., "Effects of lexicality, frequency, and spelling-to-sound consistency on the functional anatomy of reading," 205–18, Copyright (1999), with permission from Elsevier.

reading high frequency inconsistent words (e.g. *have*) and high-frequency consistent words (e.g. *gave*). Both the Dual Route and Connectionist models are consistent with these robust behavioral results (see also Goswami, Petitto, & Wolf in this volume).

Cognitive neuroscientists look for neural correlates of cognitive processes. In an imaging study Fiez *et al.* (1999) identified an area in the brain's left medial frontal region, the activation of which parallels the behavioral data. There is an interaction between word frequency and consistency and very high activation when subjects read low-frequency inconsistent words.

Does this result provide additional converging evidence in favor of one of the cognitive models? No. Both models, as well as the left medial frontal activation, are consistent with the behavioral data. On the Dual Route Model activity in the left front area is consistent with that area being involved in the processing route in which we use knowledge of letters and sounds to "sound out" pronounceable non-words. On a connectionist model (no lexicon) the area's activation is consistent with its instantiating a hidden layer in the model that computes orthographic to phonological transformation. (See arrows in Figure 3.4.)

However, the story becomes more interesting when one brings other converging imaging and neuropsychological data into the discussion. These data show that the left frontal region *is active* in phonological tasks that *do not* require orthographic to phonological transformation (e.g., maintaining items in verbal working memory). Other brain-based data show that the left frontal region *is not active* when subjects read high-frequency words, a phonological task that *does* require phonological processing. Therefore, the left frontal medial area has a more general function than the reading-specific functions the Dual Route and Connectionist models attribute to it; but, it also has a more specific function than phonological processing. Thus, Fiez *et al.* (1999) conclude that when behavioral, neuropsychological, and imaging data are fully taken into account neither model can adequately account for the data. Cognitive neuroscience suggests that we must refine our cognitive models.

How might we best do this? Franck Ramus (2001) has argued that the best strategy for model revision might be for cognitive psychologists and cognitive neuroscientists to take phonology – an established, mature behavioral science – seriously. Phonology posits a hierarchy of representations and processes at the lexical and sub-lexical levels that are required to account for how we use sound patterns to convey meaning. Cognitive psychologists and neuroscientists have only scratched the surface of what phonology can contribute to the refinement of their models of word recognition.

Following Ramus's suggestion our general neuroeducation research strategy might best be to attempt to refine our cognitive models via recursive interactions between behavioral, neuropsychological, and cognitive neuroscientific studies (see Fischer & van Geert & Steenbeek, this volume). Such a program could eventually have educational implications. We believe, for example, that phonological deficits cause dyslexia. But, which specific phonological deficits are the causes?

Conclusion

I have tried to present some guidelines or principles for an integrated mind-brain- education research program. In my first article on this topic, I introduced the bridge-building metaphor. That metaphor also applies here. We must build a better bridge between developmental neurobiology and the learning sciences. This will require discussion of the extent to which the visual system provides a model for learning and neural plasticity across the life span. We should be aware of the bridge, too infrequently traveled, that currently exists between cognitive psychology and education. Finally, we should understand how cognitive neuroscience can assist in building bridges between mind and brain science and contribute to the refinement of cognitive models. This must be an interactive, recursive interaction between behavioral, cognitive, and neurobiological scientists. Remember, we are building bridges, not looking for foundations.

References

Bachevalier, J. and Mishkin, M. (1984). An early and a late developing system for learning and retention in infant monkeys. *Behavioral Neuroscience*, 98(5), 770–778.

Bailey, D. B., Bruer, J. T., Symons, F. J., and Lichtman, J. W. (2001). *Critical Thinking about Critical Periods*. Baltimore: Paul H. Brookes Publishing Co.

Bruer, J. T. (1994). *Schools for Thought: A Science of Learning in the Classroom*. Cambridge, MA: MIT Press.

(1997). Education and the Brain: A Bridge Too Far. *Educational Researcher*, 26(8), 1–13.

(1999). *The Myth of the First Three Years: A New Understanding of Early Brain Development and Life Long Learning*. New York: The Free Press.

(2002). Avoiding the pediatrician's error: how neuroscientists can help educators (and themselves). *Nature Neuroscience*, Nov. 5, Suppl., 1031–1033.

Chugani, H. T., Phelps, M. E., and Mazziota, J. C. (1987). Positron emission tomography study of human brain function development. *Annals of Neurology*, 22, 487–497.

Chugani, H. (1998). A critical period of brain development: studies of cerebral glucose utilization with PET. *Preventive Medicine* 27, 184–188.

Cynader, M. (2000). Perspectives: neuroscience. Strengthening visual connections. *Science*, 287(5460), 1943–1944.

Dehaene, S. (1992). Varieties of numerical abilities. *Cognition*, 44(1–2), 1–42.

(1996). The organization of brain activations in number comparison: event related potentials and the additive-factors method. *Journal of Cognitive Neuroscience*, 8, 47–68.

Fiez, J. A., Balota, D. A., Raichle, M. E., and Petersen, S. E. (1999). Effects of lexicality, frequency, and spelling-to-consistency on the functional anatomy of reading. *Neuron*, 25, 205–218.

Giedd, J. N., Blumenthal, J., Jeffries, N. O., Castellanos, F. X., Liu, H., Zijdenbos, A., Paus, T., Evans, A. C., and Rapoport, J. L. (1999). Brain development during childhood and adolescence: a longitudinal MRI study. *Nature Neuroscience*, 2(10), 861–863.

Greenough, W., Black, J. and Wallace, C. (1987). Experience and brain development. *Child Development*, 58(3), 539–559.

Griffin, S. A., Case, R., and Siegler, R. S. (1994). Rightstart: Providing the central conceptual prerequisites for first formal learning of arithmetic to students at risk for school failure, In K. McGilly (ed.). *Classroom Lessons*, (pp. 25–50). Cambridge, MA: MIT Press.

Huttenlocher, P. R. (1979). Synaptic density in human frontal cortex – developmental changes of ageing. *Brain Research*, 163, 195–209.

  (2003). Basic neuroscience research has important implications for child developmen. *Nature Neuroscience*, 6(6), 541.

Kandell, E. and Schwartz, J. (1991). *Principles of Neural Science*. New York: Elsevier.

Lund, J. S., Boothe, R. G., and Lund, R. D. (1977). Development of neurons in the visual cortex (area 17) of the monkey (Macaca nemestrina): A Golgi study from fetal day 127 to postnatal maturity. *Journal of Comparative Neurology*, 176, 149–188.

Means, M. and Voss, J. (1985). Star Wars: A developmental study of expert and novice knowledge structure. *Journal of Memory and Language*, 24, 746–757.

Nathan, M. J. and Koedinger, K. R. (2000). Teachers' and researchers' beliefs about the development of algebraic reasoning. *Journal of Research on Mathematics Education*, 31(2), 168–190.

NIH Publication No. 01-4929 NIMH Press release Child and adolescent mental health information at www.nimh.nih.gov/publicat/childmenu.cfm.

Overman, W. H., Bachevalier J., Schuhmann, E., and Ryan, P. (1996a). Cognitive gender differences in very young children parallel biologically based cognitive differences in monkeys. *Behavioral Neuroscience*, 110(4), 673–684.

Overman, W. H., Bachevalier, J., Miller, M., and Moore, K. (1996b). Children's performance on "animal tests" of oddity: Implications for cognitive processes required for tests of oddity and delayed nonmatch to sample. *Journal of Experimental Child Psychology*, 62(2), 223–242.

Overman, W. H., Pate, B. J., Moore, K., and Peuster, A. (1996c). Ontogeny of place learning in children measured in the radial arm maze, Morris search task, and open field task. *Behavioral Neuroscience*, 110(6), 1205–1228.

Overman, W. H. (1990). Performance on traditional matching to sample, non-matching to sample, and object discrimination tasks by 12- to 32-month-old children. A developmental progression. *Annals of the New York Academy of Science*, 608, 365–385.

Pinel, P., Dehaene, S., Riviere, D., and LeBihan, D. (2001). Modulations of parietal activation by semantic distance in a number comparison task. *Neuroimage*, 14(5), 1013–1026.

Pressley, M. and McCormick, C. B. (1995). *Advanced Educational Psychology for Educators, Researchers, and Policymakers*. New York: Harper Collins College Publishers.

Rakic, P., Bourgeois, J. P., Eckenhoff, M. F., Zecevic, N., and Goldman-Rakic, P. S. (1986). Concurrent overproduction of synapses in diverse regions of the primate cerebral cortex. *Science*, 232(4747), 232–235.

Ramus, F. (2001). Outstanding questions about phonological processing in dyslexia. *Dyslexia*, 7(4), 197–216.

Resnick, L.B. (1982). Syntax and semantics in learning to subtract. In T.P. Carpenter, J.M. Moser, and T.A. Romberg (eds). *Addition and Subtraction: A Cognitive Perspective*. Hillsdale, NJ: Erlbaum.

4   Mind, brain, and consciousness

Jürgen Mittelstrass

Overview

One concern of philosophers is linking philosophical thought with scientific research and theory. Philosophy and psychology have common historical roots, and several important concepts such as consciousness have been approached from various points of views from both disciplines. Biology, especially neuroscience, is making its own path of discovery in the same realm from a different perspective. Mittelstrass argues that many reductionistic explanations in psychology have failed, such as behaviorism. Will cognitive neuroscience show similar limits? In any case contemporary philosophers mostly support a dualistic approach to the mind-brain question, while scientists typically prefer a monistic view. There are, of course, different shadings and textures in these options, but the wide use of brain imaging often leads to an assumption that psychic states are simply neurophysiological states described by local brain metabolism. One extreme position is what Vidal in his chapter calls "brainhood," the assumption that a person is entirely defined by his or her brain. A fruitful alternative may be a pragmatic dualism that values science's theoretical concepts while maintaining a dualist view.

The Editors

The relations between mind and body, brain and consciousness today lie at the centre not only of scientific, but also of philosophical interest. They were there once already, namely at the beginnings of modern thought, where we may find them within the so-called "remainder problems" of Cartesian dualism, in the guise of the problem of the relation between mind and body – *res cogitans* and *res extensa*, in Cartesian terminology. But this represented in a sense the birth pangs of a new kind of thought. Today, we look back on this beginning and try to understand it as a fundamentally new orientation in philosophy. But we also look forward to the future, in which we see these questions, in a still more pronounced manner than we find in early modern thought, as determining the common future of science and philosophy. This is true most of all of the mind-body problem. Here lies a good part of the scientific future of modern brain science, and here lies as well, it would seem, an essential component of the future of philosophical thought.

In the following, I will attempt to describe this common future somewhat more precisely. I will follow the lead of some thoughts that I developed together with Martin Carrier, and which I have labelled as "pragmatic dualism" (Carrier & Mittelstrass, 1991; see also Mittelstrass, 1998). This concept refers to the attempt to mediate in a constructive manner between the overwhelmingly dualist research programme of philosophy, and the overwhelmingly monistic research programme of natural science (which includes scientifically oriented psychology). This attempt has four parts, and I begin with a short recollection of the career of the mind-body problem. The latter begins in Greek thought as what we might term the soul-body problem.

The career of the mind-body problem

After having ascribed material properties to the soul, following the animist tradition – the soul as the breath of life, which leaves the body on death – Plato distinguishes among three parts of the soul, emphasising its immateriality, its prior existence and its immortality. These are: the thinking or rational soul, the passionate or brave soul, and the desiring soul. This tripartite division is motivated by the trichotomy of the civic estates (rulers, guardians, workers), whose ranking is supposed to gain biological validation through its correspondence to the three parts of the soul. Plato distinguishes furthermore between the soul (or life) as the principle of self-motion and matter as that which is, in some cases, "ensouled" through this motive principle. The case is different with Aristotle. He distinguishes between a vegetal soul, that is to say the capacities for material assimilation and reproduction, an animal soul, which comprises in addition the faculties of sense-perception, of desire and of locomotion, and a rational soul, which is the "bearer" of theoretical and practical reason, and which is divided once again into passive and active parts. According to Aristotle, the soul is the "first entelechy or actuality of an organic body," which moves the latter, and expires with it.

Medieval philosophy departs from both the Platonic and the Aristotelian characterizations, although in the philosophical tradition of Augustine, the real distinction of the parts of the soul is emphasized, whereas Thomas Aquinas and the Thomistic tradition insists on the unity of the human soul. Here again, albeit in a Christian context, the immortality of the soul plays a determining role. On the one hand, the idea of a super-individual and immortal soul, which is distinct of the mortal individual soul, is introduced, and on the other the claim is advanced that the soul is identical with the individual soul, and thus, because the latter is the actuality of a material body, that it also dies with the body. The beginning of modern thought leads to conceptions of the soul which make so-called rational psychology a part of philosophy.

The modern career of the mind-body problem begins in the seventeenth century with Descartes's dualism, in which the originally Aristotelian and medieval conception of a unity of body and soul is resolved in twin worlds of matter and of thought: "There are certain acts that we call *corporeal*, such as size, shape, motion (...), and we use the term *body* to refer to the substance in which they inhere. (...) There are other acts which we call *acts* of thought, such as understanding, willing, imagining, having sensory perceptions, and so on: they all fall under the common concept of thought or perception or consciousness, and we call the substance in which they inhere a *thinking thing* or a *mind*" (Descartes, 1964–1974, VII, p. 176). This conception lies at the foundation of all subsequent theories of mind and body, above all that of *consciousness*. I will concentrate on this notion here, in order to stick to my own, philosophical trade, and to avoid digging in the garden of others, namely of medicine and biology. When philosophers speak of the mind-body problem, they generally do it in the sense of Plato's thinking part of the soul, in other words they are thinking about consciousness.

As I mentioned earlier, the mind-body problem is often referred to in philosophy as a "remainder problem," because it arose from Descartes's two-substance metaphysics. This dualist metaphysics makes the question of how mind and body, thus matter and consciousness, may interact with one another into a great mystery – one which inevitably attracts philosophers. The first philosophical "solutions" of this problem – one of which was already offered by Descartes in the light of substantial contemporary criticism – are dualist in nature. That is to say, they argue for the assumption of distinct and autonomous realms, in other words a duality of mind and body, matter and consciousness (from a strict systematic point of view one would have to distinguish, within the historical context, between a soul-body problem, a mind-body or consciousness-body problem, and a matter-life problem). Descartes himself is deeply indecisive. On the one hand, he advocates an interactionist theory, which allows for organic communication between the two substances through the pineal gland (Descartes, 1964–1974, XI, p. 180); however, he also contents himself, in the light of the systematic incoherence of such an assumption, with a reference to everyday experiences (for the Cartesian attempts at a solution to the mind-body problem and the subsequent efforts in this direction within Cartesianism, as well as those of Leibniz and Kant, see Carrier & Mittelstrass, 1991, pp. 16–27).

Within the Cartesian tradition, this indecision takes the form of two alternative "solutions": so-called *influx-theories*, which assume a physical interaction between both substances, and so-called *occasionalism*, which resolves the paradox of a physical connection between physical and non-physical realms by appealing to "occasional" divine interventions, or (in order to discharge God) by means of a continuous correspondence between both substances caused by God. The latter solution is related to Leibniz's assumption of a *pre-established harmony* between mind and body (which incidentally saves the soul of philosophy from all-too-simple solutions), and to Spinoza's interpretation of both substances as attributes of a single divine one. At the same time, such attempts lie at the foundation of the later conception of *psychophysical parallelism*, which is later employed to solve the problem of the empirical correspondence between objective-physical stimuli and subjective-psychical sensations by, for instance, Gustav Fechner, Max Wundt, and Ernst Mach.

No wonder that such "solutions" gave rise in turn to *monistic* conceptions. Among the latter we may number both idealistic reductionism, such as the immaterialism proposed by the British idealist George Berkeley, as well as physical and materialist reductionism in both classical and modern forms. Examples of such physicalistic and materialistic reductions are, respectively, behaviourism, which sees the basis of all mental phenomena in human behaviour, and the so-called *identity-theory*, which claims that mental and physiological events are identical with one another. Every attempt to view mental events as controlled "from outside," that is to say as being detached from a basis in a neurological substance is seen from this point of view as a regression to philosophical naivety. This is true as well of so-called *epiphenomenalism*, at least to the extent that the latter views psychic states and processes as "side-effects" of physical or physiological states and processes, which on their own form a closed system free from psychic interventions.

Such monistic alternatives to dualist theories are sometimes supplemented by new information-theoretical approaches, in which psychic and mental processes are regarded as complex data-transformations, and mind and body, matter and consciousness are understood as distinct information structures. These approaches are equally well monistic and physico-materialistic in their structure. The brain is regarded as a computer. But here, just as in the monistic accounts just mentioned, it is quite clear how what were originally purely philosophical concerns are linked with research in neurophysiology and neuropsychology by way of the empirical connection between physical and psychical states and processes. The future of philosophy would seem to be bound up with that of science in the case of the mind-body problem as well, that is to say in the scientific analysis of philosophy's intuitions. But this is not an uncontroversial thesis, as modern versions of dualism make clear.

The self and its brain

Reductive programs of all flavors, scientific ones as well, run the risk of throwing the baby out with the bath-water. In this case, the problem is that in eliminating dualistic contradictions, we may give up on a reflective and non-speculative mind-body problem, and with it the concept of consciousness. A modern attempt to forestall this result is the reduction-critical, interactive dualism of Popper and Eccles (1977) whose central components are an anti-reductionism thesis and a realism-thesis (for systematic details see Carrier & Mittelstrass, 1991, pp. 114–125).

The *anti-reductionist thesis*, i.e., the assertion that different domains of reality such as physics, chemistry, ecology/sociology cannot be reduced to one another, is supposed to gain support from an argument by analogy from the history of science – historically, there have never been successful reductions, for what seems to be a reduction is essentially a correction – and by appeal to a evolutionary "creativity argument" – higher levels of organization lead to appearances which cannot be deduced from the processes on the lower levels. But these explanations do not, when examined carefully, represent a tenable position. The same is true of the *realism-thesis*, that is to say for the claim that there are three worlds – the "first" world of physical bodies, the "second" world of mental states, and the "third" world of "objective thoughts" (which already makes its appearance in the work of the logician and mathematician, Gottlob Frege (1966)) – and that each of these worlds is, furthermore, real on its own. The characterization of these worlds as "real" includes the claim that these worlds can influence each other causally in one and the same sense. This would have to hold as well of the relation of World 3, the world of theories, to World 2, the world of our thoughts, for a "reduction" of theories to thought cannot transpire according to this conception.

This philosophically problematic situation leads Popper and Eccles not only to advocate the dualistic independence of psychological and physical states or events and processes against the monistic point of view, but also to argue for the autonomy and identity of the self (or consciousness) as opposed to its representations – a position pointedly expressed in the phrase "the self and its brain." Moreover, according to this view, the brain belongs to the self, not the self to the brain. The self is the programmer of the computer "brain" – the pilot, not the piloted. Eccles, who views the self-conscious I, the self-conscious mind as being anchored in World 2, translates this idea into a neurobiological language. According to his hypothesis, the self controls and interprets the neuronal processes; it actively seeks brain events which lie in its domain of interest and integrates them into a unified and conscious experience. It constantly scans collective interactions of large numbers of neurons ("cortical modules"), which are open to an interaction with World 2 ("liaison brain"). The unity of conscious experience, on Eccles' central thesis, is mediated by a self-conscious mind, and not by neural machinery.

But how exactly are we to make sense of this in detail – that is to say how the supposed interaction of the self-conscious I or the self-conscious mind and its brain actually occurs –, this is left just as open as it was by Descartes. As a research program, this dualism scarcely goes beyond that advanced in the classical positions, despite the neurobiological language in which it is couched. It may be a more sympathetic program than its reductionist opponents; however, it remains to be shown that it is superior to them on their own territory, namely the explanation of neurobiological states and processes.

Identity and pragmatic dualism

In opposition to the dualistic picture, say that of Popper and Eccles, is the monistic picture on which neurophysiological and psychic states and processes are *identical*. But this position is also unsatisfying, for it cannot be supported by physical laws. The task of a monistic reduction is not completed simply because one has shown that there is a one-to-one correlation between psychic states and processes on the one hand and certain neurophysiological states and processes on the other. But monistic theories tend to rest on just such correlations, as is the case with the identity theory, that is to say the thesis that psychic states and processes are, in the final analysis, identical with physical ones. One argues that a psychic state or process a occurs if and only if the physical state or process a' is observable. Thus certain sensations are correlated with a change in the metabolic activity (observed by means of magnetic resonance imaging) in a certain region of the brain. But there is no further argument given in favour of their *identity*. The situation is much rather like that we find in the case of well-calibrated measurement instruments. Here as well there is a correlation between a state of the measurement apparatus with a state external to it. Thus the signal received by an MRI device indicates the presence of protons, but it is not identical with the latter. Similarly, the path in a cloud chamber signals the motion of a particle, but it is not identical with the latter. Only a lack of knowledge would lead us in such cases to (falsely) identify one member of each pair with the other. Furthermore, the criterion of translatability between the terminology of one theory into the terminology of another does not suffice to secure identity, for there must be in addition a translation between the corresponding laws. Thus the suggestion that psychic states and processes have been reduced to neurophysiological states and processes remains an unfulfilled promise.

Now, a proponent of identity-theoretical monism could agree to all this, and nonetheless remain a monist in the sense of being committed to the project of a reduction *program* – a program which would have, from the point of view of the sciences, the advantage of being completable without the use of philosophy. But, first, this may not be an advantage, and, second, we are still uncertain about what would constitute rigorous criteria for a promising reductive program. Reference to other reductive successes in other fields doesn't help us further. It is, to borrow Wittgenstein's expression, much like in philosophy: "A main cause of philosophical disease – a one-sided diet: one nourishes one's thinking with only one kind of examples" (Wittgenstein, 1953, § 593). That is to say, one refers to successful instances of reduction in physics, and one overlooks the failed ones in psychology itself. The fate of the behaviorist reduction program ought to give us pause. There is no obvious reason why the analogous neurophysiological reduction program ought to be more successful.

It may at this point help to interpret cognitive concepts, that is, those concepts we use to talk about human behavior in non-reductive terms, as *theoretical concepts*. Theoretical concepts are such as cannot be translated into the language of a theory-independent observation language, in other words concepts whose meaning depends on the theory as a whole, and on the condition of its empirical adequacy. This does not mean that in the particular case one lacks appropriate criteria for applying the concept. Thus in the case of psychology as well, one has to decide about the application of particular theoretical concepts in a given situation on the basis of certain behavioral indicators, without this entailing that their meaning is exhausted by the sum of these indicators. By introducing the notion of theoretical concepts into our discussion, I wish to draw attention to the fact that it is a property of fruitful scientific concepts that they have "excess meaning," in other words that their meaning extends beyond their operational content. They are open concepts, whose criteria of application may change in the course of scientific development. It would appear on the contrary that the monistic reduction program pursued by identity theorists restricts psychological concepts to a range of neurophysiological indicators. And this is, from the point of view of the philosophy of science, the position advocated in the 1920s. Why should the philosophy of biology repeat the mistakes of the philosophy of physics?

This is of course a form of argument deriving from the philosophy of science, and not a biological or neurophysiological argument. The ontological question concerning the identity of consciousness or mind with neurophysiological states and processes is transformed into a science-theoretical question, namely the question of whether or not independent psychological concepts are in principle fruitful, or whether they are to be avoided. Martin Carrier and I argued in favor of their fruitfulness, and thereby for a *pragmatic dualism*. In doing so, no grounds for a factual distinction between physical and psychic states and processes were advanced, but only grounds for the claim that it is better not to deny such a distinction from the outset. Put positively: independent psychological (cognitive) concepts can be defended on the grounds of their *explanatory value*. Whether or not these concepts have an ontological reference is a basic question in the philosophy of science concerning the reference of theoretical terms – a question which is the subject of active debate. But that means that it cannot be assumed to be settled in advance in the one, neurobiological domain.

From this point of view, the reductionist critique of dualism, according to which the mind plays the dubious role of the *deus ex machina*, is methodologically premature – all the more so when it is claimed, by both the reductionist and monistic sides, that our picture of the world is always a construction (Pöppel, 1985, pp. 66f.). For what is true of this picture must also be true of our biological knowledge of the processes of consciousness. To put it differently: If everything that we normally know about the world is at least partially a construction of the brain, then what biology knows about the brain is also unable to exist without being touched by such constructions.

This point of view is indeed shared by some neurobiological researchers, although they themselves are pursuing an essentially *reductionist* program, namely that of explaining high-level brain capacities such as sensation, intentional behavior and consciousness on the basis of a (reductionist) formulation of the laws and the interactive dynamics of distinct components of the brain. Thus the neurobiologist Otto Creutzfeld (1981) talks of the capacity of the human brain for symbolic representation, thereby emphasizing that the symbols are neither a product of the nervous system, nor are they the nervous system, nor are they the world itself. Creutzfeld himself draws a dualist conclusion, pointedly expressed in the remark that "dualism – i.e. standing opposite oneself – is the nature of consciousness" (Creutzfeld, 1981, p. 42). Clearly this is not a neurophysiological statement – it is rather a *philosophical* one. With regard to what has been said about a pragmatic dualism, it need not therefore be a meaningless or superfluous one. This is also true, though with some restrictions, of the following statements: The symbols, i.e., "the brain's symbolic representation of reality, not only refer to the world but rather independently form their own world, to which our brain in turn constantly refers: the world of the mind" (Creutzfeld, 1981, p. 42). Or: "No reductionist theory does justice to this essence of consciousness. They all grasp only one side, namely, the brain mechanisms, but not the other, the world of symbols, with which these mechanisms, and through them the brain, confront themselves, and which are as real as the natural world" (Creutzfeld, 1981, p. 43).

"The world of the mind," "the unity of consciousness" – these formulas breathe the spirit of classical philosophy, not that of the relatively sober, modern philosophy of science. Nevertheless, they are also compatible with the dualism I advocate here, with respect to the emphasis on the *constructive* character of our orientations, including scientific orientations, and the rejection of the reductionist thesis of an identity of brain mechanisms and consciousness. What is really crucial in all of this is not that pure mind is once again set above biology, but rather that the practice of biology is seen in its theoretical research programs from the perspective of methodological clarification. Whether the "unity of consciousness" or the asserted "reality" of the symbolic world has to be a part of this, is a question of secondary importance.

Consciousness and self-understanding

My discussion so far may well have given the impression that the task of philosophy in matters concerning consciousness and the mind-body problem is completed when such science-theoretical issues have been clarified, and thus that claims such as those made by Popper, Eccles, and Creutzfeld are illegitimate excursions beyond these bounds. And this may well hold in the case of Popper's and Eccles' interactionist dualism. But that does not mean that philosophy's business is restricted to the domain of the philosophy of science. Consciousness is, from the philosophical point of view, not merely a scientific concept, indeed considered historically this sense of the term is rare. Philosophy is therefore not restricted to analyzing that sense of "consciousness" which science seeks to explain. In the words of Creutzfeld, no one would "deny that our experiences and reactions are based on the ability of the nervous system to pick up certain physical stimuli, to code them as sequences of action potentials and to transform this information into appropriate sequences of the motoric systems, which gives a sufficient explanation to reductionism" (Creutzfeld, 1981, p. 33). But that is not, from the point of view of philosophy, what consciousness is in the first place.

Philosophers should not hope to solve problems that science can solve better – in other words those problems which are defined scientifically, and not as philosophical problems. Their task is to produce clarity in all domains of our self-understanding, and understanding of our situation including our scientific understanding. They undertake the latter task when they do philosophy of science. What is peculiar to philosophy here is that it accomplishes this task by *thinking*, not by *research*. This does not mean, of course, that research does not involve thinking, but that philosophical reflection is not research in the same way that science – in the light of theories and empirical methods – involves research. "Consciousness," "self-consciousness," "ego," but also "self-understanding" are titles of this specifically philosophical way of orienting oneself in thought and through thought. And this orientation is not a cultural luxury that a rational society performs alongside its everyday life of work and the formation of scientific knowledge; nor can it be performed by science itself. Pointedly formulated, Socrates' question about man's proper understanding of himself and his situation is not answered, or even rendered more easily answered, by increasing our scientific knowledge of the brain. This would, again, only mean that we believed (scientistically) that we would understand everything if we understood ourselves from a neurophysiological perspective. In this sense, the dualism advocated here is not only a dualism in *theoretical* intent, but also in *practical* intent.

Of course, this should not be taken as an invitation to all philosophers to continue gaily with talk about mind, consciousness, etc., as if neurophysiology and scientific psychology had never been invented. Scientific knowledge helps one to avoid the naivity with which philosophical opinions tend to put themselves in the place of scientific research. It is also important to remind oneself of the results within the philosophy of language concerning the mind-body problem, for instance of Wittgenstein's criticisms of the philosophical confusion between statements employing mental concepts with statements concerning the reality of a psychic world.

Unfortunately, this declaration of the mind-body problem as a pseudo-problem (for instance by Wittgenstein) is not conclusive. Were it so, we would have only the choice between uncommitted opinions or strict science. But the latter describe a life-world in which the subject can scarcely recognize himself: "The world presents itself to the brain by way of the sense organs. Already here, its unity is divided into a multiplicity of phenomenal forms, in so far as every sense-organ responds only to a limited spectrum of energy: the eye to the limited wavelength sector of 'visible' light, the ear to the narrow area of mechanical vibrations, the sense of touch to long-wave heat radiation and to lower frequency mechanical vibrations, and the senses of smell and taste to a narrowly restricted area of concentrations of certain molecules. The world, as it presents itself to us is thus limited to a narrow sector of physical and chemical phenomena. This is our life-world" (Creutzfeld, 1981, p. 34).

Is that really what our life-world is like? What I said earlier concerning pragmatic dualism and constructions of reality indicates otherwise. Furthermore, we are living beings who construct not only the world in which they live, but who also construct themselves, in that they live in and with their own self-understanding. To construct scientific knowledge of oneself, and to construct one's own self-understanding are two quite different things. And the latter construction is part of what we mean when we talk about consciousness. To this extent we can agree with Popper when he says: "How do we achieve knowledge of ourselves? Not by means of self-observation (. . .), but rather by becoming an "I," and by developing theories about oneself" (Pooper & Eccles, 1977, p. 45). Even the statement that the "I" does not belong to the brain, but rather the brain belongs to the "I" is validated when one regards it from a practical, life-world perspective, and not from that of the science-theoretical one. One has only to think of the case of someone going to his desk and telling himself to *think* (for instance because a lecture concerning the mind-body problem or the problem of consciousness must be completed). Does scientific knowledge change the problematic of this situation in any way? Certainly not. We know fairly well what we mean when we describe ourselves as masters in our own home, to which our brain belongs. "Scientific" explanations, such as those sought by dualism and monism are superfluous here.

This ought not lead to the consequence that the philosophical and scientific cultures settle on distant islands, least of all when we are concerned with questions for which each of them has an answer – but for which it turns out that each is answering a different question. Creutzfeld, who has been cited a number of times here, concludes his discussion by observing that "The neurophysiologist's answer is the beginning of the philosopher's questioning" (Creutzfeld, 1981, p. 43). This is certainly true, at least in this case – for many philosophers pretend to scientific knowledge that they do not in fact have. But it is also true that the answer to the philosopher's question should be informed by science. Otherwise, what philosophy is so often (and, unfortunately, rightly) accused of would hold: that it seeks to escape reality in speculation, instead of grasping it in thought.

References

Carrier, M. and Mittelstrass, J. (1991). *Mind, Brain, Behavior: The Mind-Body Problem and the Philosophy of Psychology*, Berlin and New York: de Gruyter.

Creutzfeld, O. (1981). Bewusstsein und Selbstbewusstsein als neurophysiologisches Problem der Philosophie, in: *Reproduktion des Menschen: Beiträge zu einer interdisziplinären Anthropologie*, Frankfurt and Berlin and Vienna (*Schriften der Carl-Friedrich-von-Siemens-Stiftung* 5), pp. 29–54.

Descartes, R. (1964–1974). *Oeuvres*, I–XII, ed. C. Adam and P. Tannery, Paris: Vrin, 1897–1910, new edn., I–XI, 1964–1974.

Frege, G. (1966). Der Gedanke: Eine logische Untersuchung (1918/1919), in: G. Frege, *Logische Untersuchungen*, ed. G. Patzig, Göttingen: Vandenhoeck & Ruprecht, pp. 30–53.

Mittelstrass, J. (1998). Das philosophische Kreuz mit dem Bewusstsein, in: M. Stamm (ed.), *Philosophie in synthetischer Absicht – Synthesis in Mind*, Stuttgart: Klett-Cotta, pp. 21–35.

Pöppel, E. (1985). *Grenzen des Bewusstseins: Über Wirklichkeit und Welterfahrung*, Stuttgart: Deutsche Verlagsanstalt.

Popper, K. R. and Eccles, J. C. (1977). *The Self and Its Brain: An Argument for Interactionism*, Heidelberg: Springer Verlag.

Wittgenstein, L. (1953). *Philosophical Investigations*, New York: Macmillan.

5 Understanding mind, brain, and education as a complex, dynamic developing system: Measurement, modeling, and research

Paul van Geert and Henderien Steenbeek

Overview

Human development and education can benefit from a framework that analyzes behavior and brain change as involving dynamic systems processes. Dynamic systems researchers build specific models focusing on processes of change in learning and teaching, beginning with individual growth patterns and including in mathematical models multiple layers and scales of casual interaction. These models shift the focus of research and assessment to individual behavior, fluctuations in time, and the combination of gradual change with periodic abrupt changes in performance and brain patterns. Dynamic systems models explain and predict important properties of learning and teaching such as non-linear change and self-organization (spontaneous increase of order and information). They readily combine apparently opposite processes in the same theory and model, such as gene versus environment or individual versus context/ culture, a characteristic called superposition. Measurements should involve the kind of assessment that teachers and schools do every day in the classroom – repeated measures of individual behavior. The models then provide ways of analyzing common educational phenomena, such as variability in performance, ambiguity of behavior, and context specificity. A dynamic approach promises to provide useful tools for understanding the complex individual changes that occur during education and child development.

The Editors

Human development constitutes a complex system. Rocha (1999) defines a complex system as "... any system featuring a large number of interacting components (agents, processes, etc.) ... whose aggregate activity is non-linear (not derivable from the summations of the activity of individual components) ... and typically exhibits ... self-organization ...". In this definition, complexity not only relates to quantitative aspects (large number of components) but also to specific qualitative aspects (non-linearity and self-organization). Our scientific endeavors are directed towards understanding this complexity, which inevitably, implies the reduction of complexity to something that is simple enough for our human minds to understand. Complex systems cannot be understood without taking the complexity into account, which means that, however much we simplify, the core qualitative features of the complex system must be preserved. These qualitative features are central to our understanding of the system.

The standard practice of simplifying the complexity of developmental and growth phenomena is to linearize the phenomena. One standard research method is to take a time span that is short enough to allow for unidirectional and linear causality. For instance, we perform an intervention and then study its immediate aftereffects, in the form of change in some variable of interest. Another method is to measure independent variables over independent subjects, e.g. in cross-sectional research. The subjects are considered representative of an underlying category, e.g. the category "five-year-olds" or "ADHD children." In this design, all variation that does not co-vary with our independent variables must be considered as noise.

By applying this linearization to the developmental phenomena we are able to simplify their complexity and obtain a considerable insight into a great number of relationships that hold in the complex system.

The crucial question is, however, *whether this form of simplification has preserved the core features of the complex and dynamic developmental system?* If it has not, how can we simplify and study the phenomenon in such a way that our approach remains faithful to these core features? In order to answer these questions we will begin by presenting a short but by no means exhaustive description of what we consider characteristic or core features of complex dynamic systems. We will then proceed by discussing, first, how these core features or characteristics of complexity affect general aspects of measurement of psychological variables in development and, second, how they affect theory- and model-building and the empirical testing of hypotheses. The discussion of these issues in separate sections is merely a matter of convenience, given that they are intricately linked. The answer to our crucial question will be that, in general, the standard practice of developmental research does not preserve the core features of complexity. However, we intend to show that – and how – it is possible to reconcile our familiar approach to studying development with those features of development that pertain to its dynamic and complex nature.

Characteristic or core features of complex systems

Non-linearity and self-organization

Non-linearity means that effects of variables or forces are not describable as the sum of functions of the causal variables. Self-organization implies that in complex systems, macroscopic order (structure, information, . . .) increases spontaneously, as a consequence of low-order energy consumption. Self-organization is intimately related to non-linearity, in that self-organization is itself a non-linear effect of the underlying causes (e.g. it may arise suddenly, with no apparent change in the underlying causal factors).

Self-organization is the opposite of transmission. For instance, if we conceive of teaching as a form of knowledge transmission, we imply that a structure (the knowledge) present in one location (the teacher) is brought over to another location (the student). Transmission is always subject to natural loss of information (increase of entropy, the second law of thermodynamics). The spontaneous loss of order or information in transmission systems requires that the transmitted information must be over-determined (repeated several times, for instance). Through such over-determination or repetition, the loss of information due to transmission may be repaired. If over-determination is not possible (which is the case in the Chomskyan model of language acquisition) the order, structure or information must be put into the system in advance, for instance in the form of innate modules.

Self-organization on the other hand, implies that certain systems, namely systems that are already highly ordered and structured (for instance a system consisting of students and a teacher, or a language learner in a normal environment), exhibit spontaneous increase of order, structure or information. Thus, in a self-organizing system, transmission of information (as in a teaching process) may lead to the construction of structures that are more complex and more complete than the transmitted information itself (e.g. the learning effect in some of the students exceeds the content of the teaching). Self-organization has now been demonstrated in a large range of developmental phenomena (see for instance Roubertoux & Carlier, 2002; Gottlieb, Wahlsten & Lickliter, 1998; Ford & Lerner, 1992).

An important question concerns the empirical indicators of self-organization. The first indicator is the presence of increase of order or structure that goes beyond the order and structure present in the "input." Increase of order and structure is the hallmark of development, but it is not easy to show that such order exceeds the order of the "input" (the teaching and learning environment). Note that in the Chomskyan approach to language development, the "poverty of the stimulus" argument potentially provides strong support to the idea that language acquisition must in fact be a process of self-organization. Unfortunately, because in the Chomskyan approach, self-organization was no feasible option, the "poverty of the stimulus" argument has been used to show that the structure of language must be innate. Finally, additional empirical indicators of self-organization are the occurrence of discontinuities in development, stages, temporary regressions, inverse U-shaped growth and so forth.

Superposition

Superposition, the second feature of complexity, means that a phenomenon is characterized by two (apparently) incompatible properties at the same time. The notion of superposition is used, in a formally defined sense, in quantum physics, where it relates to a particular kind of uncertainty, e.g. about the position or energy of a particle. In the context of the complex mind-brain-and-education system, a non-formal version of superposition exists. It often occurs in the context of questions such as "does the brain explain the mind," "is development explained by genes or by the environment, or in part by both," "is learning a matter of transmission or self-organization," "is knowledge a substance (a physical structure in the brain) or is it a process," "should people be (clinically) distinguished on the basis of categories (e.g. as in the psychiatric diagnostic manual) or on the basis of dimensions," and so forth.

These questions can be (relatively) easily answered by linearizing them, for instance by studying the association betweens genes and behavior in a large sample of independent subjects, to name just one issue. However, these solutions also easily lead to (apparent) paradoxes. For instance, if one compares differences in average intelligence between generations (e.g. the 1900 and the 1950 cohort), the differences are for the greatest part explained by (historical) environmental changes (see for instance the average increase in IQ over generations known as the Flynn effect). However, if one compares differences in intelligence between persons from the same generation, living in an environment that offers easily accessible opportunities for everybody, the differences are for the greatest part explained by genes. Thus, it is possible that for a particular person born in 1950, intelligence is at the same time (almost) completely determined by the environment and (almost) completely determined by genes. The paradoxical nature of this conclusion dwindles as soon as we realize that genes and environment are locked in a complex chain of steps over time and that they cannot be conceived of as variables that make mutually independent contributions to development.

To some extent, the empirical indicators of superposition are indirect. For instance, if certain issues, such as the gene-environment issue, remain over many years of scientific discussion and if the positions swing to and fro, it is likely that the issue entails a superposition that is not captured by the simplifications made in the solutions presented. On a much smaller scale of inquiry, if observers of behavior continue to disagree over certain categorizations that they are supposed to make, irrespective of how well they have been trained as observers, it is likely that the category itself is ambiguous, i.e. that it has properties of both the categories over which the observers cannot agree (see van Geert & van Dijk, 2003 for a discussion).

A direct empirical indicator of superposition, particularly in the context of development, are spikes in intra-individual variability. Human behavior and performance is intrinsically variable and fluctuating, but at times these fluctuations peak. Such peaks often indicate transitions from one development state, level or stage, to another and are likely to be caused by the temporal superposition of the two states, levels or stages. The superposition implies that at some moment the child functions on one state or level, and at another moment on another state. Figure 5.1 gives an example of data from a child's language development (Bassano and van Geert, 2007). Utterances were divided into groups, according to three proposed generating functions, a holophrastic generator producing one-word sentences, a combinatorial generator producing two- to three-word sentences, and a syntactic generator producing four- and more-word sentences and, by default, also sentences consisting of one to three words. The developmental pattern takes the form of overlapping curves, representing the frequencies of the utterance types. Analysis of the variability patterns showed two peaks, probably corresponding with the take-over of the holophrastic (one-word) generator by the combinatorial generator, and of the combinatorial generator by the syntactic generator.

Substance and process

A third core feature or characteristic of complex dynamic systems is that they are based on the synthesis of substance and process. "Substance" refers to the tangible, physical and permanent existence of physical objects and structures. Process refers to the temporal succession of causally linked changes in substances. Given our human, cognitive structure, it is easier to understand a substance than a process explanation and that is why substance explanations are preferred over the more ephemeral process models. The idea of a brain as a physical substance that contains the causes of behavior in some substance format currently receives major scientific interest. The substance aspect is demonstrated by the search for specific, localizable regions or parts of the brain that are responsible for some specific form of cognitive activity, for instance reading or the manipulation of numbers. However interesting such localization studies are, it should be noted that they do not offer an explanation of the reading process or the thinking with numbers (in the popular press, at least, the finding of a "brain site that does it" is often presented as an ultimate explanation of the process at issue). Moreover, the localized regions are "real" only to a certain extent, since they are the result of a considerable amount of averaging over subjects and occasions, in addition to the fact that they refer only to regions of increased activity and not to unique places where the task at issue is performed without the help of less active regions (see for instance Mazoyer & Tzouriou-Mazoyer, 2002; Beaulieu, 2000, Uttal, 2001).

Thelen and Smith's dynamic systems theory (Thelen & Smith, 1994) makes a very strong case against the substance interpretation of knowledge. They argue strongly against interpreting knowledge and concepts as some fixed "machine" in the brain that produces the behavior in which this knowledge and behavior are expressed. In their view, knowledge, concepts, skills and so forth are processes. They view these things as soft-assembled, i.e. local and temporal entities that have no existence outside the process in which they emerge. However, it is a characteristic of the complexity of human cognition, that knowledge and concepts are at the same time substance and process, that they are at the same time transient and "soft-assembled" on the one hand and causal and conditional entities of the mind on the other hand. Note that this fact is closely related to the property of superposition explained in the preceding paragraph. This relationship illustrates a more general point, namely that the properties of complexity are in fact *all* related to one another.

Are there any empirical indicators for this superposition of substance and process? An important indicator is intra-individual variability itself (note that, in the section on superposition, we focused on *peaks* in intra-individual variability as a main empirical indicator). If psychological phenomena, such as knowledge or skills, are at the same time "hard-wired" (in the brain) and the product of processes that necessarily involve contexts and environments, for any person in particular they will fluctuate or vary in characteristic ways. The amount of variability determines whether a phenomenon can be more reliably described as substance (if variability is low) or process (if variability is high).

The multi-layered and multi-scaled nature of causality

The fourth core feature or characteristic of a complex dynamic system is that it consists of many layers and many time scales, for instance the layers of the individual, group, society, culture, species and the scales of micro-genetic, ontogenetic, historical and evolutionary time. It is clear that many problems relating to the study of development can be tackled by isolating a particular layer or scale, but many others will require explicitly accounting for the interactions between the layers or scales. One of the cornerstones of the Vygotskyan program, for instance, which was formulated about eighty years ago, was the study of the interrelationships between the historical development of society and the ontogenesis of the individual (Vygotsky, 1978). The relationships between these layers of organization and between the corresponding time scales are inherently mutual.

The principle of mutual or reciprocal causality is explicitly accounted for in dynamic growth models (van Geert, 1991, 1994, 1998; Fischer & Bidell, 2006, Fischer, this volume). They conceive of development as a web of interacting components that entertain supportive, competitive, and conditional relationships. The relationships are reciprocal but not necessarily symmetrical. For instance, it is likely that an earlier linguistic strategy bears a supportive relationship to a later, more complex linguistic strategy. The latter, however, may have a competitive relationship with its predecessor (see Bassano & van Geert, 2007). By modeling such webs of reciprocal action, it is possible to understand the emergence of stages, temporary regressions, inverse U-shaped growth and so forth.

The multi-layered nature of developmental causality is also expressed in the fact that properties of complex systems are (often) distributed over many components. Things such as "concepts" or "knowledge" are definitely properties of persons. If we think about them, we cannot see them but as internal properties. However, the complexity of the task that such properties have to serve, for instance of moving about in a real world or solving a math problem, far exceeds the possibilities of an internally represented knowledge base. Hence, our knowledge and concepts heavily rely on the properties of the outside world, and in that sense, our knowledge is a so-called distributed and situated property (Clark, 1997). It is situated not only in the physical but also in the social context (e.g. computers and human collaborators). The external tools that are created to improve cognition and action, are not just external appendages that in themselves do not affect the internal processes that they support. Over the long run – and it is the long run that counts in developmental and historical processes – they will shape the form of the internal processes themselves, for instance by selecting for those internal skills that improve the use of the external tools. For instance, in the history of writing, written signs were originally just external mnemonic aids, but since then they have evolved into an entirely new kind of cognitive skill, evolutionarily speaking, namely reading and writing. These skills have been "adopted" by regions of our brains that could handle them (see Dehaene, this volume, and Wolf, this volume). However, it is highly likely that the evolution of reading and writing itself has been shaped by the properties of the brain functions by which these skills were adopted.

What are the empirical indicators of the multi-layered and multi-scaled nature of development? A direct indicator is the finding of a difference between the mechanisms that govern the short-term evolution of a process and those that govern its long-term change. Another indicator is the finding of a difference between structures discovered by analyzing differences *between* individuals in a population (e.g. the factor structure of personality or intelligence) and structures found by analyzing differences *within* an individual (for instance as a result of a dynamic factor analysis of repeated measures in a single individual, see Molenaar, 2004). The problem is that there is only so much research on individual trajectories and thus the evidence on such differences is scarce (an exception is the study on perceived control and academic performance by Musher-Eizenman *et al.* (2002)).

We have now reviewed four core features or characteristics of complex dynamic systems, namely non-linearity and self-organization, super-position, substance and process and finally, the multi-layered and multi-scaled nature of causality. We have suggested empirical indicators, i.e. properties that indicate the presence of these features in a process or phenomenon. We will now apply these features or characteristics to an important aspect of developmental research, namely the measurement of development.

Aspects of complexity in developmental measurement

Fuzziness and ambiguity versus uncertainty

Most of the phenomena that we are interested in – a child's cognitive level, reading ability, social cognition, and so forth – are in themselves complex variables, i.e. variables that inherit all or many of the properties of the complex systems in which they feature. We already mentioned an interesting group of empirical indicators of complexity, which was pri-marily related to the characteristic of superposition, namely ambiguity and apparent paradoxicalness. These characteristics are directly related to the issue of developmental measurement.

For instance, if we score emotional expressions during an interaction between children, we will often be confronted with the fuzzy or even ambiguous nature of such emotions, which we solve by imposing simplify-ing assumptions upon them, such as reducing them to a one-dimensional variation from negative to positive expressions (see for instance Steenbeek & van Geert, 2002). Another example is the interpretation of syntactic categories in early child language, such as prepositions and verbs. In general, there exists no sharp boundary between a word that is and one that is not yet a preposition, for instance (van Dijk & van Geert, 2005, van Geert & van Dijk, 2002, 2003). The fact that, in this example, a word is something in-between a verb and a preposition, is an example of fuzziness: a categorical distinction that seems to involve mutual exclusiveness (a word is either a preposition or not a preposition) involves gradualness (there is a gradual transition between a non-preposition and a preposition). This gradual transition can be quantified, i.e. fuzziness can be accounted for in a formal way (van Geert & van Dijk, 2003). The gradual transition between categories creates ambiguity, e.g. if a word represents something between a verb and a preposition, it is both a verb and a preposition and at the same time it is neither one. Thus, the word is ambiguous in terms of syntactic categorization.

The fuzziness and ambiguity of variables is often interpreted as the result of a lack of information. In this view, the phenomenon is clearly determined, it is either this or that, but the observer still lacks the information (or the skill) to determine which of the two it is. Put differently, fuzziness and ambiguity are nothing else but uncertainty. It is clear that there are many instances where fuzziness and ambiguity, resulting for instance in disagreement among observers, is indeed caused by insufficient information or lack of expertise in the observers and can be solved by obtaining more information or by further observer training. However, if fuzziness and ambiguity are part of the very nature of the phenomena that we study, we must try to make a distinction between observations where fuzziness is real and observations where it indeed amounts to a lack of information. In situations where fuzziness is real, we must try to objectify it by trying to quantify it (in the same way as uncertainty is quantified by specifying a confidence interval). For instance, instead of using inter-rater disagreement as an indicator of measurement error (the more disagreement, the more error), the disagreement among well-informed and trained observers who share the same set of criteria and rating skills can be used as quantifiable information about the intrinsic ambiguity and fuzziness of the categories they have to rate (see van Geert & van Dijk, 2003, for an application in the field of language development).

In clinical assessment, uncertainty – we would however call it real fuzziness – is often an issue, for instance uncertainty about a child "having" or "not having" ADHD. Would the uncertainty – or the fuzziness, for that matter – be solved if the behavioral indicators can be linked with objective ones, such as particular regions of the brain that are more active in "real" ADHD children, for instance? In our discussion of the third characteristic of complex dynamic systems, the superposition of substance and process, we have already argued that the identification of a substance property, such as a particular region of the brain, does not solve the problem of what ADHD – for instance – really is, how it develops, how it differs among persons and how it varies over the life span. Knowledge of the brain adds another piece to the complexity puzzle and will thus contribute to solving the puzzle; it does not replace the puzzle by the real picture.

Dynamic aspects of psychological variables

In our discussion of the fourth characteristic of complex dynamic systems, the multi-layered and multi-scaled nature of such systems, we have seen that whatever we measure as a variable, e.g. the child's developmental level on a cognitive reasoning task, in fact results from the dynamic interplay between person abilities and context affordances (see Thelen & Smith, 1994; Fischer *et al.*, 1993; van Geert, 2002; Clark, 1999, Fischer, this volume). Although it is statistically possible to separate context- and person-aspects, such separation requires the assumption of independence of persons and contexts. This assumption is untenable under a dynamic interpretation of performance. On a short time scale, context affordances and person abilities result from the real-time interaction between the two and are, therefore, inherently dependent on one another. On a longer time scale, persons tend to actively select and manipulate the contexts in which they function, whereas contexts in their turn help shape the person's characteristics and abilities. Given a person's characteristic internal features and also given the person's range of characteristic contexts (which are different for a child and an adult, for instance), the person's scores on the variable in question will show a characteristic dynamic. It is this characteristic dynamic that should be the target of psychological measurement. In order to capture the properties of that dynamic, measurement must comply with the following requirements.

First, measurement must be repeated with such frequency (intervals between the measurements) that the characteristic variability of a person can be observed, i.e. the characteristic range within which the person's scores will vary. This range is the product of the person's characteristic context variation, but also of the inherent variability of internal conditions (see for instance De Weerth, van Geert & Hoitink, 1999; de Weerth & van Geert, 2002a, 2002b; Li *et al.*, 2001, 2004; Granic *et al.*, 2003; Eizenman *et al.*, 2004; Schmitz & Skinner, 1993; Kernis *et al.*, 1993; Butler *et al.*, 1994; Rabbit *et al.*, 2001; Alibali, 1999; Bassano & van Geert, 2007). Research on developmental discontinuities – for instance the sudden emergence of a new cognitive principle such as conservation – has also strongly focused on the meaning of increasing variability as a predictor of the coming discontinuity (van der Maas & Molenaar, 1992; van der Maas, 1993; Hosenfeld, van der Maas & van den Boom, 1997; Jansen & van der Maas, 2002; Wimmers, 1996).

Secondly, the measured variable is distributed across the person and the person's characteristic contexts (a property that we have discussed in the section on the multi-layered nature of complex systems). The distributed nature often coincides with the person functioning in characteristic modes. Thus, measurement implies that the characteristic modes of operation are explored, in the form of multiple testing in various (characteristic) contexts. Examples are the functional and optimal mode resulting from Fischer's testing, with and without support or cooperation, with more competent others being one of the characteristic contexts of cognitive operation, especially in developmental and educational contexts (Fischer *et al.*, 1993; Fischer, this volume). Other examples relate to states in the vicinity of a discontinuous shift, e.g. between different types of language production (Bassano & van Geert, 2007), from non-conservation to conservation understanding in the sense of Piaget (van der Maas & Molenaar, 1992) or when discontinuous stages are represented by means of distinct modes of operation (e.g. verbal and nonverbal modes, see Goldin-Meadow *et al.*,1993). The brain of a person who (eventually temporarily) operates in these two distinct modes shows an example of superposition. It is a brain that features both on a developmental level A and a developmental level B, for instance. This superposition does not amount to a logical paradox. It is possible because the brain in question functions in a complex system – and is itself a complex system.

Aspects of complexity in developmental theory building and hypothesis testing: A case study

What are the consequences of the features of complexity for the way we do research on developmental processes? How can we capture aspects such as non-linearity and self-organization, superposition and the multi-layered nature of causality? Can we understand the course of processes if we do not actually follow these processes in real time? It seems that the adoption of a complexity and dynamic systems approach requires an entirely new developmental methodology. Does it mean that our current methods are not suitable for understanding the dynamic and complexity aspects of development? In this section, we will argue that the standard methodology and standard designs of developmental psychology allow us to capture at least a significant part of the complex and dynamic nature if we are prepared to take a slightly different look at our data. In order to illustrate how this can be done we present an example of one of our own research projects.

The relationship between properties of interaction and sociometric status

Already at the age of six to seven years, children show specific preferences for their classmates. By means of sociometric techniques, it is possible to divide children from the same school class in to various sociometric statuses, for instance popular, average, and rejected. Earlier research has shown that in social interaction with peers, popular children show a higher amount of positive emotional expressions and more directedness toward peers than children from other statuses (Black & Logan, 1995; Rubin *et al.*, 1998). In a longitudinal research project at the University of Utrecht, children of popular and rejected status were put together with a child of average status and then videotaped during a pretend play session with various sets of toys, lasting for ten minutes. The results did not confirm the earlier findings of a positive linear association between status and positive emotional expression (de Koeijer, 2001). The problem is, however, that the finding of an association between variables in a sample or population – and eventually the inability to replicate such findings – tells us nothing about the causal process that relates features of sociometric statuses in children with their actual expression of positive emotions and interactions with other children.

A dynamic model of emotional expression and interaction

General properties of the model

In our own study, we started from a dynamic model of emotional expression and directedness in social interaction (*directedness* is all activity that is directed towards another person, if it is responded to by the other person we call it *coherence*; Steenbeek & van Geert, 2005; Steenbeek & van Geert, 2007a, b). The model of social interaction is based on a general, highly simplified model of human action and is strongly inspired by the functional theory of emotions, introduced among others by Frijda (1986) and Campos *et al.* (1994). We speculated that action – and behavior in general – is based on two components. One component refers to the person's *concerns*, i.e. the "interests" that the person tries to realize. The other component that we call *reciprocity*, refers to the inherently adaptive nature of social exchange, which means that people will tend to reflect each other's behavior. If applied to a play situation involving two children, the concerns are reduced to two basic concerns. One is an interest in Involvement (the class of actions of playing together, including all actions directed towards the other person with the intention of trying to involve that person in the interaction). The other is an interest in Autonomy (the class of actions of playing alone, without interchange with the other person). Emotions are evaluations of the degree to which concerns are realized, i.e. satisfied. For instance a positive emotional expression communicated to the play partner signals both to the child himself and to the play partner that the current situation satisfies the child's involvement concern (see Figure 5.2 for a graphical representation of the model).

A play session, like any other form of social interaction, is a structure of iterative actions. That is, an action (such as verbally directing oneself to the other person) is answered, in some way or another, by the other person, and this response of the other is again followed by an action from the person, and so on (see Figure 5.2, at the bottom). This iterative or recursive aspect is an explicit part of the model. It implies, among others, that the interacting persons constitute each other's interaction context. Moreover, it is a context that is partly created by the child himself and partly by the play partner. In this sense, the context is not an added, static frame that can be conceived of as an "independent" variable that can be freely varied over individuals. The rules of the actions and responses in a particular context are defined by the concern aspect and by the reciprocity aspect.

Sociometric status is incorporated into the model in the following way. First, we assume that the child's concern for Involvement is higher if the play partner has a higher sociometric status. Second, the literature suggests that popular children are more socially effective than their nonpopular peers: they have a higher impact on the behavior of their peers and they are better able to discriminate between situations in which action is effective and situations in which it is not (effectiveness is defined in function of the realization of their concerns).

This basic conceptual model has been transformed into two kinds of dynamic models. The first is a so-called agent model, which models the interaction process in a more detailed way (see Steenbeek & van Geert, 2005, 2007a, b). The second is a highly simplified mathematical formulation of the above-mentioned interaction principles, captured in the form of a pair of coupled differential equations. This model was used to calculate predictions regarding directedness and emotional expressions in children of popular and rejected sociometric status playing with a peer of average

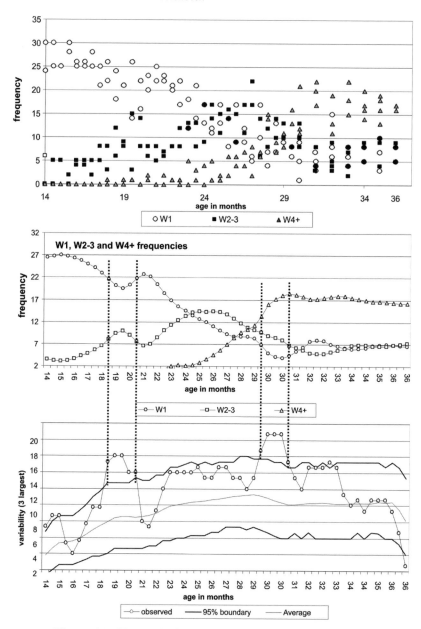

Figure 5.1 Changes in frequency of 1-word, 2–3 word and 4- and more word utterances in a French-speaking girl between the ages of 14 and 36 months. The utterance groups refer to presumed underlying generators: holophrastic, combinatorial, and syntactic.

status. The predictions did not pertain to the actual course of the interaction process, but concerned only global measures, such as average amounts and intensities of expressions over the entire interaction course. Before discussing these predictions and their empirical testing, we will first address the question of how the current procedure of starting from a dynamic model is consistent with the complexity approach discussed in this chapter.

Aspects of complexity in the simple dynamic interaction model

Instead of using a model of linear associations between variables over independent subjects, we used a dynamic model that specifies the interaction properties as a result of a process in real time. The dynamic model is used to specify predictions about global, average properties of interaction sessions and can thus be tested by means of a standard cross-sectional design, based on independent cases (the dyads). The model also specifies the simplest possible case of self-organization: for each set of parameter values, it stabilizes onto a fixed value. Thus, the amount of positive emotions and directedness of the children towards each other is

---

Figure 5.1 (continued)

Top: Raw data, based on sub-sessions counting 30 utterances each. A complete observation session consisted of either 60 (before month 22) or 120 utterances (after month 22) and was subdivided in sub-sessions of 30 utterances in order to study within-session variability.

Middle: Smoothed frequency curves, based on a Loess smoothing technique, which estimates (changing) central values for the three types of utterances and follows local regressions or other deviations from a main trend.

Bottom: Within-session variability, defined as the average of three maximal values of within-session variability over a period of five consecutive comparisons. Variability peaks around month 19, simultaneous with a temporary regression in 1-word utterances and a temporary peak in the 2- and 3-word sentences. A second peak occurs around month 30, which is the moment of consolidation of 4- and more word utterances. It is likely that 1- and 2–3 words utterances ocurring after month 30 are increasingly generated by the new syntactic generator. The observed variability peaks are compared with a range of variability, estimated on the basis of a multinominal model: since the smoothed frequencies of the three utterance types can be conceived of as multinominal probability functions, the statistically expected variability can be computed, for instance in the form of 95 percent-band. The peaks in variability differ significantly from the statistically expected peaks ($p < 0.01$).

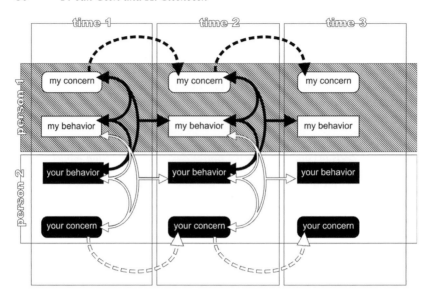

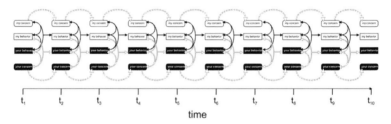

Figure 5.2 A basic model of behavioral short-term change in a social interaction situation. Both persons (e.g. two children) have a concern regarding doing things together or alone (playing together or playing alone). Mathematically, the concern takes the form of a preferred ratio of playing together over playing alone. The next level in a person's behavior (e.g. at time 2) is based on an evaluation of the difference between the person's own behavior (either playing together or playing alone), the other person's behavior and the person's concern. The model is symmetrical for both persons. In this simplified model, concerns are not adapted over the short term (dashed arrows represent the fact that the concerns remain the same over time). Whereas the figure at the top represents only three time steps, the figure at the bottom provides a better idea of the iterative character of the process.

not conceived of as the product of a certain internal and relatively static tendency of a child towards positive emotions. It is modeled as the outcome of a dynamic interaction process and thus incorporates aspects of the subject(s) and of the context. In this sense, the levels of emotion and directedness are the result of a distributed process, i.e. a process distributed over the participants of the interaction.

The property of superposition, characteristic of complex systems, clearly features in the way the notions of context and subject are defined. In view of the iterative nature of the interaction, the context, namely the play partner's actions and properties, is at the same time a product of the child's own action and a cause of those actions. Similarly, the properties of the child are to a considerable extent determined by the context (e.g. the child's concerns). Thus, although context and subject can be separated at any time, the subject is the creator of the context and the context is the creator of the subject. This form of superposition is not vague or metaphorical: it is entirely defined by the equations specified in the model.

The aspect of substance and process takes the form of an explicit choice between those parts of the model that are conceived of as "fixed" internal properties, for instance the social effectiveness of the child, and those parts that result from the processes that the model describes (the concerns, the emotions, etc.). The choice for a "substance" or fixed aspect (a property of the person, for instance) does not entail a generalizable claim about the nature of the fixed aspect as "fixed." In a model that tries to explain this aspect, e.g. the social effectiveness, it is likely that the fixed aspect takes the form of a process.

However, the current model still falls short in a final aspect of complex dynamic systems, namely the multi-layered and multi-scaled nature of processes. The model specifies the short-term dynamics of social interaction, corresponding with a play session of ten minutes, for instance. It should be complemented by a model of the long-term dynamics of social interaction, explaining how and why the parameters distinguished in the model change in the course of development, partly as a consequence of social interaction itself (see Steenbeek and van Geert, 2007b for an example).

Testing dynamic systems hypotheses in a standard sample design

Subjects, procedure, and predictions

Grade 1 pupils with mean age of 6.5 years, with an upper limit of 8.8 years and a lower limit of 5.8 years participated in this study. From a group of 83 children (47 boys and 36 girls), 24 dyads were selected on the basis of their sociometric status, determined by means of a rating test, Ssrat (Maassen, Akkermans & van der Linden, 1996). The dyads were videotaped three times, with intervals of approximately one and a half months. An interaction consisted of a ten-minute play session. Changes in expressiveness and responsiveness of each videotaped child were coded for every one-tenth of a second (event sampling).

Model predictions were generated by calculating all possible outcomes for a parameter space corresponding with the postulated properties of rejected and popular children, in terms of their hypothesized concerns and hypothesized effectiveness. The predictions that the model made were as follows. In his own dyad, the popular child will show less directedness towards the play partner than the rejected child and also show less positive emotional expressions. In the popular child, the positive emotions will be more effectively distributed; the popular child will also show more negative emotions than the rejected child. Irrespective of the differences between dyads, we expect more similarity between the child and his play partner than should be expected on the basis of chance. The model predicted that the involvement of the play partner of a popular child would not differ from the involvement of the play partner of a rejected child. The play partner of the rejected child will show more negative expressions than the play partner of the popular child. Finally, the model predicts less shared involvement in the popular-average dyad than in the rejected-average dyad. No differences are expected between popular dyads and rejected dyads in the amount of shared negative expressions. Note that these predictions, based on a dynamic model of real-time interaction, are crucially different from the prediction made on the basis of earlier research (that found a positive association between popularity, positive emotions and directedness).

The fact that the numbers of popular and rejected children are small and also given the labor-intensive scoring procedure, resulted in small samples of rejected-average, average-average, and popular-average dyads (13, 14, and 14 respectively). For this reason and also because we have no idea about the expected distribution of the variables on the population level, we applied a non-parametric random permutation test (see Manly, 1997; Good, 1999; Toddman & Dugard, 2001) for each operational variable. A major advantage of this statistical procedure is that virtually any prediction can be tested, as long as the null hypothesis is clearly formulated and the test can take the form of a statistical simulation.

Finally, what is characteristic of a group, e.g. of rejected children, is not necessarily something that occurs in all the members of the group and not even in the majority of the group members. Thus, it is likely that differences between groups occur in the extremes and not necessarily in the averages, or that the differences in the averages are in fact due to differences in extremes. For this reason, we not only tested differences in terms of group averages, but also inspected the properties of the extremes (in fact the upper or lower 20 percent of the group).

Results and discussion

In short, our data confirmed almost all our predictions. In particular, rejected children are inclined to show an *overflow* with regard to positive expressions, in the sense that they show many positive expressions that are not reflected by reactions of the play partner. It is likely that this overflow is a consequence of their hypothesized high concern for Involvement, in this particular context of playing with a child of a higher status. The overflow is also an indicator of their relative lack of effectiveness, in the sense that much of their effort is not shared.

The positive expressions shown by the popular children, which, as predicted, were less frequent than with rejected children, are more often accompanied by a positive expression of the play partner. This association suggests that popular children are more effective than rejected children in establishing an intersubjective framework. In addition, popular children are effective in their interaction, in the sense that they invest less effort and nevertheless generate high levels of effort in the play partner. This effort is demonstrated by the play partner's many initial verbal and nonverbal turns. The differences we found between average-status play partners, whether playing with a rejected or with a popular child, were not statistically significant (and this absence of difference was predicted). There was one exception, namely if a play partner of a rejected child expresses a negative emotion, this emotion is more intense.

In addition, besides examining differences between status groups, we also looked at differences between child and play partner of each dyad separately. In both types of dyads a process of adjustment emerges, i.e. child and play partner develop a characteristic level of concordance. This concordance is demonstrated among others by the fact that the play partner of the rejected dyad is remarkably positive, both in directedness and positive expressions.

Visual inspection of the data suggests that in most variables, the lower part of the distributions of the status groups is similar, whereas differences appear in the upper part, including the extremes, of the distribution.

In some variables, we found differences in extremes that were not found in the analyses of the averages.

Aspects of complexity

Our data illustrate the fact that behavior must not be treated as a fixed property of a person, but as the result of adaptive action in a context that is partly the product of the person's action itself. The data also illustrate non-linearity in that the association between a property and a sociometric status is not linearly distributed across the status group or sample. Differences are often due to a characteristic subgroup that represents the "typical" patterns on the basis of which the groups or statuses are identified, but do not necessarily represent the majority in the group. Moreover, the characteristic patterns found in rejected and popular dyads show a superposition of (apparently) contradictory properties: the child has a rejected status but nevertheless shows high-intensity interaction and positive emotions that are shared by the play partner. Thus, the complexity of being popular or rejected in a group is related to the diverse ways in which interaction among children can occur and the fact that action is functional, i.e. geared towards realizing concerns.

Finally, the fact that our findings so strongly supported our predictions, lends additional credibility to the dynamic systems model from which the predictions were inferred.

Conclusion: Simplifying the reality of development must preserve its complexity

In this chapter, we discussed four core features of complex dynamic systems that apply directly to human development. Human development cannot be properly understood if these features are not taken into account. Unfortunately, in its quest for necessary reduction and simplification of the object of study, much of the current methodology discards those properties and by doing so creates an inadequate image of the fundamental aspects of human development. In our discussion of psychological measurement, we have attempted to show that features such as ambiguity, fuzziness, variability and context specificity should be put at the heart of the measurement process, instead of being abandoned as mere measurement error. In an example of a study on the relationship between sociometric status, emotional expression and directedness in social interaction, we have tried to demonstrate that with relatively few alterations, a standard research design can provide interesting insights into the complexity and dynamics of the behavior of young children.

References

Alibali, M. (1999). How children change their minds: strategy change can be gradual or abrupt. *Developmental Psychology*, 35(1), 127–145.
Bassano, D. and van Geert, P. (2007). Modeling continuity and discontinuity in utterance length: a quantitative approach to changes, transitions and intra-individual variability in early grammatical development. *Developmental Science*, 10(5), 588–612.

Beaulieu, A. (2000). *The space inside the skull: digital representations, brain mapping and cognitive neuroscience in the decade of the brain.* Groningen: Doctoral Dissertation.

Black, B. and Logan, A. (1995). Links between communication of mother-child, father-child, and child-child peer interactions and children's social status. *Child Development*, 66, 255–271.

Butler, A., Hokanson, J., and Flynn, H. A. (2004). A comparison of self-esteem lability and low trait self-esteem as vulnerability factors for depression. *Journal of Personality and Social Psychology*, 66, 166–177.

Campos, J. J., Mumme, D. L., Kermoian, R., and Campos, R. G. (1994). A functionalist perspective on the nature of emotion. *Monographs of the Society for the Study of Child Development*, 59 (2–3), 284–303.

Clark, A. (1997). *Being There: Putting Brain, Body and World Together Again.* Cambridge, MA: MIT Press.

De Koeijer, I. (2001). *Peer Acceptance, Parent-child Fantasy Play Interactions, and Subjective Experience of the Self-in-relation; A Study of 4- to 5-year-old Children.* Veenendaal: Universal Press.

De Weerth, C. and van Geert, -P. (2002). Changing patterns of infant behavior and mother-infant interaction: Intra- and interindividual variability. *Infant Behavior and Development*. 24(4), 347–371.

De Weerth, C. and van Geert, P. L. C. (2002). A longitudinal study of basal cortisol in infants: intra-individual variability, circadian rhythm and developmental trends. *Infant Behavior and Development*, 25, 340–374.

De Weerth, C., van Geert, P., and Hoijtink, H. (1999). Intraindividual variability in infant behavior. *Developmental Psychology*, 35 (4), 1102–1112.

Eizenman, D. R., Nesselroade, J. R., Featherman, D. L., and Rowe, J. W. (2004). Intra-individual variability in perceived control in an older sample: the macArthur Successful Aging Studies. *Psychology and Aging*, 12, 489–502.

Fischer, K. W. and Thomas R. Bidell (2006). Dynamic development of action, thought and emotion. In R. M. Lerner and W. Damon W. (eds.), *Handbook of Child Psychology. Vol 1: Theoretical Models of Human Development* (6 edn pp. 313–399). New York: Wiley.

Fischer, K. W., Bullock, D. H., Rotenberg, E. J., and Raya, P. (1993). The dynamics of competence: how context contributes directly to skill. In R. H. Wozniak and K. W. Fischer (eds.), *Development in Context: Acting and Thinking in Specific Environments*. Hillsdale, NJ: Erlbaum, pp. 93–117.

Ford, D. and Lerner, R. (1992). *Developmental Systems Theory: An Integrative Approach*. London: Sage.

Frijda, N. H. (1986). *The Emotions: Studies in Emotion and Social Interaction.* Cambridge: Cambridge University Press.

Goldin-Meadow, S., Alibali, M. W., and Breckinridge Church, R. (1993). Transitions in concept acquisition: Using the hand to read the mind. *Psychological Review*, 100(2), 279–297.

Good, P. I. (1999). *Resampling Methods: A Practical Guide to Data Analysis.* Boston: Birkhauser.

Gottlieb, G., Wahlsten, D., and Lickliter, R. (1998). The significance of biology for human development: a developmental psychobiological systems view. In

W. Damon & R. Lerner (eds.), *Handbook of Child Psychology* (pp. 233–273). New York: Wiley.

Granic, I., Hollenstein, T., Dishion, Th. J., and Patterson, G. R. (2003). Longitudinal analysis of flexibility and reorganization in early adolescence: A dynamic systems study of family interactions. *Developmental Psychology*. 39(3):, 606–617.

Hosenfeld, B., Maas, H. L. J. van der Boom, D. C. (1997). Indicators of discontinuous change in the development of analogical reasoning. *Journal of Experimental Child Psychology*, 64, 367–395.

Jansen, B. R. J. and van der Maas, H. L. J. (2002). The development of children's rule use on the balance scale task. *Journal of Experimental Child Psychology*, 81, 383–416.

Kernis, M. H., Cornell, D., Sun, C.-R., Berry, A., and Harlow, T. (1993). There's more to self-esteem than whether it is high or low: the importance of stability of self-esteem. *Journal of Personality and Social Psychology*, 65, 1190–1204.

Li, S.-C., Lindernberger, U., Hommel, B., Aschersleben, G., Prinz, W., and Baltes, P. (2004). Lifespan transformations in the couplings among intellectual abilities and constituent cognitive processes. *Psychological Science*, 15(3), 155–163.

Li, S.-C., Aggen, S. H., Nesselroade, J. R., and Baltes, P. B. (2001). Short-term fluctuations in elderly people's sensori-motor functioning predict text and spatial memory performance: the MacArthur successful aging studies. *Journal of Gerontology*, 47, 100–116.

Manly, B. F. (1997). *Randomization, Bootstrap and Monte Carlo Methods in Biology (2nd edition)*. Boca Raton: Chapman and Hall.

Maassen, G. H., Akkermans, W. and van der Linden, J. L. (1996). Two-dimensional sociometric status determination with rating scales. *Small Group Research*, 27(1), 56–78.

Mazoyer, B. and Tzouriou-Mazoyer, N. (2002). Variabilité anatomique et fonctionelle des aires du langage. In J. Lautrey, B. Mazoyer, and P. van Geert (eds.), *Invariants et variabilités dans les sciences cognitives* (pp. 55–68). Paris: Editions de la Maison des Sciences de l'Homme.

Molenaar, P. C. M. (2004). A manifesto on psychology as idiographic science: bringing the person back into scientific psychology – this time forever. *Measurement*, 2 (4), 201–219.

Musher-Eizenman, D. R., Nesselroade, J. R., and Schmitz, B. (2002). Perceived control and academic performance: a comparison of high- and low-performing children on within-person change-patterns. *International Journal of Behavioral Development*, 26, 540–547.

Rabbitt, P., Osman, P., and Moore, B. (2001). There are stable individual differences in performance variability, both from moment to moment and from day to day. *The Quarterly Journal of Experimental Psychology*, 54A, 981–1003.

Rocha L. M. (1997). *Evidence Sets and Contextual Genetic Algorithms: Exploring Uncertainty, Context, and Embodiment in Cognitive and Biological Systems*. New York: Binghampton University Doctoral dissertation.

Roubertoux P. L. and Carlier, M. Invariants et variants génetiques: les apports de la génomique dans l'étude des processus cognitifs. In J. Lautrey, B. Mazoyer, and P. van Geert (eds.), *Invariants et variabilités dans les sciences cognitives*. (pp. 25–40). Paris: Editions de la Maison des Sciences de l'Homme.

Rubin, K. H., Bukowski, W. M., and Parker, J. G. (1998). Peer interactions, relationships, and groups. In W. Damon (Series ed.) and N. Eisenberg (Vol. ed.), *Handbook of Child Psychology: Vol. 3. Social, Emotional, and Personality Development* (5th edn., pp. 619–700). New York: Wiley.

Schmitz, B. and Skinner, E. (1993). Perceived control, effort and academic performance: interindividual, intraindividual en multivariate time-series analyses. *Journal of Personality and Social Psychology*, 64, 1010–1028.

Steenbeek, H. and van Geert, P. (2002). Variations on dynamic variations. *Human-Development*. May–Jun; Vol. 45(3), 167–173.

Steenbeek, H. and van Geert, P. (2005). A dynamic systems model of dyadic interaction during play of two children. *European Journal of Developmental Psychology*, 2(2), 105–145.

Steenbeek, H. and van Geert, P. (2007a). A dynamic systems approach to dyadic interaction in children's emotional expression, action, dyadic play, and sociometric status. *Developmental Review*, 27(1), 1–40.

Steenbeek, H. and van Geert, P. (2007b). The empirical validation of a dynamic systems model of interaction: do children of different sociometric status differ in their dyadic play interactions? *Developmental Science* (in press).

Thelen, E. and Smith L. B. (1994). *A Dynamic Systems Approach to the Development of Cognition and Action*, Cambridge, MA: MIT Press.

Todman, J. B. and Dugard, P. (2001). *Single-case and Small-n Experimental Designs: A Practical Guide to Randomization Tests*. Mahwah, NJ: Erlbaum.

Uttal, W. M. (2004). *The New Phrenology: The Limits of Localizing Cognitive Processes in the Brain*. Cambridge, MA: Cambridge University Press.

Van der Maas, H. (1993). *Catastrophe analysis of stagewise cognitive development, model method and applications*. Dissertation, University of Amsterdam.

van der Maas, H. and Molenaar, P. (1992). A catastrophe-theoretical approach to cognitive development. *Psychological Review*, 99, 395–417.

van Dijk, M. and van Geert, P. (2005). Disentangling behavior in early child development: Interpretability of early child language and its effect on utterance length measures. *Infant Behavior and Development*, 28, 99–117.

Van Geert, P. and van Dijk, M. (2002). Focus on variability: New tools to study intra-individual variability in developmental data. *Infant Behavior and Development*, 25, 1–35.

(2003). Ambiguity in child language. The problem of inter-observer reliability in ambiguous observation data. *First Language*, 23(3), 259–284.

Van Geert, P. (1991). A dynamic systems model of cognitive and language growth. *Psychological Review*, 98, 3–53.

(1994). *Dynamic Systems of Development*. New York and London: Harvester Wheatsheaf.

(1998). A dynamic systems model of basic developmental mechanisms: Piaget, Vygotsky and beyond. *Psychological Review*, 105, 5, (4), 634–677.

(2002). Developmental dynamics, intentional action and fuzzy sets. In N. Granott and J. Parziale (eds.), *Microdevelopmental Clues: Transition Processes in Development and Learning*, (pp. 319–343), Cambridge: Cambridge University Press.

Vygotsky, L. S. (1978). *Mind in Society*. Londen: Harvard University Press.

Wimmers, R. H. (1996). *Grasping Developmental Change: Theory, Methodology and Data*. Doctoral Dissertation: Free University of Amsterdam.

Part II

Brain development, cognition, and education

6   Epigenesis and brain plasticity in education

Wolf Singer

Overview

Some robust results in neurobiology can explain characteristics of the neuronal representation of knowledge in humans. The functional architecture of the brain depends not only on genes but on epigenetic mechanisms (developmental processes) based on the stabilization of connections among neurons for specific tasks. "Neurons that fire together wire together" is the basic rule, not only in the embryonic period but also after birth. Babies are endowed with an incredible wealth of information already accessible in their brains, as illustrated by other chapters such as those by Dehaene and Petitto. Education does not start from a blank slate but develops from a priori knowledge about the internal and external environment. During the early periods of development some windows of development occur, well documented for the visual areas of the cortex, where sensory deprivation may alter forever the consolidation of cortical circuits. After puberty any learning is constrained by invariant neuronal architectures, but learning continues to occur because of functional modifications in the connectivity of the brain system, as described by Bruer in his chapter. Educational programs will benefit from knowledge of the way new neuronal circuits develop during learning.

The Editors

Considerations on the optimization of educational strategies should take into account knowledge on brain development and learning mechanisms that has been accumulated by neurobiological research over the past decades. The vast amount of data precludes a comprehensive overview of potentially relevant aspects in the format of this presentation. Therefore, emphasis will be on general aspects of knowledge acquisition and representation. In this context the following questions are of particular importance: First, how knowledge is represented in the brain. Second, whether, at birth, brains already possesses knowledge about the world in which they are going to evolve, or whether they should be considered as a freely programmable tabula rasa. Third, whether and how experience and education interfere with brain development. Fourth, to what extent the developing brain has control over the processes that mediate its development and knowledge acquisition. Fifth, whether, and if so, how, learning processes in the developing brain differ from those in the mature organism.

The neuronal representation of knowledge

Unlike computers that consist of an invariant hardware which performs fixed operations, the sequence of which can be freely programmed by appropriate software, there is no dichotomy between hard- and software in the brain. The way in which brains operate is fully determined by the integrative properties of the individual nerve cells and the way in which they are interconnected. It is the functional architecture, the blueprint of connections and their respective weight, that determines how brains perceive, decide and act. Hence, not only the rules according to which brains process information but also all the knowledge that a brain possesses reside in its functional architecture. It follows from this that the connectivity patterns of brains contain information and that any learning, i.e. the modification of computational programs and of stored knowledge, must occur through lasting changes of their functional architecture. Such changes can be obtained by altering the integrative properties of individual neurons, by changing the anatomical connectivity patterns, and by modifying the efficacy of excitatory and/or inhibitory connections. Thus, search for the sources of knowledge is equivalent to the search for processes that specify and modify the functional architecture of the brain.

Three main processes can be distinguished: Evolution, ontogenetic development and learning. Although these processes differ remarkably in their time course and the underlying mechanisms they are equally responsible for the specification of the functional architecture of the brain. Hence, they can be considered as mechanisms underlying knowledge acquisition, or in more general terms, as cognitive processes.

Evolution as a cognitive process

The architectures of brains have evolved according to the same principles of trial, error and selection as all the other components of organisms. Organisms endowed with brains whose architecture permitted realization of functions that increased their fitness survived and the genes specifying these architectures were preserved. Through this process of selection, information about useful computational operations was implemented in brain architectures and stored in the genes. Every time an organism develops, this information is transmitted from the genes through a complicated developmental process into specific brain architectures which then translate this knowledge into well adapted behavior.

Because evolution is conservative, basic features of the functional architecture of nervous systems have been preserved once they have proven their efficacy. Thus, the integrative properties of nerve cells and the main principles of information processing have remained unchanged since the very first emergence of simple nervous systems in invertebrates. This implies that computational strategies, as for example the learning mechanism that associates temporally contingent signals, have remained virtually unchanged throughout evolution. We continue to utilize the knowledge that primitive organisms have acquired about computational algorithms that have proven useful for the evaluation of sensory signals and the preparation of well adapted responses. The only major change that nervous systems have undergone during evolution is a dramatic increase in complexity. This complexity is due to a massive increase in the number of nerve cells and even more so to a stunning increase of connections. The human brain consists of about 10^{11} nerve cells and 10^{14} connections. A cubic millimeter of cerebral cortex contains approximately 60,000 neurons. Each of these contacts between 10,000 and 20,000 other neurons and receives inputs from a comparable number of nerve cells. The majority of the interactions mediated by these connections occur among nerve cells located in close vicinity, but there are also numerous long-range connections that link nerve cells that are distributed across remote areas of the brain. Most of these connections are highly selective and their trajectories are genetically specified.

Thus, an enormous amount of information is stored in the functional architecture of highly evolved brains, and one of the sources of this information is evolutionary selection. Important in the present context is the fact that most of the genetically determined features of brain architecture are readily expressed by the time of birth. This implies that babies are born with brains that have stored in their architecture a substantial amount of knowledge about useful strategies of information processing. While the functional specialization of sense organs determines which signals from the environment are to be captured by the organism for further evaluation, the functional architecture of the nervous system determines, how these signals are to be processed, recombined, stored, and translated into action patterns. Inborn knowledge defines how we perceive and interpret sensory signals, evaluate regularities and derive rules, associate signals with one another and identify causal relations, attach emotional connotations to sensory signals, and finally how we reason. Human babies are born with an immense knowledge base about the properties of the world in which they are going to evolve, and this knowledge resides in the genetically determined functional architecture of their brains (see Koizumi, Dehaene and Singer, this volume).Thus, their brains are far from being a freely instructable *tabula rasa*.

For obvious reasons we have no conscious recollection of the acquisition of this knowledge. It is a priori in nature and determines the basic operations of our brains including the subsequent acquisition of further knowledge by learning. It is implicit knowledge that specifies how we perceive the world and categorize phenomena as alike or different. We cannot question this knowledge nor can we override, by conscious deliberations, the computational results provided by our inborn brain architecture. Even though we know that vibrations with frequencies below and above 18 Hz differ only quantitatively in physical terms, our sensory systems arbitrarily subdivide this continuum into vibrations and sounds, respectively. Examples for such arbitrary category formation according to a priori inferences set by the architecture of our nervous system are numerous. These inborn preconceptions can also be more subtle and then are less easily identified as such. They appear as non-questionable convictions about the nature of the world in which we evolve. Current research on primates and babies is aimed at revealing this innate knowledge base. Because this a priori knowledge provides the framework for all subsequent learning processes it needs to be taken into account in any attempts to improve early educational efforts.

Experience-dependent development

Despite the substantial determination of brain architecture by genetic factors human babies are born with extremely immature brains that continue to develop structurally until the end of puberty. At the time of birth, all neurons are in place and the basic connections, especially those bridging long distances, are formed. However, the majority of neurons in the cerebral cortex are not yet fully connected. It is only after birth and during the following years that the functional architecture of the brain attains its final complexity. This developmental process is characterized by a continuous turnover of connections. Nerve cells extend the processes which receive contacts from other nerve cells (their dendrites) and the processes with which they distribute their activity to other nerve cells (axons) and establish contacts. Once formed, these connections are subject to a functional test and are then either consolidated for the rest of life or they are removed irreversibly. This validation process is controlled by neuronal activity. Connections among neurons that have a high probability of displaying temporally correlated activity tend to become consolidated while connections among neurons that have a lower probability of being activated in a correlated manner tend to become removed.

"Neurons wire together if they fire together." After birth, the activity of neuronal networks is of course influenced to a large extent by the now available sensory signals. This implies that sensory experience has access to a developmental process that leads to the specification of functional architectures. Through this process experience can shape neuronal connectivity (for review of literature on experience-development see Singer, 1990; 1995).

What makes this process so important in the context of considerations on educational strategies is its irreversibility. As mentioned above, this process of circuit formation and selection according to functional criteria persists until the end of puberty – but it occurs within precisely timed windows that differ for different structures. For areas of the cerebral cortex that accomplish low level processing of sensory signals such as the primary sensory areas this experience-dependent maturation of circuitry begins shortly after birth and comes to an end within the first two years of life. For areas which are devoted to the processing of language, the developmental window starts later and is also open for a longer period of time. And even later are the developmental windows for the maturation of the centers which serve the management of declarative memory, the representation of the self, and the embedding of the individual in social systems.

Once the respective developmental windows close, neurons stop forming new connections and existing connections can no longer be removed. This is why the windows during which brain maturation is susceptible to experience-dependent influences are termed "critical periods" (see Bruer for a discussion on critical periods, this volume). It is only during these critical periods that brain architectures can be modified and optimized according to functional criteria. Once the respective critical period is over, the circuitry in the concerned area of the neocortex is no longer modifiable. Connections that are lost cannot be recovered and inappropriate connections cannot be removed. The only way to induce further modifications in the now cristallized architecture is to change the efficacy of the existing connections. These functional modifications are assumed to be the basis of adult learning and after puberty are constrained by the then invariant anatomical architectures.

The important role that experience plays in these postnatal maturation processes is underlined by the dramatic consequences of sensory deprivation. In the preantibiotic area babies have often suffered from perinatally acquired infections of their eyes which caused opacities of the cornea or the lense. Hence, these babies had no contour vision. They were unable to receive high-contrast signals from contour borders and could perceive only diffuse brightness changes. Because of pre-specified response properties that are tuned to contrast borders, neurons in the cerebral cortex cannot respond well to such global changes in brightness, and as a consequence, activity between interconnected neurons along the transmission cascade from the eye to cortical neurons is only poorly correlated. Due to these poor correlations initially formed connections become disrupted and those which happen to persist are exempt from functional validation and have a high chance to be inappropriate. Because of the lack of normal contour vision, the circuitry in the visual cortex cannot develop normally, circuits cannot be selected according to functional criteria, and the developmental process stalls at an immature, non-functional level. Once the critical period is over, which in cats lasts about three months and in human babies about a year after birth, these deficits in the connectivity can no longer be restored. Surgical interventions that restore the optical media of the eyes are then in vain because the brain is now unable to appropriately process the signals conveyed by the eyes. Animal experiments revealed that the retinae are functioning normally despite early deprivation but the neuronal networks in the visual cortex are unable to appropriately process the incoming activity patterns. Babies that have undergone such late restoration of their sight, remain functionally blind, and at best develop some rudimentary perception of luminance changes.

Although, for obvious reasons, there are no systematic studies on deprivation effects on higher cognitive functions such as language acquisition and social integration, it appears legitimate to conclude by extrapolation that there are critical windows for the acquisition of such higher functions as well and that deprivation effects will be equally detrimental.

Despite the likely importance of developmental windows for the acquisition of higher cognitive functions rather little is known about their onset and duration. As knowledge about these time courses would be highly valuable for a better management of educational curricula research in developmental psychology will gain increasing importance in the field of pedagogics.

The adaptive value of epigenetic circuit selection

The dramatic effects that deprivation has on the maturation of brain architectures raise the question why nature has implemented developmental mechanisms that expose the maturing brain to the hazards of sensory experience. It is likely that opening the developmental process to epigenetic influences allows the realization of functions that could not have been attained through genetic instructions alone and overcompensate the possible hazards of deprivation. Considerations on the development of visual functions provide support for this notion.

Animals including human beings with frontal eyes have the ability to fuse the images generated on the two retinae into a single percept. This has at least two great advantages: First, it permits a significant improvement of signal-to-noise ratios through comparison of two independent sensory channels. Second, it allows for stereoscopic vision, the ability to extract precise depth information through comparison of the disparities between the two retinal images. In order to realize these functions which undoubtedly increase the fitness of the organism, connections between the two eyes and cortical neurons have to be specified in a very precise manner. It needs to be assured that ganglion cells which code signals from the same point in visual space – provided that the animal fixates with both eyes – converge on exactly the same cortical neurons. In technical terms, it needs to be assured that afferents from corresponding retinal loci terminate at the same cortical cells. Several arguments suggest that such precise connectivity patterns cannot be achieved with genetic instructions alone. Which retinal loci will actually be corresponding in the mature system depends on a number of factors such as the interocular distance, the precise size of the eye balls, and the precise location of the eye balls in the orbita. These variables depend themselves on a number of epigenetic factors such as nutrient-dependent growth processes in utero and other epigenetic interferences. Thus, they cannot be anticipated with sufficient precision by the genetically determined developmental process. There is, however, an elegant strategy to identify a posteriori which of the connections actually come from corresponding retinal loci, and this is to rely on correlated activity. Per definition, afferents originating from corresponding retinal sites are activated by exactly the same contours in visual space. Therefore, they convey highly correlated activation patterns when the organism fixates a pattern with both eyes. Thus, a mechanism that is capable of selecting among many different afferents those which convey the best correlated activity assures selective stabilization of inputs from corresponding retinal loci. This is exactly the mechanism according to which afferents from the eyes to cortical cells are selected during development. In this particular case there is, thus, a good reason to include experience as a shaping factor in circuit development.

Related arguments apply for other developmental processes in which selection of cortical circuits depends on experience. Through the selective stabilization of connections that link neurons exhibiting correlated activity frequently occurring correlations in the outer world can be translated into the architecture of connections. Thus, the system can learn about statistical contingencies in its environment and can store this knowledge in its processing architectures. This knowledge can then be used to formulate educated hypotheses about the specific properties of the world in which the organism evolves. Through epigenetic shaping of the brain's functional architecture the organisms can adapt their neuronal architectures to the environment in which they happen to be born, and this economizes greatly the computational resources that have to be invested in order to cope with the specific challenges of the respective environments (see Dehaene, this volume).

An impressive illustration of such experience-dependent adaptation of cognitive processes is provided by language acquisition. Exposure to the mother language induces irreversible changes in the processing architectures required for the decoding and reproduction of this language. Thus, children develop specific schemata for the prosody of their mother language and for characteristic phonemes. This allows them to rapidly and automatically segment the continuous stream of sounds produced by speakers. This is not the case for second and third languages if they are acquired only at later stages of development. In this case, segmentation is no longer automatic but requires attentional control which is the reason why effort is required to follow multi-speaker conversations in late acquired foreign languages. A particularly striking example for the irreversible shaping of processing architectures is the inability of speakers of Asian languages to distinguish the consonants "R" and "L". They are actually unable to hear the difference between these consonants because Asian languages melt them into a single phoneme category (see Goswami, this volume). Evidence indicates that it is exceedingly difficult – if not impossible – to reinstall these phoneme boundaries by learning once developmental windows for the acquisition of the mother language have come to an end.

The option to open the development of the brain's functional architecture to epigenetic, experience-dependent modifications has thus two major advantages over developmental processes that depend uniquely on genetic instructions. First, by including signals from the environment it permits functional validation and fine tuning of connections to an extent that cannot be achieved by genetic instructions alone. This permits the realization of functions that could not have been developed otherwise. Second, the inclusion of environmental influences in the developmental process permits the specific adaptation of processing architectures to the actual demands of the environment in which they happened to be born. These options obviously overcompensate the risks that are associated with the epigenetic modification of brain architectures.

The control of experience-dependent development by internal gating systems

As one might expect, the developing brain has mechanisms to protect itself against inappropriate epigenetic modifications of its architecture. Obviously, it has no possibility to defend itself against deprivation because lack of information cannot be compensated for. However, nature has implemented powerful mechanisms which allow the brain to exclude environmental signals from the shaping of its architecture that are identified as inappropriate or conflicting. For the induction of activity-dependent modifications of developing circuits, their consolidation or disruption, complex cascades of molecular interactions need to be triggered by neuronal activity. This highly complex chain of molecular processes is in turn controlled by signals of multiple sources that enable or disable the translation of neuronal activity into lasting anatomical modifications. These gating signals are derived from feedback projections originating in other processing areas and from modulatory systems that control global brain states and whose activity is modulated by factors such as attention, reward value of stimuli and behavioral relevance. These control systems assure that only those signals from the environment can induce circuit modifications that match the expectancies and the needs of the developing brain.

The experience-dependent selection of corresponding retinal afferents is again a good example. This selection can only be successful if it is confined to epochs in which the baby does not move its eyes but fixates a target with both eyes. It is only in those instances that activity from corresponding retinal loci is actually correlated. Thus, it needs to be assured that circuit selection is confined to episodes in which the baby has its eyes properly adjusted. In order to assure this, nature has implemented several parallel control mechanisms. Based on genetic instructions, coarse correspondence between the afferents of the two eyes is already established before the critical period of experience-dependent fine tuning starts. The consequence is that network activity resonates better if the images on the two eyes are roughly corresponding than if the eyes are not properly aligned. As strong and resonant activity induces circuit modifications more effectively than weak and incoherent activity, circuit modifications are more likely to occur when the eyes are already in a close to optimal position. Furthermore, there is input from the stretch receptors of the extraocular muscles that signal whether the eyes are at rest or move. These signals, too, have a role in gating the use-dependent selection of afferent connections. Finally, the activity of several modulatory systems is required whose activity is regulated as a function of arousal and attention. The activity of these modulatory systems guarantees that only those signals can induce lasting changes in circuitry that are attended to by the organism and attributed behavioral significance (see Posner *et al.* in this volume). Thus, the a priori knowledge that resides in the genetically determined architectures of the brains is used to select the environmental signals that are appropriate for the epigenetic shaping of brain architectures. The developing brain knows about the nature of the signals that can be used for the optimization of its circuitry. Thus, the developing brain engages in active search for signals that it needs in order to support its own development. Depending on the time course of the various developmental windows, the nature of required signals changes. Accordingly, only those inputs are considered for circuit changes that match the needs of the actual developmental process. It follows from this that the developing brain has the initiative in all processes of experience-dependent development. It poses specific questions at specific developmental stages, directs its attention selectively to the special input patterns, and accepts only those signals for circuit optimization that match pre-wired expectancies (for review of pertinent literature see Singer, 1990).

These notions have far reaching consequences for the design of educational curricula. It is obvious that deprivation will have disastrous consequences at all stages of development. However, it is also obvious that there is no point in offering as many stimuli as possible over as long a time as possible. The developing brain will utilize only those signals that it actually needs, and there is the risk that offering too many and too diverse stimuli has a distractive effect and makes it difficult for the brain to concentrate on those signals that it needs. A more effective strategy is probably to carefully observe the spontaneous behavior of the children, to find out what their needs and interests are at the various developmental stages, and to then provide as comprehensive and non-ambiguous answers as possible. What the children are actually looking for and require for successful development can easily be deciphered from their emotional attitudes. They are not only searching spontaneously for the stimuli they need but they will respond to the availability of the requested stimuli with positive emotions. As the time courses of the various developmental windows may show considerable interindividual variability it is important to find out when a particular child needs which information in order to promote its brain development. This can be achieved by carefully observing which activities attract that child's attention and raise its interest.

The importance of rest and sleep in experience-dependent brain development

It has long been known that sleep has beneficial effects on the consolidation of memories. Over the last decades this general notion has received robust support by well controlled experimental studies. Sleep appears as a highly structured active process by which memory traces that have been accumulated throughout the day become reorganized and consolidated.

Neurophysiological studies suggest that activity patterns induced by learning trials are repeated during particular sleep phases, and it is believed that this rehearsal promotes consolidation of memory traces (Louie & Wilson, 2001; Hoffman & McNaughton, 2002). Interestingly, not only the consolidation of declarative, i.e. consciously stored memories requires sleep but also the acquisition of abilities that are acquired through procedural learning, i.e. through practice. A well examined example is perceptual learning. If subjects practice discrimination of certain visual features such as the orientation of contours their performance increases over time in a way that is highly specific for the particular task. This improvement of an instrumental ability that relies on modifications of response properties of neurons in the visual cortex also requires consolidation through sleep. If subjects are sleep-deprived after the training sessions performance does not improve (Ahissar & Hochstein, 1997).

Even more surprising is the increasing evidence that also the experience-dependent modifications of neuronal architectures that occur during brain development require sleep for their expression and consolidation. The evidence comes again from deprivation experiments in the visual system. In early experiments it was found that visual experience had more profound effects on the response properties of cortical neurons of kittens when these were exposed to the visual environment for only brief periods, and subsequently allowed to rest in the dark, than when they were exposed to the same environment for a similar period of time uninterruptedly (Mioche & Singer, 1989). Another study showed that circuit changes did not occur despite exposure to visual conditions that normally induce drastic changes when animals were anesthetized following exposure and thus were prevented from natural sleep (Rauschecker & Hahn, 1987). A more recent study provided direct evidence that interference with a particular sleep phase, the so-called paradoxical or rapid eye movement sleep, is sufficient to disrupt experience-dependent circuit selection. Thus, experience-dependent developmental processes seem to depend on sleep in very much the same way as the formation of memories by conventional learning (see Cardinali, this volume).

This evidence from animal experimentation should have consequences for the organization of occupation schedules in day-care centers. It is to be expected that children require episodes of rest and presumably also sleep after phases during which they had particular intense experiences. Thus, one should consider organizing day-care centers in a way that allows the children to retreat and have a nap according to their individual needs. To the best of my knowledge there are no systematic studies on the relation between sleep patterns, learning and brain maturation in children – but the data from animal experiments suggest strongly that rest and sleep play a pivotal role even in developmental processes.

Mechanisms of adult learning

As mentioned above, it is generally assumed that adult learning relies on changes in the efficacy of excitatory and/or inhibitory connections. The mechanisms that mediate these learning-induced changes in the coupling strength among neurons closely resemble those which mediate the activity-dependent circuit changes during experience-dependent development. Excitatory connections among neurons strengthen if these neurons discharge in a correlated way while they weaken if the activity of the cells is temporally unrelated. The molecular processes that evaluate the temporal correlations among neuronal firing patterns and translate these into lasting modifications of coupling strength are by and large the same as those promoting activity-dependent circuit selection during development (for review see Singer, 1995). The only major difference is that in the adult, weakening of connections is no longer followed by their removal and that no new connections are formed. However, there are a few exceptions. Over the past years evidence has become available that in a few distinct brain regions, parts of the hippocampus and the olfactory bulb neurons continue to be generated throughout life, and these neurons form new connections and become integrated in existing circuitry (Kempermann *et al.*, 1997 for review). Thus, in these distinct areas of the brain, developmental processes persist throughout life, and it is presently unclear why this is only the case in these particular regions and not in the cerebral cortex, where most of the learning-related modifications are supposed to take place.

Adult learning resembles experience-dependent developmental processes also with respect to its dependence on attentional mechanisms, on reward systems and on sleep. Thus, all the strategies that have been developed in order to improve learning processes in the adult are likely to be helpful also for the promotion of experience-dependent developmental processes in the young. What is required now is the transfer of knowledge about experience-dependent developmental processes that has been accumulated with neurobiological experimentation to educational programs. This necessitates intensification of research in developmental psychology and the incorporation of non-invasive techniques for the assessment of brain processes in children. Such methods are now available and can be applied to children as for example electroencephalographic or magneto-encephalographic recordings together with functional magnetic resonance tomography (for other techniques such as Near Infrared Spectroscopy

NIRS – Optical Topography, OT – see Koizumi & Petitto, this volume). Such approaches may help to define more precisely the critical periods of the development of particular brain functions and to design adapted strategies for the optimization of experience-dependent developmental processes.

References

Ahissar, M. and Hochstein, S. (1997). Task difficulty and the specificity of perceptual learning. *Nature* 387, 401–406.

Hoffman, K. L. and McNaughton, B. L. (2002). Coordinated reactivation of distributed memory traces in primate neocortex. *Science*, 297, 2070–2073.

Kempermann, G., Kuhn, H. G. and Gage, F. H. (1997). More hippocampal neurons in adult mice living in an enriched environment. *Nature*, 386, 493–495.

Louie, K. and Wilson, M. A. (2001). Temporally structured replay of awake hippocampal ensemble activity during rapid eye movement sleep. *Neuron*, 29, 145–156.

Mioche, L. and Singer, W. (1989). Chronic recordings from single sites of kitten striate cortex during experience-dependent modifications of receptive field-properties. *J. Neurophysiol.*, 62, 185–197.

Rauschecker, J. P. and Hahn, S. (1987). Ketamine-xylazine anaesthesia blocks consolidation of ocular dominance changes in kitten visual cortex. *Nature*, 326, 183–185.

Singer, W. (1990). The formation of cooperative cell assemblies in the visual cortex. *J. Exp. Biol.*, 153: 177–197.

(1995). Development and plasticity of cortical processing architectures. *Science*, 270, 758–764.

7 Chronoeducation: How the biological clock influences the learning process

Daniel P. Cardinali

Overview

Neuroscience research can be of great help in improving school performance in children and adolescents. We know, for instance, that sleep deprivation significantly impairs memory and the acquisition of many skills, and disturbs emotional and cognitive performance as well. By inducing sleep deprivation in many people in most urban environments, modern 24-hour society can become a threat to healthy behavior. Adolescents, in particular, tend to sleep less during school time because of late bedtime (work or entertainment) and early schooling. This current cultural pattern is out of phase with the body's internal clock and the circadian rhythms that are the result of millions of years of biological adaptation in mammals. People certainly are not prepared to be awake when our body temperature is at a minimum, for instance. Moreover the cyclical pattern of sleeping and waking changes with age. Adolescents show a shift toward a more owl-like behavior and their optimal time of the day is generally in the evening. This is the reason why they can be sleepy in the morning and become more alert when their classes are mostly over. By paying attention to these facts of chronoeducation, schools can improve student learning by creating a better connection between diurnal rhythms and the school schedule.

The Editors

Many biological functions wax and wane in cycles that repeat each day, month, or year. Such patterns do not reflect simply organism's passive response to environmental changes. Rather, they reflect the organism's biological rhythms, that is, its ability to keep track of time and to direct changes in function accordingly.

Because the Earth rotates on its axis, it presents two environments, i.e. light and darkness; because the Earth's axis of rotation is tilted, durations of daily periods of darkness and light vary systematically during the course of the year. Through Evolution, animals responded to these environmental changes by preferentially adapting to them (see Koizumi, this volume).

The circadian clock is one of the most indispensable biological functions

This is the origin of biological rhythms that repeat approximately every 24 hours, called circadian rhythms (from the Latin *circa*, for around, and *dies*, for day), and of rhythms that oscillate annually, following the recursive appearance of the seasons. Thus when animals switch between diurnal, nocturnal or seasonal modes of their behavior, they are not simply responding passively to changes in external lighting conditions. They are responding to signals generated by a circadian pacemaker which is written in their genes that is synchronized with the cycles of the Earth's rotation, anticipates the transitions between day and night, and triggers appropriate changes in behavioral state and physiological substrates. In this way, the circadian pacemaker creates a day and night within the organism that mirrors approximately the world outside.

During the past decade, enormous progress has been made in determining the molecular components of the biological clock. The molecular mechanisms that underlie the function of the clock are universally present in all the cells and consist of gene-protein-gene feedback loops in which proteins can down-regulate their own transcription and stimulate the transcription of other clock proteins (Hastings, Reddy, & Maywood, 2003).

Although circadian rhythms are anchored genetically they are synchronized by (entrained) and maintain certain phase relationships to external (exogenous) factors, especially the sleep portion of the light-dark schedule. These rhythms will persist with a period different from 24 h when external time cues are suppressed or removed, such as during complete social isolation or in constant light or darkness.

Research in animals and humans has shown that only a few such environmental cues, like light dark cycles, are effective entraining agents for the circadian oscillator ("Zeitgebers"). An entraining agent can actually reset, or phase shift, the internal clock. Depending on when an organism is exposed to such an entraining agent, circadian rhythms can be advanced, delayed, or not shifted at all. Therefore, involved in adjusting the daily activity pattern to the appropriate time of day is a rhythmic variation in the influence of the Zeitgeber as a resetting factor (Murphy & Campbell, 1996; Cardinali, 1998; Asayama *et al.*, 2003).

In mammals, a hierarchically major circadian oscillator is located in the suprachiasmatic nuclei (SCN) of the hypothalamus. The SCN circadian master clock acts like a multifunctional timer to adjust the homeostatic system, including sleep and wakefulness, hormonal secretions and various other bodily functions, to the 24-hour cycle (Rusak & Zucker, 1979; Murphy *et al.*, 1996; Cardinali, 1998; Hastings *et al.*, 2003).

Circadian mechanisms are active in modern humans

Our hominid ancestor, *Homo erectus*, used caves as shelters and may have used fire as early as 1.5 million years ago. *Homo sapiens* began to construct artificial dwellings (which could block out the rays of the sun) as early as 45,000 years ago, and to make lamps (which could be used to extend the daily period of illumination into nighttime hours) as early as 28,000 years ago. In the past 200 years, humans have developed increasingly efficient lamps and inexpensive sources of energy to power them. At the same time, they have increasingly moved their activities from countryside to city and from outdoors to indoors, where natural light may not penetrate. Consequently, humans have increasingly insulated themselves from the natural cycles of light and darkness that have shaped the endogenous rhythms of life on this planet for billions of years.

However, light, when appropriately applied, can have profound effects on the human circadian clock. In normal volunteers, bright light exposure during the first part of the night delays the phase of the circadian cycle; a comparable light change near the end of the night, advances it. At other times during the day light exposure has no phase-shifting influence (Rusak et al., 1979; Murphy et al., 1996; Cardinali, 1998; Hastings et al., 2003).

Melatonin, a hormone produced by the pineal gland and that is the endogenous chemical code of the night, showed an opposite phase response curve to light, producing phase advances during the first half of the night and phase delays during the second (Cardinali, 1998). Indeed, melatonin is the endogenous prototype of a class of compounds that can reset the biological clock, called "chronobiotics." Melatonin use in a number of pathologies that present circadian disruption, like blindness (Skene, 2003) or Alzheimer's disease (Cardinali, Brusco, Liberczuk, & Furio, 2002), is now warranted.

Among the innumerable periodic changes that underlie and support the overt physiologic rhythms, the peak values occur in a characteristic sequence over the day ("phase map") in human healthy subjects. Such a sequence and spacing reflects the order and temporal relationships of cause-effect in the normal interactions of the various bodily processes and is the very indicative of organism's health (Cardinali, Jorda Catala, & Sanchez Barcelo, 1994). Phase maps may undergo transitory disruptions when humans are compelled to make a rapid phase adjustment as, for example, after a rapid move to a new geographic longitude or as a consequence of shift work or after sudden changes from diurnal to nocturnal habits, like those observed among adolescents.

Under such circumstances the various individual 24-h components comprising the circadian phase map do not reset their phases to the new environmental times at the same rate, and become somewhat displaced in their relations to one another. To reset them to the new local time requires several days of exposure to the local phase setters. This phenomenon is quite familiar to persons who have traveled long distances rapidly through several time zones. The resultant rhythmic dislocation and the need for gradual adjustment over two to ten days at the end of such a trip is known as "jet-lag" (Hastings *et al.*, 2003).

Sleep-wakefulness is the most conspicuous circadian rhythm in humans

Sleep is an essential process in life. It is a behavioral state defined by: (i) characteristic relaxation of posture; (ii) raised sensory thresholds; and (iii) distinctive electroencephalographic (EEG) signs (Figure 7.1).

Two main, though not mutually exclusive, hypotheses have been predominant in interpreting sleep: (i) sleep is restorative for brain metabolism; (ii) sleep serves memory consolidation and the learning process.

One difficulty in understanding sleep is that it is not a unitary state but composed of two sub-states. One is characterized by rapid eye movements (REM sleep); the other, where there are no rapid eye movements, is known as non-REM (NREM) or slow-wave sleep (Fig. 7.1 and 7.2). In any typical sleep episode the two sub-states alternate: in adult humans, the NREM-REM sleep cycle has a period of 90–100 min (Fig. 7.2 and 7.3) (Hobson & Pace-Schott, 2002; Pace-Schott & Hobson, 2002).

Four stages of NREM sleep are distinguished in the EEG. Stage 1 is shallow sleep, with low-amplitude, high frequency activity. Stage 2 is characterized by the occurrence of spindles and is more superficial than stages 3 and 4, which are dominated by slow-wave activity (Fig. 7.1). During human REM sleep, the EEG resembles the low-amplitude, high frequency pattern of stage 1 NREM sleep. The tone in most voluntary muscles is minimal but the autonomic nervous system and the eye muscles are phasically active, giving REM sleep some resemblance to the wake state, for which reason it is sometimes referred to as "paradoxical" sleep. In all mammals, sleep is initiated by NREM and is interrupted by REM at regular intervals. In mature humans the average nocturnal sleep period consists of four to five such cycles. After a prolonged period of wake activity (as in humans) the first cycles are characterized by a preponderance of high-voltage, slow wave activity (i.e., the NREM phase is enhanced) while the last cycles show more low-voltage, fast wave activity (i.e., the REM phase is enhanced) (Figs. 7.2 and 7.3) (Hobson *et al.*, 2002; Pace-Schott *et al.*, 2002).

The recurrent cycles of NREM and REM sleep are accompanied by major changes in all physiological systems of the body. Indeed it can be

Awake, REM sleep

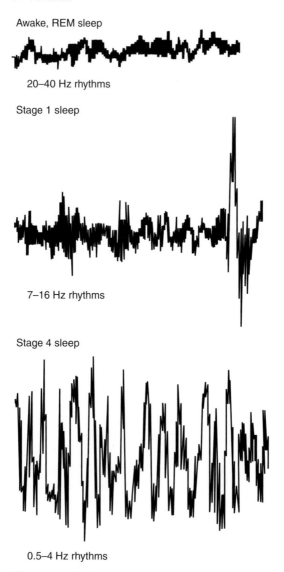

20–40 Hz rhythms

Stage 1 sleep

7–16 Hz rhythms

Stage 4 sleep

0.5–4 Hz rhythms

Figure 7.1 Typical electroencephalographic recording from wakefulness and sleep phases.

said that we live sequentially in "three different bodies": that of wakefulness, that of NREM and that of REM. For an adult living 75 years, approximately 50 years are lived in wakefulness, 19 years in NREM sleep and 6 years in REM sleep. Striking physiological differences

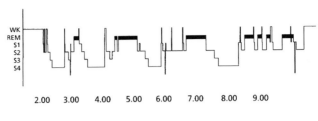

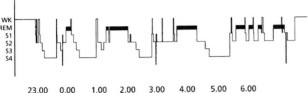

Figure 7.2 Sleep architecture as assessed polygraphically in a young adolescent showing a delayed phase sleep syndrome (upper panel) as compared to a normal adult (lower panel). W: wakefulness, REM: REM sleep (dark bars), S1-S4: Stage 1 to Stage 4 of non Rem sleep. In abcissas, clocktime.

between these three stages (or "bodies") have been documented. During NREM sleep there are decreases in blood pressure, heart rate, and respiratory rate, and occurrence of a pulsatile release of anabolic hormones like growth hormone together with a general increase of immune function. The concomitance of these events gives credence to the notion that NREM sleep is functionally associated with anabolic and cytoprotective processes. The brain itself is hypoactive as indicated by a 20–30 percent reduction in oxygen consumption, resembling what is seen in a light anesthesia. Several neurotrophic factors are synthesized during NREM sleep (Mazzoni et al., 1999; Peigneux, Laureys, Delbeuck, & Maquet, 2001).

In contrast, REM sleep is associated with an "antihomeostatic" stage. The regulatory mechanisms controlling the cardiovascular, respiratory and thermoregulatory functions become grossly inefficient. Heart rate and blood pressure increase, and respiratory rate becomes irregular. Penile erection in males and clitoral engorgement in females accompany the brain and autonomic activation of this phase and the somatic musculature is actively inhibited. Awakening from activated or REM sleep typically yields detailed reports of hallucinoid dreaming, even in subjects who rarely or never recall dreams spontaneously. This indicates that the brain activation of this phase of sleep is sufficiently intense and organized to support complex mental processes and again argues against a rest function for most of the brain in REM. Indeed, several areas of the

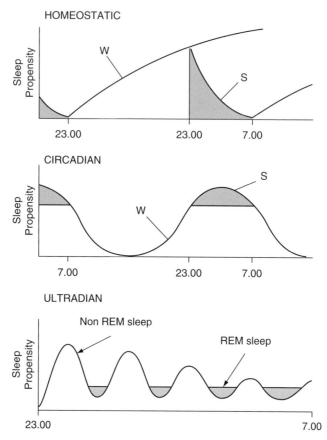

Figure 7.3 Three interacting processes regulate the timing, duration and depth, or intensity, of sleep: a homeostatic process that maintains the duration and intensity of sleep, a circadian rhythm that determines the timing of sleep, and an ultradian rhythm given by non REM sleep-REM sleep sequence.

brain, e.g. the limbic system, are more active than during wakefulness (Hobson *et al.*, 2002; Pace-Schott *et al.*, 2002).

A significant physiological concomitant of REM sleep is the loss of temperature regulation. If ambient or core temperature begins to fall, sleep is interrupted, but thermoregulatory processes cannot be brought into play during REM sleep. Thus the notion that we humans are home-othermic animals is no longer tenable. We resemble snakes, at least in part of our life! The logic of somatic and autonomic disconnection is that if acted, this period of sleep could be damaging for individual's survival.

There are several aspects of sleep including the continuity, timing, and patterning of different stages of sleep that are necessary for the restorative process to occur. For example, if subjects are permitted to sleep *ad libitum* for 8 to 10 hours but are awakened every 15 minutes for brief periods, the following day they will report tiredness, fatigue, and emotional changes similar to having obtained insufficient amounts of sleep. Similarly, if subjects are permitted *ad libitum* amounts of sleep but are selectively deprived of one sleep stage, such as rapid eye movement (REM) or slow sleep, they also report daytime attentional deficits (Hobson *et al.*, 2002; Pace-Schott *et al.*, 2002).

Three interacting processes regulate the timing, duration and depth, or intensity, of sleep: a homeostatic process that maintains the duration and intensity of sleep within certain boundaries, a circadian rhythm that determines the timing of sleep and an ultradian rhythm given by non REM sleep – REM sleep alternance (Fig. 7.3). The homeostatic process depends on immediate history: the interval since the previous sleep episode and the intensity of sleep in that episode. This drive to enter sleep increases, possibly exponentially, with the duration since the end of the previous sleep episode. It declines exponentially once sleep has been initiated. This reinforces the cyclical nature of sleep and wakefulness and equates sleep with other physiological needs such as hunger or thirst. The homeostatic sleep drive controls NREM sleep rather than REM sleep.

In contrast, the phase and amplitude of the circadian rhythm are independent of the history of previous sleep but are generated by the major pacemaker, the SCN. The circadian variation of human sleep propensity is roughly the inverse of the core body temperature rhythm: maximum propensity for sleep and the highest continuity of sleep occur in proximity to the minimum temperature (Fig. 7.3).

Adaptive drives, including a variety of mechanisms that influence sleep but which are independent of the time spent awake and of circadian rhythms, should be also considered in sleep regulation. Adaptive factors modify the sleep-wake cycle according to changes in the environment, which are significant for the individual. They include behavioral factors, like motivation, attention and other psychological responses to the environment (e.g. bed comfort, social activity), noise, environmental temperature, physical exercise and food intake (Hobson *et al.*, 2002; Pace-Schott *et al.*, 2002).

The circadian system is influential in the educational process

A very important general principle about the circadian system relevant to learning is that it adapts slowly to changes in sleep/wake schedules. Thus, adolescents who rapidly shift sleep/wake schedules between school nights and weekends or vacations can face circadian consequences (Sadeh, Gruber, & Raviv, 2003; Shin, Kim, Lee, Ahn, & Joo, 2003; Carskadon, Acebo, & Jenni, 2004). Another important general principle about the circadian timing system relevant to education is that the circadian system adapts more easily to delays in the sleep/wake schedule rather than to advances. This is why it is naturally easier to stay up later and sleep in later on weekends and why it is easier to travel 2–3 time zones to the west rather than to the east (Cardinali *et al.*, 1994; Hastings *et al.*, 2003).

The relevance of these principles to adolescent sleep patterns is straightforward. Many adolescents have abrupt changes in the timing of their sleep between regular school schedules, requiring early morning awakening, and the late bedtimes, with quick shifts back to late bedtimes and sleeping in on weekends and vacations. For example a typical Argentine adolescent going to bed at 3:00 am on weekends and sleeping in until noon will phase-delay their circadian system during the vacation time to be awakened till 3 am within a few days. However, the shift to an earlier time after ending the vacation period, compatible with going to school early in the morning, will require several days of a stable schedule to shift the temperature and hormone rhythms completely.

Therefore, many adolescents, particularly those who oversleep or miss an occasional day of school during the middle of the week may experience jet lag-like symptoms of fatigue, difficulty in falling asleep at night, and difficulty in awakening in the morning. In the most severe version of this problem, labeled delayed sleep phase syndrome, adolescents and their families often battle for months about late night bedtimes and great difficulties awakening on school days (Fig. 7. 2). Indeed, the adolescents are trying to awaken during their body temperature minimum, when their body is not prepared to be awake and active. An important principle to be considered is that slow, steady, and consistent changes in the sleep/wake timing will permit the circadian system to realign to a more appropriate pattern.

Sleep strongly influences education

When sleep is considered within the educational context several relevant aspects emerge. One deals with the association of learning processes with sleep. Several studies have shown augmentation in sleep amounts or sleep architecture following learning tasks (Carskadon *et al.*, 2004). For example, positive correlations between the number of NREM sleep cycles and memorization of word lists were reported (Mazzoni *et al.*, 1999). Maze learning has been shown to increase stage 2 sleep and EEG slow wave activity in subsequent sleep (Peigneux *et al.*, 2001) and similar increases in EEG spindles are reported following memorization of word lists (Gais, Plihal, Wagner, & Born, 2000) and are positively correlated with memory performance. Interestingly, stage 2 NREM sleep, which is particularly rich in EEG slow wave activity, is reported to be positively correlated with the acquisition of several skills.

Another central principle about sleep, which is of particular relevance to aspects of human development, is the close link between sleep and perceptions of threat/safety. Sleep, at a behavioral level, involves the loss of awareness and responsiveness to the external environment. During sleep, most exteroceptive information stops at the level of the thalamus, preventing perception of (and behavioral response to) potential threats in the environment. As a result, most species have evolved mechanisms to ensure that sleep behavior is limited to niches relatively safe from predators. It also makes sense that any perception of threat and the accompanying increased arousal is the opposite to going to sleep. This link between sleep and safety has clinical relevance to sleep problems.

In the human ancestral environment, a close-knit social group provided protection against predators. The human brain evolved under conditions in which this sense of social belonging was crucial for safety. Natural tendencies in the modern human brain continue to reflect these links, such that social stressors evoke powerful feelings of threat and sleep disruption, but feelings of love, caring, and social connection create a sense of safety and promote sleep. This is important to consider how safety/threat perception and its capability to disrupt sleep change during development. The development of the vigilance or threat perception and response system shows a significant increase across puberty probably because adolescents were making the physical preparations to take on adult roles, with increased demands on threat appraisal.

Another aspect to be considered is the shortening of sleep time caused by the "24-hour society." Since modern humans use artificial light to extend their period of wakefulness and activity into the evening hours, they adhere to a short-night sleep schedule throughout the year for most of their lives. In these circumstances, individuals fall asleep shortly after lying down and sleep without interruption until they arise in the morning. This type of sleep, which we tend to regard as our only normal type of sleep, is highly consolidated and efficient, occupying almost all of the nightly period of bed rest. However, modern humans probably obtain less than their full quota of nightly sleep. At steady state in artificial long nights, normal volunteers sleep an average of 8.25 hour/night, which is more than most humans obtain in modern life. This finding raises the possibility that modern humans are sleep-deprived and less fully awake in

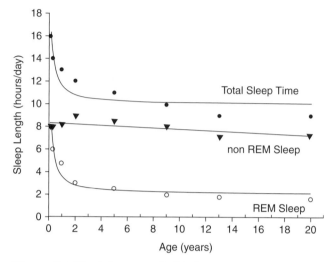

Figure 7.4 Total sleep, non REM sleep and REM sleep duration from birth to late adolescence.

the daytime than would otherwise be the case (Hobson *et al.*, 2002; Pace-Schott *et al.*, 2002).

Differing from man, the sleep of most other animals is polyphasic, exhibiting multiple bouts per day. In fact, most people would probably regard sleep in polyphasic bouts that alternate with periods of quiet wakefulness as abnormal and undesirable if it occurred. However, sleep studies of voluntaries in long nights indicate that human sleep can also be polyphasic. In long nights, periods of quiet rest and contemplation often begin after transitions to wakefulness from periods of REM sleep (and dreaming) that are particularly intense. It is tempting to speculate that in prehistoric times this arrangement provided a channel of communication between dreams and waking life that has gradually been closed off as humans have compressed and consolidated their sleep. If so, then this alteration might provide a physiological explanation for the observation that modern humans seem to have lost touch with the wellspring of myths and fantasies.

Age-related (developmental) processes exert profound influences on sleep regulation

Total sleep decreases from 14–16 hour/day in the newborn to approximately 8 hour/night by age 18 years (Fig. 7.4). One-year-old children sleep 11–12 hours/night with another 2.5 hours of sleep obtained in two separate daytime naps. By age 3 years, the average child gets 10.5 hours of sleep each night with one 1.5-hour nap. In Argentina, a typical child ceases daytime naps at about 4 to 5 years of age. It is also important to emphasize that there is considerable individual variation in sleep requirements as well as cultural influences on sleep and napping behavior; for example, daytime naps continue through adulthood in Latin American cultures.

What are the major changes of sleep during adolescence? The major changes found are: (i) there is a decrease in the duration and depth of NREM (stages 3 and 4) and REM sleep, (ii) more adult-like pattern of REM sleep develops, (iii) there are increases in daytime sleepiness, (iv) there is a shift in the circadian pattern toward a more owl-like tendency for later bedtimes and wake-up times (Fig. 7.2). There is also a decrease in the threshold of arousal from infancy through adolescence (Fukuda & Ishihara, 2001; Quine, 2001; Paavonen, Fjallberg, Steenari, & Aronen, 2002; Sadeh, Gruber, & Raviv, 2002). Adolescent maturation is also associated with a relative shortening of the interval from sleep onset to the first REM period (shorter REM latency) and a decrease in the REM density (rate of eye movements occurring within REM).

Adolescents typically get by on less sleep (at least on school nights). However, there are several reasons to believe that this decrease occurs independent of biology. In studies of adolescents in natural environments (when adolescents obtain less sleep than in the laboratory situations), dramatically elevated levels of daytime sleepiness are often observed. In many cases, the levels of sleepiness in high school students are near the threshold seen in sleep disorders such as narcolepsy or sleep apnea. Flexible educational practices and irregular way of life were associated with the shortest duration of sleep and the least performant attentional capacities (Billon-Descarpentries, 1997). Therefore, parental educational errors resulting in a poor nyctohemeral waking-sleeping time distribution and chronic sleep debt appear to be a cause of school underachievement.

School schedules also affect adolescent sleep patterns, seen most commonly as imposing earlier rise times as the school day begins earlier during the adolescent years (Carskadon et al., 2004). Ironically, the school starting time moves earlier as children's grade advances. Although school starts earlier, children cannot adjust their bedtime accordingly, and this could result in sleep deprivation (Dexter, Bijwadia, Schilling, & Applebaugh, 2003; Sadeh et al., 2003). Subsequently, they are sleepy during the morning and become more alert in the afternoon when school is almost over (Andrade, Benedito-Silva, & Menna-Barreto, 1992; Andrade, Benedito-Silva, Domenice, Arnhold, & Menna-Barreto, 1993). The circadian phase shift could also influence children's school performance through asynchrony between their preferred time of day and the time at which classes are taught. According to the synchrony effect, younger and older adults perform better on a number of cognitive tasks at their optimal time of day than at their non optimal time of day (which happens to be different for the two groups). For example, younger and older adults are less distractible at their optimal times, their recognition of newly learned information is better at their optimal times and their control over strong but inappropriate responses is better at their optimal times (Heuer, Spijkers, Kiesswetter, & Schmidtke, 1998; Roberts & Kyllonen, 1999; Alapin *et al.*, 2000; Eliasson, Eliasson, King, Gould, & Eliasson, 2002). As well, and of special relevance to classroom learning, is evidence that shows dramatic differences in memory performance for younger and older adults tested at optimal versus at non optimal times.

Since children's time of day preference shifts toward eveningness as they get older, their cognitive functioning is likely to be at its peak more toward the afternoon than in the morning. Thus, if important basic classes such as reading and mathematics are taught in the morning, older school children will be learning this critical material at their less-preferred, or non optimal time of day, resulting in poorer school performance than might be found were the courses in greater synchrony with circadian arousal rhythms (Roberts, Roberts, & Chen, 2002). It is interesting that in recent study on sleep habits and school outcomes in middle-school children (Drake *et al.*, 2003), participants who reported low school achievement, high rates of absenteeism, low school enjoyment, low total sleep time, and frequent illness reported significantly higher levels of daytime sleepiness compared to children with better school-related outcomes. Giannotti *et al.* examined the relationship among circadian preferences, regularity of sleep patterns, sleep problems, daytime sleepiness and daytime behavior (Giannotti, Cortesi, Sebastiani, & Ottaviano, 2002). Eveningness was associated with later bedtime and wake-up time, especially on weekends, shorter time in bed during the week, longer weekend time in bed, irregular sleep-wake schedule, subjective poor sleep. Moreover, evening types used to nap more frequently during school days, complained of daytime sleepiness, referred more attention problems, poor school achievement and more injuries and were more emotionally upset than the other chronotype (Giannotti *et al.*, 2002).

Besides inadequate sleep, a separate but related factor is tiredness. Tiredness can be defined as the feeling of fatigue that makes it difficult to motivate or initiate certain types of behavior, particularly those behaviors associated with long-term goals or negative consequences. Tiredness and symptoms of fatigue can be prominent in adolescents, even if they remain awake; these symptoms may also contribute to longer-term consequences. In addition, part-time employment has a significant impact on the sleep patterns of teenagers: those who work more than 20 hours each week sleep less, go to bed later, are more sleepy, and drink more caffeine and alcohol (Dexter et al., 2003; Shin et al., 2003).

Another important domain of sleep deprivation effects is in relation to mood (Carskadon et al., 2004). Sleep deprivation may impair the ability to perform both a cognitive and emotional task at the same time. Although these may seem to be relatively subtle effects, the foundation of social competence, an area of major struggle for adolescents, requires fluency in performance in such tasks. In particular, the ability to concentrate on a long-term goal or consequence while regulating emotional reactions in social situations is precisely the territory that many adolescents are struggling to navigate in their day-to-day lives. If sleep deprivation results in impairment in this domain, it may have very significant consequences.

Concluding remarks

Consciousness, defined by the English philosopher John Locke as "the perception of what passes in a man's own mind," depends heavily on the levels of alertness and therefore exhibits significant circadian fluctuations. Particular types of performance peak at different times during the circadian cycle, depending on perceptual involvement, the use of memory, and the amount of logical reasoning required. Performance of tasks involving manual dexterity, simple recognition, and reaction time parallels the circadian rhythm of body temperature, peaking when body temperature is highest, in the late afternoon. Verbal reasoning peaks earlier in the circadian cycle and may adjust more quickly than other types of performance to such disruptions as jet lag or shift work. In addition, when subjects are asked to indicate their level of alertness, weariness, happiness, or other moods on a visual scale at regular times throughout the course of the day, consistent circadian patterns emerge.

Many aspects of human performance decline to minimal levels at night, reflecting not only the influence of the circadian pacemaker, but also the lack of sleep. Sleep deprivation, even for one night, is one of the most important disrupting factors of human mental and physical function. The circadian clock also leads to a nighttime minimum in many types of performance. Thus, sleep deprivation combined with the influence of the circadian pacemaker can severely curtail performance at night. These factors have important implications for any educational system in our "24-hour society," that superimposes an increasing demand for wakefulness on our grossly inadequate physiological design, unable to keep unmodified levels of alertness regardless of time of day.

Transition to an earlier school start time, along with pubertal phase delay, significantly affects teenagers' sleep quality, sleep/wake schedule, and daytime behavior. The combination of the phase advance, late-night activities or jobs, and early-morning school demands can significantly constrict hours available to sleep. The available community and school-based studies examining the prevalence of sleep disturbances in youths indicate that symptoms of insomnia and hypersomnia are common. Indeed in non-clinical populations 20–30 percent of children and adolescents have been found to have complaints or difficulties related to sleep that are regarded as significant.

Acknowledgements

Work in the author's laboratory was supported in part by the Agencia Nacional de Promoción Científica y Tecnológica, Argentina, the University of Buenos Aires, Consejo Nacional de Investigaciones Científicas y Técnicas (CONICET), Argentina, Fundación Bunge y Born, Buenos Aires and Fundación Antorchas, Buenos Aires.

References

Alapin, I., Fichten, C. S., Libman, E., Creti, L., Bailes, S., and Wright, J. (2000). How is good and poor sleep in older adults and college students related to daytime sleepiness, fatigue, and ability to concentrate? *J.Psychosom.Res.*, 49, 381–390.

Andrade, M. M., Benedito-Silva, A. A., Domenice, S., Arnhold, I. J., and Menna-Barreto, L. (1993). Sleep characteristics of adolescents: a longitudinal study. *J Adolesc.Health*, 14, 401–406.

Andrade, M. M., Benedito-Silva, A. A., and Menna-Barreto, L. (1992). Correlations between morningness-eveningness character, sleep habits and temperature rhythm in adolescents. *Braz.J.Med.Biol.Res.*, 25, 835–839.

Asayama, K., Yamadera, H., Ito, T., Suzuki, H., Kudo, Y., and Endo, S. (2003). Double blind study of melatonin effects on the sleep-wake rhythm, cognitive and non-cognitive functions in Alzheimer type dementia. *J.Nippon Med.Sch*, 70, 334–341.

Billon-Descarpentries, J. (1997). [Influence of parental educational practices on the sleep and attentional performances in children]. *Arch.Pediatr.* 4, 181–185.

Cardinali, D. P. (1998). The human body circadian: How the biologic clock influences sleep and emotion. *Ciencia e Cultura*, 50, 172–177.

Cardinali, D. P., Brusco, L. I., Liberczuk, C., and Furio, A. M. (2002). The use of melatonin in Alzheimer's disease. *Neuroendocrinol.Lett.*, 23 Suppl 1, 20–23.

Cardinali, D. P., Jorda Catala, J., and Sanchez Barcelo, E. J. (1994). *Introducción a la Cronobiología. Fisiología de los Ritmos Biológicos.* [Introduction to

Chronobiology. Physiology of Circadian Rhythms]. Caja Cantabria, Santander: Editorial Universidad de Cantabria.

Carskadon, M. A., Acebo, C., and Jenni, O. G. (2004). Regulation of adolescent sleep: implications for behavior. *Ann.N.Y.Acad.Sci*, 1021, 276–291.

Dexter, D., Bijwadia, J., Schilling, D., and Applebaugh, G. (2003). Sleep, sleepiness and school start times: a preliminary study. *WMJ*, 102, 44–46.

Drake, C., Nickel, C., Burduvali, E., Roth, T., Jefferson, C., and Pietro, B. (2003). The pediatric daytime sleepiness scale (PDSS): sleep habits and school outcomes in middle-school children. *Sleep*, 26, 455–458.

Eliasson, A., Eliasson, A., King, J., Gould, B., and Eliasson, A. (2002). Association of sleep and academic performance. *Sleep Breath*, 6, 45–48.

Fukuda, K. and Ishihara, K. (2001). Age-related changes of sleeping pattern during adolescence. *Psychiatry Clin.Neurosci.*, 55, 231–232.

Gais, S., Plihal, W., Wagner, U., and Born, J. (2000). Early sleep triggers memory for early visual discrimination skills. *Nat.Neurosci.*, 3, 1335–1339.

Giannotti, F., Cortesi, F., Sebastiani, T., and Ottaviano, S. (2002). Circadian preference, sleep and daytime behaviour in adolescence. *J.Sleep Res.*, 11, 191–199.

Hastings, M., Reddy, A. B., and Maywood, E. S. (2003). A clockwork web: circadian timing in brain and periphery, in health and disease. *Nat Rev Neurosci*, 4, 649–661.

Heuer, H., Spijkers, W., Kiesswetter, E., and Schmidtke, V. (1998). Effects of sleep loss, time of day, and extended mental work on implicit and explicit learning of sequences. *J.Exp.Psychol.Appl.*, 4, 139–162.

Hobson, J. A. and Pace-Schott, E. F. (2002). The cognitive neuroscience of sleep: neuronal systems, consciousness and learning. *Nat.Rev Neurosci*, 3, 679–693.

Mazzoni, G., Gori, S., Formicola, G., Gneri, C., Massetani, R., Murri, L. *et al.* (1999). Word recall correlates with sleep cycles in elderly subjects. *J.Sleep Res.*, 8, 185–188.

Murphy, P. J. and Campbell, S. S. (1996). Physiology of the circadian system in animals and humans. *J. Clin Neurophysiol*, 13, 2–16.

Paavonen, E. J., Fjallberg, M., Steenari, M. R., and Aronen, E. T. (2002). Actigraph placement and sleep estimation in children. *Sleep*, 25, 235–237.

Pace-Schott, E. F. and Hobson, J. A. (2002). The neurobiology of sleep: genetics, cellular physiology and subcortical networks. *Nat.Rev Neurosci*, 3, 591–605.

Peigneux, P., Laureys, S., Delbeuck, X., and Maquet, P. (2001). Sleeping brain, learning brain. The role of sleep for memory systems. *Neuroreport*, 12, A111–A124.

Quine, L. (2001). Sleep problems in primary school children: comparison between mainstream and special school children. *Child Care Health Dev.*, 27, 201–221.

Roberts, R. D. and Kyllonen, P. C. (1999). Morningness-eveningness and intelligence: early to bed, early to rise will likely make you anything but wise! *Pers.Individ.Dif.*, 27, 1123–1133.

Roberts, R. E., Roberts, C. R., and Chen, I. G. (2002). Impact of insomnia on future functioning of adolescents. *J.Psychosom.Res.*, 53, 561–569.

Rusak, B. and Zucker, I. (1979). Neural regulation of circadian rhythms. *Physiol. Rev*, 59, 449–526.

Sadeh, A., Gruber, R., and Raviv, A. (2002). Sleep, neurobehavioral functioning, and behavior problems in school-age children. *Child Dev.*, 73, 405–417.

(2003). The effects of sleep restriction and extension on school-age children: what a difference an hour makes. *Child Dev.*, 74, 444–455.

Shin, C., Kim, J., Lee, S., Ahn, Y., and Joo, S. (2003). Sleep habits, excessive daytime sleepiness and school performance in high school students. *Psychiatry Clin.Neurosci.*, 57, 451–453.

Skene, D. J. (2003). Optimization of light and melatonin to phase-shift human circadian rhythms. *J.Neuroendocrinol.*, 15, 438–441.

8   Dynamic cycles of cognitive and brain development: Measuring growth in mind, brain, and education

Kurt W. Fischer

Overview

Since the seminal work of Jean Piaget on the relation between knowledge and general biology, researchers have started to understand the basic neurocognitive processes in the unfolding of human development. In particular, recent dynamic growth models illuminate the complex, interrelated changes that take place during brain growth, cognitive development, and learning. Neurocognitive development should be conceived not as a ladder of successive stages but as a complex network of interactions and attractors, convergent and divergent paths, nested cycles, stabilities and instabilities, progressions and regressions, clusters of discontinuities and stable levels of performance. Cycles of cortical development and cycles of cognitive performance seem to be related. In particular the relationship becomes most visible with optimal functioning of the cognitive system, such as when a good teacher or textbook supports a student's performance. A series of discontinuities in optimal cognitive growth define a ten-level developmental scale, which has many potential educational implications. More generally, the systematic growth cycles of cognition and brain have many implications for education, which are sometimes not straightforward. It is essential to the future of education that teachers become involved in neurocognitive research and neuroscientists discover the great theoretical and practical challenge of working in schools.

The Editors

Most scientists and teachers find it obvious that cognitive development and brain development go together, and the enterprise of connecting mind, brain, and education starts with that assumption, as evident in most chapters of this book. Knowledge of brain development is growing at a phenomenal rate (Coch, Fischer, & Dawson, in press; Dawson & Fischer, 1994), and knowledge of cognitive development and learning is extensive, deep, and still building (e.g., Case, 1998; Fischer & Bidell, 1998; Fischer & Bidell, 2006; Piaget, 1983; Siegler, 1997). Yet understanding of how cognitive and brain development relate has been

127

minimal. Many brain characteristics – number of neurons and synapses, brain mass, myelination, brain activity, and so forth – change systematically as children grow up. Simultaneously children's actions, speech, concepts, problem solving, social skills, motivation, and emotions develop. All these various changes are globally correlated, but the correlations are not very informative because everything is changing in parallel. Scientists who seek to understand brain-behavior relations and educators who want to use cognitive neuroscience to improve education need ways of finding and analyzing meaningful connections between changes in brain and behavior, moving beyond the finding that characteristics go generally up (some go generally down) with age. Despite these limitations of scientific knowledge, public expectations about relating brain science to educational practice are running far ahead of the realities of scientific knowledge (chapter by Bruer; Fischer, Immordino-Yang, & Waber, 2006).

Meaningful approaches to relating brain and cognitive development are beginning to emerge, however. In one promising arena, the new tools of dynamic systems analysis have combined with the discovery of growth cycles in cognitive and brain development to provide a foundation for moving beyond the difficulties of analyzing brain-behavior relations. Dynamic systems theory provides tools for analyzing complex patterns of change in individual people, in contrast to traditional tools that focus on analyzing average patterns of change for groups, which smooth out the interesting complexities of individual change (chapter by van Geert & Steenbeck). Research shows that individuals grow in complex patterns, showing not linear change but cycles of jumps and drops (Dawson-Tunik, Commons, Wilson, & Fischer, 2005; Fischer & Bidell, 2006; Molenaar, 2004). These discontinuities and complex patterns provide valuable tools for analyzing development of brain and behavior because scientists can examine relations between the patterns. Evidence is accumulating for cycles of brain growth, cycles of cognitive development, and cycles in learning. All three cycles seem to involve a common process of growth, and one outcome of the research on these growth patterns is the discovery of a general ruler for development and learning that has many uses in educational assessement and practice.

Growth cycles and rulers for brain and behavior

In living organisms, growth generally occurs through cycles. A prime example is the growth of the cortex, which grows six layers in a cyclical process of neuron generation and migration, as described by Rakic (1971; 1988). A single growth process thus produces six distinct layers in which cells for different layers end up with vastly different functions, even though they are all created by the same process. The process begins as the germinal layer in the embryo's ventricular zone grows new cells in large numbers, and each cell migrates along a ladder created by a glial cell to its destination. The first cells to migrate stop at the first layer of the cortex (dubbed layer six because it is the sixth layer from the top of the cortex, although it is the first one in development of the embryo). After that layer fills up, the cells continue to a higher point to become the second layer, which in turn becomes filled. The next cells then stop at what becomes the third layer, which again becomes filled. This process continues until the six layers of the cortex are all laid down. In this way one growth process creates cortical layers that end up with very different properties and functions. Within a cortical column, the six layers relate to each other hierarchically, with the lower layers (5 and 6 by conventional numbering) performing more basic functions, such as dealing with basic sensory and motor inputs and outputs, and the higher layers (1 and 2) performing functions that combine, integrate, or differentiate the signals from the lower ones.

Analogous growth cycles seem to occur in brain and cognitive development over time, based on the still young research on growth patterns of brain activity and the more mature evidence on cognitive performance. One of the simplest indexes of the cyclical pattern is that growth occurs with a series of discontinuities – spurts or drops in the simplest case, such as the widely documented spurts in language in the second year (Reznick & Goldfield, 1992). In a study of spontaneous language production in Dutch children Ruhland and van Geert (1998) found that most children showed rapid jumps in performance for specific word categories in the vicinity of 24 months of age, such as the spurt produced by Tomas for use of personal pronouns, shown in Figure 8.1.

This spurt at around 24 months comprises one pass through the *growth cycle for cognitive development*, which moves through a series of spurts in performance starting in early infancy and continuing into the 20s (Fischer & Bidell, 2006), as shown for the upper line in Figure 8.2. Infants, children, adolescents, and young adults all move through periods when their skills are leaping forward at a fast pace, especially under conditions that support optimal performance (upper line). In more ordinary performance, where they are not pushing the limits of their capacity, they commonly show either linear growth or unsystematic change (lower line). The graph presents a summary portrait of the growth patterns for the advanced abstract skills that develop during adolescence and early adulthood (Fischer, Yan, & Stewart, 2003).

These complex growth patterns combined with methods from dynamic systems theory provide powerful tools for use in research on brain

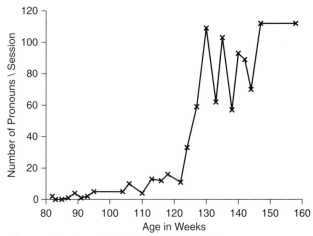

Source: Data from Ruhland & van Geert, 1998

Figure 8.1 Developmental spurt in use of personal pronouns by Tomas, a Dutch boy.

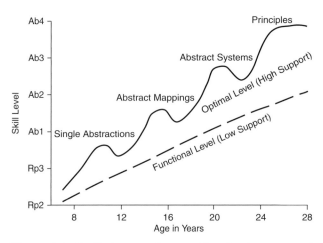

Figure 8.2 Cyclical spurts for cognitive development under optimal conditions.

development and education, because they follow a common scale across domains. Skills in different domains demonstrate discontinuities along the same scale (Dawson-Tunik *et al.*, 2005; Fischer & Bidell, 2006). The results are especially strong and clear for cognitive development and learning, where research has clearly demonstrated a single common scale for skill complexity across diverse contents and with different methods for assessing patterns of change. Cognitive development moves along this scale whatever the domain, just as temperature follows one scale whether the object measured is a sick child, a glacier, a boiling pot of water, a volcano, or the surface of the sun. The complexity scale provides a useful ruler for educational assessments, applying for different domains, for learners and teachers, for tests and curricula (Bidell & Fischer, 1992; Dawson-Tunik & Stein, in press). It has proved useful even for tracking the ups and downs of learning a specific task, which is commonly called microdevelopment (Granott, Fischer, & Parziale, 2002).

Understanding the growth patterns behind the scale requires first addressing a common misconception about development. Most people assume unconsciously that development involves progression along a ladder from one stage to the next. However, children and likewise adults develop not along a ladder but along a web of many strands. The common complexity scale across domains does not mean that development occurs in ladder-like stages. Figure 8.3 illustrates the web for three domains of development in adolescents and young adults – mathematics, self-in-relationships, and reflective judgment (Fischer *et al.*, 2003). An individual constructs separate skills for each domain, including several different strands within each. All strands move along the same complexity scale, but the skills in one strand are independent of those in another. Sometimes strands differentiate into new, separate strands, and at other times they combine to form a new integrated strand. For some purposes skills in different domains such as reflective judgment and conceptions of self can be treated as simply separate, but as development proceeds, people often combine strands from different domains, connecting for example conceptions of self as a student with conceptions about how they know that something is true (the bases of knowledge – reflective judgment). In either case, the same complexity scale characterizes development along each strand, even though the strands involve separate skills. The same ruler measures the complexity, but this common ruler does not imply that all the skills are the same, any more than a common temperature reading means that a person with a given temperature contains the same heat energy as a summer day with that temperature.

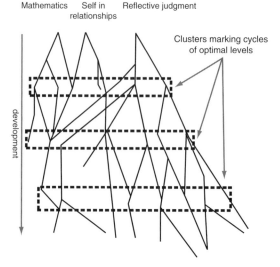

Mathematics   Self in   Reflective judgment
relationships

Clusters marking cycles
of optimal levels

development

Figure 8.3 A developmental web of many strands with clusters of discontinuities for three skill levels.

The growth cycle of skill construction appears in the web as *clusters of discontinuities* – angles, joinings, and separations of lines within the boxes marking the zones in which three new optimal levels emerge. These clusters capture changes for optimal performance, while ordinary, non-optimal performance takes place at lower points along the strands. That is, the same person in the same domain or strand shows a different developmental level depending on whether he or she is performing at optimal or functional level (as shown in Figure 8.2). People do not act consistently at one level, even for a familiar domain such as conceptions of self. Their skills vary in complexity from minute to minute depending on contextual support, motivation, fatigue, and other factors.

Cycles of cognitive development

Cognitive development moves through ten levels between 4 months of age and early adulthood. The levels from childhood to adulthood, which are most relevant for education, are summarized in Table 8.1. Among the simplest, most compelling evidence for the levels is the spurts and drops in performance that occur for optimal performance at specific ages. Research on arithmetic, self concepts, reflective judgment, moral reasoning, classification, conservation, and many other tasks shows these

Table 8.1 *Developmental levels during the school years: optimal & functional.*

Level	Optimal	Functional[*]
Rp1 Single Representations	2 years	2 to 5 years
Rp2 Representational Mappings	4	4 to 8
Rp3 Representational Systems	6	7 to 12
Rp4/Ab1 Single Abstractions	10	12 to 20
Ab2 Abstract Mappings	15	17 to 30
Ab3 Abstract Systems	20	23 to 40, or never for many domains
Ab4/P Single Principles	25	30 to 45, or never for many domains

[*]Ages for functional levels vary widely & are coarse estimates, based on research by Dawson, Fischer, Kitchener, King, Kohlberg, Rest, & others. Levels are highly related to education.

spurts and drops marking the onset of capacities to build skills at each of the levels.

In a study of concepts for arithmetic operations, adolescents demonstrated spurts under optimal conditions for three levels – single abstractions, abstract mappings, and abstract systems (Fischer, Kenny, & Pipp, 1990). Students between 9 and 20 years of age from diverse schools as well as a university in a mid-Western American city performed a set of arithmetic problems, such as $7 + 7 + 7 = 21$, $3 \times 7 = 21$, $5 + 9 = 14$, and $14 - 9 = 5$. They then answered questions that required them to explain the operations of addition, subtraction, multiplication, and division, and then the relations between the pairs of operations, such as addition and multiplication, or addition and subtraction. What is multiplication, and how do the problems that were calculated fit the definition of multiplication? How does multiplication relate to addition, and how do the problems involve that relation? Students first did the calculations and offered the explanations under low-support conditions, simply answering the questions on their own. Then they were provided with good, prototypic answers to the questions about the operations (high support), which they were asked to explain in their own terms. At the end of the session they were told that they would return in two weeks to do the problems again, and they should think about the questions. When they returned, they again did the problems and answered the questions first with low support and then with high support.

Students showed dramatic jumps in performance under optimal conditions at specific ages, as shown in Figure 8.4 for mappings relating pairs of arithmetic operations. The spurts were especially abrupt in the second session, two weeks after the first one, when students had not only high

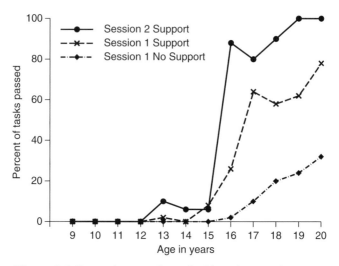

Figure 8.4 Spurts for mappings of arithmetic operations.

support but also days to practice and think about the questions. Students were asked to explain the relations between addition and subtraction, addition and multiplication, multiplication and division, and subtraction and division (two versions of each question for a total of eight tasks). When they were simply asked, without any support or practice (Session 1 No Support), they showed very low levels of performance – near zero until age 16 and reaching only 32 percent correct at age 20. However, when they were given support (Session 1 Support), their performance jumped sharply between 15 and 17 years. The opportunity to think about the problems for two weeks led to an even more abrupt spurt, from 6 percent at age 15 to 88 percent at age 16 (Session 2 Support). This study was the first test of a spurt predicted solely from dynamic skill theory without any prior evidence, and Figure 8.4 shows that the finding was strong and unambiguous.

Besides the spurt for mappings, the graph also shows another developmental phenomenon with strong educational relevance – *later-level consolidation*: A new kind of skill, such as relations of arithmetic operations or concepts for determining truth, emerges at one level; but it is only consolidated to produce consistent performance at a later level several years later, when the various components can be coordinated and interconnected. In the arithmetic study, the two curves showing spurts both leveled out for a few years after 16 and then spurted again to even better performance at about age 20. Such a second spurt occurs commonly in cognitive development, reflecting the emergence of the next level, which in this case is abstract systems (Ab3). When a new level emerges, performance jumps above zero, but it typically jumps to much less than perfect performance. For example, with reflective judgment (explaining the bases of knowledge in complex dilemmas), students' performance jumped to only about 50 percent correct with the first emergence of a level (Kitchener, Lynch, Fischer, & Wood, 1993). Only five years later, with emergence of the next level, did performance approach 100 percent.

The series of discontinuities in cognitive growth define a ten-level *developmental scale* – three levels of sensorimotor actions plus the seven levels in Table 8.1. In addition, a different set of methods have produced independent evidence of the same scale of seven levels in Table 8.1. Theo Dawson (Dawson & Wilson, 2004; Dawson-Tunik *et al.*, 2005) pioneered this research, using Rasch analysis to scale item difficulty in extensive data sets based on interviews, standardized tests, essays, and other written materials. Rasch scaling detected exactly the same seven-level scale in these data sets, demonstrating clustering of items by complexity level and gaps along the complexity scale between the clusters. The clustering holds even for adults, where age is not a factor in the ordering of items.

The successive levels that develop as shown in Table 8.1 indicate one kind of growth cycle, a recurring cluster of spurts in performance with emergence of each new cognitive level. Analogous to the growth cycle that produces successive layers of cortex through the common process of neuron generation and migration, the cognitive levels build over time based on a common growth process, producing a qualitatively new skill structure at each level.

Within these levels a second kind of growth cycle appears as well – a repetitive pattern of types of coordination of components that groups the levels into what are called *tiers*. This cycle first became evident in research when coders made common errors that mixed up, for example, a 5-year-old's simple relations of concrete roles with the more abstract relations of a 15-year-old (Fischer & Elmendorf, 1986). Five-year-olds relate roles of mother with child or of doctor with patient, as when they tell stories with standard specific interactions between mother and child. Fifteen-year-olds relate instead broad, abstract roles of mother with child or doctor with patient. They describe the mother and child roles in society, for example, instead of limiting themselves to a specific, prototypical mother-child interaction. This combination of similarity and difference reflects a repetitive cycle of skill levels, a tier.

In general, development moves through at least three repetitive cycles from early infancy to adulthood. In each cycle or tier, a child or adult first controls a single unit of behavior – a single action, representation, or

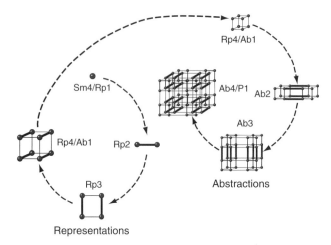

Figure 8.5 Developmental cycles for tiers of representations and abstractions.

abstraction for the sensorimotor, representational, and abstract tiers, respectively (Fischer, 1980; Fischer & Bidell, 2006). Then the person relates at least two such units to form a mapping of actions, representations, or abstractions. Next the person coordinates at least two mappings to form a system. Finally with the fourth level in a tier, the person integrates at least two systems to form a system of systems, which generates a new kind of unit: Action systems generate single representations. Representational systems generate single abstractions. Abstract systems generate single principles. (There is no evidence to date of emergence of new levels beyond single principles.) Figure 8.5 illustrates this cycle for the representational and abstract tiers with the metaphor of building blocks, in which the simple blocks for representations eventually create a new kind of more complex building block to begin the capacity to think abstractly. I suspect that growth cycles of this kind are pervasive in cognitive and brain development, and I will propose several cycles for brain development that by hypothesis are related to these cycles of cognitive development.

Cycles of cortical development

Most research on the structure and development of the brain has focused on local, microscopic anatomy and physiology, such as how single neurons and synapses function. For connecting to education, the big picture of how the brain functions and changes with development is more obviously relevant. Although research on the brain system has been relatively sparse, it is growing rapidly, and there are sufficient findings to establish some key facts about brain development and to build initial models of cycles of brain growth (Fischer & Rose, 1994).

The first established fact about brain development – of which many scientists and educators remain unaware – is that the brain and its parts generally grow in spurts, as do other body systems (Blinkov & Glezer, 1968; Fischer & Rose, 1994; Lampl, Veldhuis, & Johnson, 1992; Noonan, Farnum, Leiferman, Lampl, Markel, & Wilsman, 2004; Thatcher, 1994). The smooth growth curves shown on pediatric charts work only for averages of many children. Individual children grow in fits and starts.

These discontinuities are evident in many different measures of brain anatomy and activity, including cortical thickness, synaptic density, cortical electrical activity, and cortical connectivity. One of the simplest characteristics that shows this pattern of spurts and drops is the energy in the electroencephalogram (EEG), which is measured by calculating the area under the curves generated by electrical activity. In a classic study Matousek and Petersén (1973) measured EEG for people between 1 and 21 years of age in Sweden. The relative energy (energy in one frequency band for a cortical region divided by energy in all bands for that region) showed highly systematic growth curves, as shown in Figure 8.6 for the alpha band measured in the occipital-parietal region. Growth proceeds consistently upward, but there are recurring spurts (marked by the black dots in Figure 8.6), plateaus, and slight drops, reminiscent of the growth curves for development of arithmetic, reflective judgment, and other cognitive skills (Figures 1, 2, and 4). (Note that for some frequency bands (notably theta and delta) the growth curves go consistently downward, moving in similar fits and starts. Also, the form of the growth curves varies depending on the cortical region; for example, spurts during adolescence are much stronger in the prefrontal region than in the occipital region (Hudspeth & Pribram, 1992).)

Remarkably the ages of the spurts for EEG energy correspond closely with the ages for cognitive spurts, as evident in comparisons of Figure 8.6 and Table 8.1. The correspondence is so close that it suggests a linkage between the two dynamic growth processes. This finding first inspired the simple form of the *brain growth hypothesis*: that cortical growth spurts reflect the emergence of new skill levels. However, most studies that show these spurts in brain or cognitive development measure only one – brain or cognition – not both, which means that few data exist to test whether the two in fact relate in developing individuals. Fortunately a

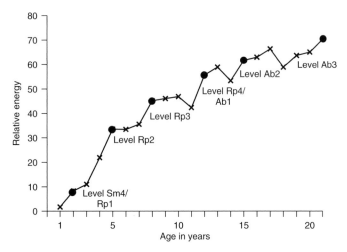

Figure 8.6 Development of relative energy in alpha EEG in occipito-parietal area.

small number of studies do measure both brain and cognitive develop-ment, and they support the brain growth hypothesis (Bell & Fox, 1994; Bell & Fox, 1996; Stauder, 1999; van der Molen & Molenaar, 1994), but clearly more research is required to test the correspondence fully.

These phenomena suggest a simple growth model of correlated suc-cessive spurts in cortical activity and cognitive capacity, but they raise questions about the nature of the brain reorganizations with each spurt as well as the relation to the cognitive reorganizations in the growth cycles shown in Figure 8.5. My colleagues and I have created a model of growth of cortical networks – the network-growth hypothesis – based on existing research, especially the findings of Thatcher (Hanlon, Thatcher, & Cline, 1999; 1992; 1994), Matousek and Petersén (1973), Hudspeth and Pribram (1990; 1992), and Somsen (Somsen, van 't Klooster, van der Molen, van Leeuwen, & Licht, 1997). Besides EEG energy, the other most important measures from these findings involve EEG coherence, the correlation between electrical wave patterns in two regions. Correlated wave patterns indicate an active connection between two regions. Uncorrelated wave patterns indicate no active connection.

Explanation of the neural-network model requires describing the general layout of cortical areas assessed by EEG and other brain imaging tech-niques. Figure 8.7 diagrams the brain viewed from the top, with the nose marking the front of the head and the gray area indicating the prefontal cortex, which plays an especially important role in cortical networks. The

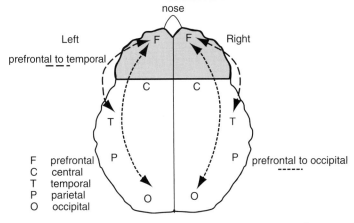

Figure 8.7 Top view of cortex illustrating some network connections.

regions of the cortex are given standard names listed in the diagram: left and right hemispheres, and within each hemisphere areas called prefrontal (F), central (C), temporal (T), parietal (P), and occipital (O). Neural fibers (axons) connect parts of the cortex even across long distances, such as the prefrontal-occipital connections marked by the long arrows. Shorter connections are also important in neural networks, such as the prefrontal-temporal connections marked by the shorter arrows as well as connections within a cortical region, such as prefrontal-prefrontal connections (not shown). Evidence indicates that the large majority of active network connections occur within a hemisphere, as indicated by the arrows.

According to the *network-growth hypothesis*, the changes in energy shown in Figure 8.6 arise from developmental changes in neural networks in the brain, developments that come about through a cyclical process of rewiring and retuning networks. This growth process moves around the cortex systematically in a manner similar to that suggested by Thatcher (Hanlon *et al.*, 1999; 1994) and illustrated in Figure 8.8 for the cognitive levels Rp3 and Ab1 that emerge at about 6 and 10 years. The prefrontal cortex leads the way, since empirical evidence indicates that the large majority of systematic changes with age in networks involve connections between the prefrontal cortex and other regions. Thatcher's data suggest that growth dominates in one part of the cortex at a given time, but it undoubtedly occurs less saliently in other places as well. Also, the diagram represents the hypothesized normative pattern, but different people are likely to show different patterns in the growth cycle. Research clearly shows, for instance, differences between males and females (Hanlon *et al.*, 1999).

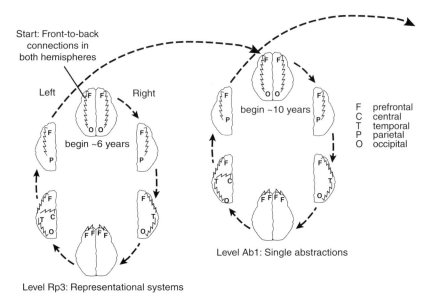

Figure 8.8 Cortical network cycle for two successive cognitive levels.

At the top of the diagram, front-back (prefrontal-occipital) connections grow more strongly than other connections as the level of representational systems Rp3 begins to develop. Gradually over several years the leading edge of growth of connections moves around the cortex, starting with the right hemisphere, where it becomes more local over time, tuning shorter connections. Halfway through the cycle, at the bottom of the diagram, the leading edge moves to the prefrontal cortex, as growth of local connections there predominate. Next it moves into the left hemisphere, starting more local and gradually moving toward longer connections until it returns to the longest, frontal-occipital connections. Here it begins the process over again, as the level of single abstractions Ab1 starts to develop. Eventually the cycle repeats, restructuring the network for the capacity of single abstractions, until eventually it completes, and the next level begins, abstract mappings Ab2.

According to the hypothesis, the network cycle corresponds to periods when particular types of learning and developmental changes occur, such as spurts in a major skill. In two studies, Martha Ann Bell has shown exactly such a relation – spurts and drops in coherence for specific cortical regions related to growth of major skills in infancy (Bell, 1998; Bell & Fox, 1996). In her ambitious study of the onset of crawling, infants who were beginning to crawl displayed high coherence connecting frontal, occipital, and parietal regions, especially in the right hemisphere. As the infants became skilled crawlers, coherence dropped. Similarly, in a case study an infant showed high frontal-temporal coherence, especially in the left hemisphere, as she focused on babbling to produce many syllable-like sounds. The left temporal region plays an important role in language in most older children and adults.

For the minority of people who use the right hemisphere more prominently for language, the growth pattern for coherence should be different, of course. Likewise in general, individual differences in abilities and patterns of learning with age should correspond to cycle differences, based on the network-growth hypothesis. Just as infants who crawl late show a later spurt in frontal-occipital and frontal-parietal coherence, children who develop abstract thinking (Ab1 and beyond) late or learn to read late or suddenly begin to work hard at learning a sport should show parallel changes in growth of coherence in particular regions.

For cognitive development, the cycle that produces cognitive levels is nested within the wider cycle for tiers (Figure 8.5). Likewise, by hypothesis, the cycle for growth of networks shown in Figure 8.8 is nested within a larger cycle of growth of energy, coherence, and other brain characteristics that relate to tiers – the *nested network hypothesis*. For example, prefrontal energy seems to surge when a new tier emerges according to the analyses of EEG energy by Hudspeth and Pribram (1990; 1992). Also, the highest spurts in energy move around the cortex systematically, according to the evidence to date. In addition, the oscillation patterns of coherence for specific cortical connections shift in correspondence with the movement into a new cortical-network cycle (Thatcher, 1994). Presumably, as yet unspecified shifts in network connections and other brain properties co-occur with the peak shifts.

According to the nested network hypothesis, the peak energy in specific cortical regions shifts systematically as cortical network cycles change through a tier of levels, as shown in Figure 8.9. Note that the cortical network cycle is nested inside the peak-energy cycle in the diagram. The peak energy begins in the prefrontal cortex and then gradually moves around the cortex over long age periods as children grow new levels. The model in Figure 8.9 fits reasonably with the few data that are available: Growth of peak energy moves gradually from prefrontal to occipital, parietal, central, temporal, and then back to central, parietal, occipital, and prefrontal. A reasonable hypothesis is that the first peaks (right side of the diagram) are concentrated in the right hemisphere, and the later ones in the left hemisphere; but most of the published data do not contain

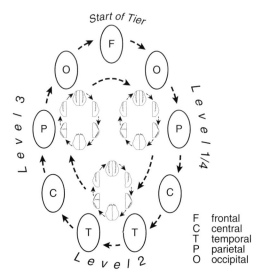

Figure 8.9 Peak energy cycle for tier, with nested network cycles.

the information for testing this specification. This nested cycle, like the network-growth cycle in Figure 8.8, presumably also corresponds to particular behavioral patterns, such as focusing on some skill domain or social-emotional issue.

Cycles of learning: Backwards growth and microdevelopment

The skill scale and the dynamic growth patterns that accompany it create several avenues for research on mind, brain, and education. Not only do they make possible research relating cognitive change with brain development, but they also provide a scale for measuring learning, teaching, curriculum, and other cognitive performances and products – a scale that has wide-ranging uses in educational assessment, evaluation, and practice (Dawson-Tunik & Stein, in press; Schwartz & Fischer, 2005). To illustrate this range of uses, I will focus on analysis of classroom learning as microdevelopment – growth of skill in school-related time periods, such as minutes, hours, days, and weeks during which students are supposed to learn.

When analyzed in terms of levels of constructed skill, students' performances show dynamic changes, with lots of increases and drops.

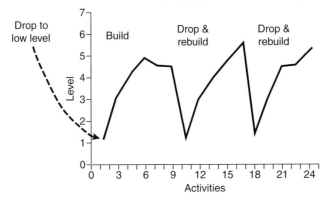

Figure 8.10 Building a new skill through repeated reconstruction, or scalloping. (Levels 1 to 3 involve actions, 4 to 6 involve representations, and 7 and above involve abstractions.)

These patterns of change reflect a cyclical process of skill construction, in which task characteristics interact with the student's level of expertise in the domain, among other things. The patterns also demonstrate that building of general knowledge (as opposed to learning specific "facts") is slow and hard. Much research shows that the kinds of knowledge taught in many high school and college courses – causes of the Civil War, the concept of energy in physics, analyzing evidence for evolution, writing a convincing essay – take much longer than a semester or a year to master (Fischer *et al.*, 2003; Salomon & Perkins, 1989).

The skill scale provides a method for measuring performance and learning across all these tasks and in any other domain and thus makes possible the assessment of any performance on a single metric as well as the comparison of performances across domains and tasks on that metric. In research on students learning over several months (middle school science students learning about magnetism, graduate students learning how to use a computer for statistical analysis, etc.) we found that learning occurs in recurring waves or scallops (Granott, 2002; Schwartz & Fischer, 2005; Yan & Fischer, 2002): A student starts with a low level of understanding a task or performance, such as using the computer to do a statistical analysis, and gradually builds up the skill in one situation, moving from actions to representations or from representations to abstractions, as shown in Figure 8.10. But the understanding collapses because of a change in the situation or for any of a hundred reasons. The student then builds up the understanding again and sustains it briefly, but once more it collapses. This process repeats itself many times as the

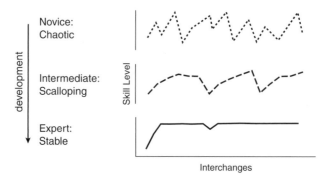

Figure 8.11 Growth curves for learning a task: novice, intermediate performers, and experts.

student learns a new skill or understanding, producing what is called a scalloping pattern in learning.

The collapses do not indicate difficulties. Instead they are normal and required, reflecting the need to build and rebuild a skill with variations so that the person can eventually sustain it in the face of changes in context and state. Commonly, mastering a task requires moving down to primitive levels of representations or even actions (similar to those of infants) as shown in Figure 8.10, so that the person can figure out the action characteristics of the task or situation. The human capacity to move down to such elementary levels provides enormous flexibility for intelligent adaptation, because people can learn new patterns of sensori-motor action required for success in a different kind of task. Moving to a low cognitive level for a new task comprises an essential part of intelligence.

The scalloping pattern only occurs some of the time in learning situations, however. It reflects the midpoint in the learning process, as shown in Figure 8.11. When students are novices – not familiar or comfortable with tasks that they need to do – their performance is even more variable than that in Figure 8.10 (Yan & Fischer, 2002). Instead of building to a higher level skill over several activities, any relatively complex skill that they build quickly falls apart. Their performance vacillates up and down chaotically, as in the upper growth curve in Figure 8.11. As they acquire some knowledge of the task, they move from this chaotic pattern to the intermediate pattern of scalloping (the middle curve in Figure 8.11 and the curve in Figure 8.10), where they can sustain a higher level skill for a longer time but are still subject to abrupt, periodic collapse.

After working at the task for some time (typically months or even years), they become experts who can sustain a stable, high level performance, as shown in the lower curve in Figure 8.11. Experts often require an initial period of exploring the task to understand its properties ("figure it out") before reaching a stable level, which leads to a gradual rise in level, as shown in the curve. Also, they occasionally encounter some event that leads to a drop in complexity level, which is typically shortlived.

In this way, learning involves not monotonic growth to higher levels of understanding but an extended cyclical process, in which a student repeatedly builds and rebuilds a performance. He or she moves from chaotic variation in skill level to repeated, gradual rebuilding of a skill (scalloping) and eventually to a relatively stable level of expertise. This analysis provides one example of how the skill complexity scale can illuminate learning and other educational activities. Perhaps it will also become possible to analyze brain activity as learning progresses, to ask how changes in brain activity relate to degree of skill and expertise. It is possible that some of the brain growth cycles described earlier will be evident as learning progresses in microdevelopment.

Moving from growth cycles to educational implications

The research relating cognitive developmental cycles and scaling to educational assessment is but one of many instances in which cognitive science findings contribute straightforwardly to educational research and practice. Connections between the cycles of brain development and education, however, are further from fruition. Eventually research directly connecting brain growth cycles with patterns of learning will illuminate the processes of learning, especially differences across individuals and contexts. For example, by hypothesis, differences in cortical network cycles relate to differences between children in both motivation to learn and effectiveness of learning in specific domains, such as spatial reasoning, mathematics, and literacy.

At present, however, efforts to link brain development research to education raise serious concerns because of carelessness and excess in "application" (chapter by Bruer this volume; Fischer *et al.*, 2007). Journalists, educators, and even brain scientists too readily leap from a brain research finding to an "implication" for education – which is typically nothing more than seat-of-the-pants speculation. An important case of this kind of excess and its dangers took place in the 1970s and 1980s, when a few scientists uncovered the first evidence of head growth spurts (Epstein, 1974) and then brain activity growth spurts (Fischer & Rose, 1994; John, 1977). Within a few years some scientists and educators were leaping to conclusions wholly unwarranted by the data, such as that students could not learn anything new during plateau periods between brain growth spurts. They recommended to a number of school districts that curricula be changed to introduce no new concepts during the normative age periods of brain growth plateaus, because no new learning would occur then, they asserted (Epstein, 1978; Fischer & Lazerson, 1984). The cognitive evidence, including data on school performance and learning, never supported this speculation, but a number of school systems in North America took the recommendations seriously because the proponents claimed that they came from brain science. Several of us fought against these specious claims for several years until finally the troublesome efforts faded away.

Another common error has been to leap from evidence of critical periods in brain development – a limited window of time during which a specific experience shapes brain function – to implications about when people can and cannot learn to speak, read, do arithmetic, etc. (Bailey, Bruer, Symons, & Lichtman, 2001; Snow & Hoefnagel-Hohle, 1978). These claims too represent illegitimate conclusions that are not supported by careful research evidence.

Researchers and educators in mind, brain, and education need to use normal scientific caution in drawing conclusions for educational practice. That includes refraining from leaps to educational implications from brain research until there is direct evidence assessing learning and performance – evidence that links brain to behavior and behavior in turn to practice. For example, there is great promise that cycles of brain and cognitive growth will illuminate learning and educational practice, providing powerful new tools for analyzing students' learning patterns and differences and optimizing educational interventions. Already the research on cognitive growth cycles is bearing fruit in assessing and comparing learning patterns across domains and individuals as well as relating them to teaching and curriculum. However, the current state of knowledge does not allow direct extrapolation from brain growth cycles to educational practice. Building links among mind, brain, and education requires building reciprocal relations among cognitive science, biology, and education based in inter-actions of researchers and practitioners. As those links grow, questions and insights from educational practice will inform and enrich brain and cognitive science just as much as scientific findings will inform and enrich educational practice.

References

Bailey, D. B., Jr., Bruer, J. T., Symons, F. J., and Lichtman, J. W. (eds.) (2001). *Critical Thinking About Critical Periods*. Baltimore, MD: Paul H. Brookes Publishing.

Bell, M. A. (1998). The ontogeny of the EEG during infancy and childhood: Implications for cognitive development. In B. Garreau (ed.) *Neuroimaging in Child Psychiatric Disorders* (pp. 97–111). Berlin: Springer-Verlag.

Bell, M. A. and Fox, N. A. (1994). Brain development over the first year of life: Relations between electroencephalographic frequency and coherence and cognitive and affective behaviors. In G. Dawson & K. W. Fischer (eds.), *Human Behavior and the Developing Brain* (pp. 314–345). New York: Guilford Press.

(1996). Crawling experience is related to changes in cortical organization during infancy: Evidence from EEG coherence. *Developmental Psychobiology*, 29, 551–561.

Bidell, T. R. and Fischer, K. W. (1992). Cognitive development in educational contexts: Implications of skill theory. In A. Demetriou, M. Shayer, & A. Efklides (eds.), *Neo-Piagetian Theories of Cognitive Development: Implications and Applications for Education* (pp. 9–30). London: Routledge & Kegan Paul.

Blinkov, S. M. and Glezer, I. I. (1968). *The Human Brain in Figures and Tables*. New York: Plenum Press.

Case, R. (1998). The development of conceptual structures. In D. Kuhn and R. S. Siegler (eds.), and W. Damon (Series ed.), *Handbook of Child Psychology: Vol. II. Cognition, Perception, and Language*. New York: Wiley.

Coch, D., Fischer, K. W., and Dawson, G. (eds.) (2007). *Human Behavior, Learning and the Developing Brain: Normal Development* (2nd edn.). New York: Guilford.

Dawson, G. and Fischer, K. W. (eds.) (1994). *Human Behavior and the Developing Brain*. New York: Guilford Press.

Dawson, T. and Wilson, M. (2004). The LAAS: A computerizable scoring system for small- and large-scale developmental assessments. *Educational Assessment*, 9, 153–191.

Dawson-Tunik, T. L., Commons, M., Wilson, M., and Fischer, K. W. (2005). The shape of development. *European Journal of Developmental Psychology*, 2, 163–195.

Dawson-Tunik, T. L. and Stein, Z. (in press). Cycles of research and application in science education. In K. W. Fischer & T. Katzir (eds.), *Building Usable Knowledge in Mind, Brain, and Education*. Cambridge: Cambridge University Press.

Epstein, H. T. (1974). Phrenoblysis: Special brain and mind growth periods. *Developmental Psychobiology*, 7, 207–224.

(1978). Growth spurts during brain development: Implications for educational policy and practice. In J. S. Chall and A. F. Mirsky (eds.), *Education and the Brain (Yearbook of the NSSE)*. Chicago: University of Chicago Press.

Fischer, K. W. (1980). A theory of cognitive development: The control and construction of hierarchies of skills. *Psychological Review*, 87, 477–531.

Fischer, K. W. and Bidell, T. R. (1998). Dynamic development of psychological structures in action and thought. In R. M. Lerner (ed.) and W. Damon (Series ed.), *Handbook of Child Psychology: Vol. I. Theoretical Models of Human Development* (5th edn., pp. 467–561). New York: Wiley.

(2006). Dynamic development of action, thought, and emotion. In R. M. Lerner (ed.) and W. Damon (Series ed.), *Handbook of Child Psychology: Vol. I. Theoretical Models of Human Development* (6th edn., pp. 313–399). New York: Wiley.

Fischer, K. W. and Elmendorf, D. (1986). Becoming a different person: Transformations in personality and social behavior. In M. Perlmutter (ed.), *Cognitive Perspectives on Children's Social Development. Minnesota Symposium on Child Psychology*, 18, 137–178. Hillsdale, NJ: Erlbaum.

Fischer, K. W., Immordino-Yang, M. H., and Waber, D. P. (2007). Toward a grounded synthesis of mind, brain, and education for reading disorders: An introduction to the field and this book. In K. W. Fischer, J. H. Bernstein, & M. H. Immordino-Yang (eds.), *Mind, Brain, and Education in Reading Disorders* (pp. 3–15). Cambridge, UK: Cambridge University Press.

Fischer, K. W., Kenny, S. L., and Pipp, S. L. (1990). How cognitive processes and environmental conditions organize discontinuities in the development of abstractions. In C. N. Alexander and E. J. Langer (eds.), *Higher Stages of Human Development: Perspectives on Adult Growth* (pp. 162–187). New York: Oxford University Press.

Fischer, K. W. and Lazerson, A. (1984). Research: Brain spurts and Piagetian periods. *Educational Leadership*, 41(5), 70.

Fischer, K. W. and Rose, S. P. (1994). Dynamic development of coordination of components in brain and behavior: A framework for theory and research. In G. Dawson and K. W. Fischer (eds.), *Human Behavior and the Developing Brain* (pp. 3–66). New York: Guilford Press.

Fischer, K. W., Yan, Z., and Stewart, J. (2003). Adult cognitive development: Dynamics in the developmental web. In J. Valsiner and K. Connolly (eds.), *Handbook of Developmental Psychology* (pp. 491–516). Thousand Oaks, CA: Sage.

Granott, N. (2002). How microdevelopment creates macrodevelopment: Reiterated sequences, backward transitions, and the zone of current development. In N. Granott and J. Parziale (eds.), *Microdevelopment: Transition Processes in Development and Learning* (pp. 213–242). Cambridge: Cambridge University Press.

Granott, N., Fischer, K. W., and Parziale, J. (2002). Bridging to the unknown: A transition mechanism in learning and problem-solving. In N. Granott and J. Parziale (eds.), *Microdevelopment: Transition Processes in Development and Learning* (pp. 131–156). Cambridge: Cambridge University Press.

Hanlon, H. W., Thatcher, R. W. and Cline, M. J. (1999). Gender differences in the development of EEG coherence in normal children. *Developmental Neuropsychology*, 16, 479–506.

Hudspeth, W. J. and Pribram, K. H. (1990). Stages of brain and cognitive maturation. *Journal of Educational Psychology*, 82, 881–884.

Hudspeth, W. J. and Pribram, K. H. (1992). Psychophysiological indices of cerebral maturation. *International Journal of Psychophysiology*, 12, 19–29.

John, E. R. (1977). *Functional Neuroscience*. Vol. II: *Neurometrics*. Hillsdale, NJ: Erlbaum.

Kitchener, K. S., Lynch, C. L., Fischer, K. W., and Wood, P. K. (1993). Developmental range of reflective judgment: The effect of contextual support and practice on developmental stage. *Developmental Psychology*, 29, 893–906.

Lampl, M., Veldhuis, J. D., and Johnson, M. L. (1992). Saltation and stasis: A model of human growth. *Science*, 258, 801–803.

Matousek, M. and Petersén, I. (1973). Frequency analysis of the EEG in normal children and adolescents. In P. Kellaway and I. Petersén (eds.), *Automation of Clinical Electroencephalography* (pp. 75–102). New York: Raven Press.

Molenaar, P. C. M. (2004). A manifesto on psychology as idiographic science: Bringing the person back into scientific psychology, this time forever. *Measurement*, 2, 201–218.

Noonan, K. J., Farnum, C. E., Leiferman, E. M., Lampl, M., Markel, M. D., and Wilsman, N. J. (2004). Growing pains: Are they due to increased growth during recumbency as documented in a lamb model? *Journal of Pediatric Orthopedics*, 24, 726–731.

Piaget, J. (1983). Piaget's theory. In W. Kessen (ed.) and P. H. Mussen (Series ed.), *Handbook of Child Psychology:* Vol. I. *History, theory, and methods* (pp. 103–126). New York: Wiley.

Rakic, P. (1971). Guidance of neurons migrating to the fetal monkey neocortex. *Brain Research*, 33, 471–476.

  (1988). Specification of cerebral cortical areas. *Science*, 241, 170–176.

Reznick, J. S. and Goldfield, B. A. (1992). Rapid change in lexical development in comprehension and production. *Developmental Psychology*, 28, 406–413.

Ruhland, R. and van Geert, P. (1998). Jumping into syntax: Transitions in the development of closed class words. *British Journal of Developmental Psychology*, 16(Pt 1), 65–95.

Salomon, G. and Perkins, D. N. (1989). Rocky roads to transfer: Rethinking mechanisms of a neglected phenomenon. *Educational Psychologist*, 24, 185–221.

Schwartz, M. S. and Fischer, K. W. (2005). Building general knowledge and skill: Cognition and microdevelopment in science learning. In A. Demetriou and A. Raftopoulos (eds.), *Cognitive Developmental Change: Theories, Models, and Measurement*. Cambridge, UK: Cambridge University Press.

Siegler, R. S. (1997). *Children's Thinking* (3rd edn.). Englewood Cliffs, NJ: Prentice-Hall.

Snow, C. E. and Hoefnagel-Hohle, M. (1978). The critical period for language acquisition: Evidence from second language learning. *Child Development*, 49, 1114–1128.

Somsen, R. J. M., van 't Klooster, B. J., van der Molen, M. W., van Leeuwen, H. M. P., and Licht, R. (1997). Growth spurts in brain maturation during middle childhood as indexed by EEG power spectra. *Biological Psychology*, 44, 187–209.

Stauder, J. E. A. M., Peter, C. M., and van der Molen, M. W. (1999). Brain activity and cognitive transition during childhood: A longitudinal event-related brain potential study. *Child Neuropsychology*, 5, 41–59.

Thatcher, R. W. (1992). Cyclic cortical reorganization during early childhood. Special Issue: The role of frontal lobe maturation in cognitive and social development. *Brain & Cognition*, 20(1), 24–50.

(1994). Cyclic cortical reorganization: Origins of human cognitive development. In G. Dawson and K. W. Fischer (eds.), *Human Behavior and the Developing Brain* (pp. 232–266). New York: Guilford Press.

van der Molen, M. W. and Molenaar, P. C. M. (1994). Cognitive psychophysiology: A window to cognitive development and brain maturation. In G. Dawson and K. W. Fischer (eds.), *Human Behavior and the Developing Brain* (pp. 456–490). New York: Guilford.

Yan, Z. and Fischer, K. W. (2002). Always under construction: Dynamic variations in adult cognitive development. *Human Development*, 45, 141–160.

9 Brain mechanisms and learning of high level skills

Michael I. Posner, Mary K. Rothbart, and M. Rosario Rueda[1]

Overview

Two significant scientific contributions, brain images and gene sequences, are helping scientists and educators to understand individual differences in the acquisition of cognitive and emotional skills. Research on brain mechanisms of attention in children and adults shows three independent neuronal networks for alerting, orienting, and executive control in conflict resolution. The authors' attention network test evaluates the efficiency of each of these three systems and reveals clear individual differences, which relate to evaluations of children's ability to regulate their own behavior. Among factors affecting this capacity for regulation are two genes related to the neurotransmitter dopamine, which relate to both performance and activation of a node of the attention network in the anterior cingulate. From early childhood, effortful control of attention plays a role not only in learning but also in socialization and empathy. Understanding attention regulation and its relation to learning will clearly be informative to teachers and parents.

The Editors

Two major developments have greatly altered the prospects for making a connection between common networks of the human brain and theories of how people differ. First, with the development of neuroimaging, we could glimpse inside the human brain as people think (Posner & Raichle, 1994). When combined with electrical or magnetic recording from outside the skull, it was possible to see in real time the circuits involved in computing aspects of a task. Although some parts of this technology had been around for a long time, only in the past fifteen years did it become clear that we could create local images of the functioning anatomy of the human brain.

[1] This research was supported in part by a James S. McDonnell 21st Century Grant and by NSF Grant BCS 9907831, NIMH Grant MH43361, and a fellowship from La Caixa Fellowship Program (Spain).

At the beginning of the twentieth century, Santiago Ramón y Cajal (1937) was able for the first time to observe individual nerve cells. Our current ability to see into the human brain depends on the operation of these nerve cells. When neurons are active, they change their own local blood supply. This makes it possible to trace areas of the brain that are active during cognitive processes by measuring local changes in aspects of the brain blood supply.

The second major development at the end of the twentieth century was the sequencing of the entire human genome (Venter, Adams, Myers, Li, *et al.*, 2001). Now it was possible not only to study the functional anatomy of brain networks, but also to examine how genetic differences might lead to individual variation in the potential to use these networks in the acquisition and performance of skills. However, the route from genetic endowment to performance would be neither simple nor separate from an understanding of the brain networks themselves. Taken together, these developments open up the opportunity to examine the networks that underlie the self-regulation of thoughts, emotions, and behavior needed to succeed in school.

Attention networks

Functional neuroimaging has allowed many cognitive tasks to be analyzed in terms of the brain areas they activate, and studies of attention have been among the most often examined in this way (Corbetta & Shulman, 2002; Driver, Eimer, & Macaluso, 2004; Posner & Raichle, 1994). Imaging data have supported the presence of three networks related to different aspects of attention. These networks carry out the functions of alerting, orienting, and executive control (Posner & Raichle, 1994). A summary of the anatomy and transmitters involved in the three networks is shown in Table 9.1.

Alerting is defined as achieving and maintaining a state of high sensitivity to incoming stimuli; orienting is the selection of information from sensory input; and executive control involves the mechanisms for monitoring and resolving conflict among thoughts, feelings, and responses. The alerting system has been associated with thalamic as well as frontal and parietal regions of the cortex. A particularly effective way to vary alertness has been to use warning signals prior to targets. The influence of warning signals on the level of alertness is thought to be due to modulation of neural activity by the neurotransmitter norepinephrine (Marrocco & Davidson, 1998).

Orienting involves aligning attention with a source of sensory signals. This may be overt, as when eye movements accompany movements of

Table 9.1 *Anatomical structures and neuromodulators related to each of the three attentional networks.*

Function	Structures	Modulator
Orient	Superior parietal Temporal parietal junction Frontal eye fields Superior colliculus	Acetylcholine
Alert	Locus Coeruleus Right frontal and parietal cortex	Norepinephrine
Executive attention	Anterior cingulate Lateral ventral prefrontal Basal ganglia	Dopamine

attention, or may occur covertly without any eye movement. The orienting system for visual events has been associated with posterior brain areas including the superior parietal lobe and temporal parietal junction and in addition, the frontal eye fields (Corbetta & Shulman, 2002). Orienting can be manipulated by presenting a cue indicating where in space a target is likely to occur, thereby directing attention to the cued location (Posner, 1980). Event related functional magnetic resonance imaging (fMRI) studies have suggested that the superior parietal lobe is associated with orienting following the presentation of a cue (Corbetta & Shulman, 2002). The superior parietal lobe in humans is closely related to the lateral intraparietal area (LIP) in monkeys, which is known to produce eye movements (Andersen, 1989). When a target occurs at an uncued location, and attention has to be disengaged and moved to a new location, there is activity in the temporal parietal junction (Corbetta & Shulman, 2002). Lesions of the inferior parietal lobe and superior temporal lobe have been consistently related to difficulties in orienting (Karnath, Ferber, & Himmelbach, 2001).

Executive control of attention is often studied by tasks that involve conflict, such as various versions of the Stroop task. In the Stroop task, subjects must respond to the color of ink (e.g. red) while ignoring the color word name (e.g. blue) (Bush, Luu, & Posner, 2000). Resolving conflict in the Stroop task activates midline frontal areas (anterior cingulate) and lateral prefrontal cortex (Botvinick, Braver, Barch, Carter, & Cohen, 2001; Fan, Flombaum, McCandliss, Thomas, & Posner, 2003). There is also evidence for the activation of this network in tasks involving conflict between a central target and surrounding flankers that may be congruent or incongruent with the target (Botvinick *et al.*, 2001; Fan *et al.*, 2003). Experimental tasks may also provide a means of fractionating the functional contributions of different areas within the executive attention network (McDonald, Cohen, Stenger, & Carter, 2000). Recent neuroimaging studies have provided evidence that the executive attention network is involved in self-regulation of positive and negative affect (Beauregard, Levesque, & Bourgouin, 2001; Ochsner Kosslyn, Cosgrove, Cassem *et al.*, 2001) as well as in a wide variety of cognitive tasks that underlie intelligence (Duncan, Seitz, Kolodny, Bor *et al.*, 2000).

Individuality

Almost all studies of attention have been concerned with either general abilities or with the effects of brain injury or pathology on attention. However, it is clear that normal individuals differ in their ability to attend to sensory events and even more clearly in their ability to concentrate for long periods on internal trains of thought. To study these individual differences we have developed an attention networks test (ANT, see Figure 9.1) that examines the efficiency of the three brain networks we have described above (Fan, McCandliss, Sommer, Raz, & Posner, 2002).

The data provide three numbers representing the skill of each individual in the alerting, orienting, and executive networks. In a sample of forty normal persons, we found each of these indexes to be reliable over repeated testing; in addition, no correlation was found among the three networks scores.

The ability to measure individual differences in attention among adults raises the question of the degree to which attention is heritable. To address this issue, we used our attention network test to study twenty-six pairs of monozygotic and twenty-six pairs of dizygotic same sex twins (Fan *et al.*, 2001). We found strong correlations between the monozygotic twins for the executive network measure. This led to an estimate of heritability of the executive network of 0.89. Because of the small sample, the estimate of 95 percent confidence interval for heritability is between 0.3 and 0.9. Nonetheless, these data support a role for genes in the efficacy with which the executive network is put into action.

As a way of searching for candidate genes that might relate to the efficiency of these networks, we used the association of the executive network with the neuromodulator Dopamine (DA) (Fossella, Sommer, Fan, Wu *et al.*, 2002). To do this, we ran 200 persons in the ANT and genotyped them to examine frequent polymorphisms in genes related to their respective neuromodulators. We found significant association of two genes related to dopamine, the DRD4 and MAOA genes. We then conducted a neuroimaging experiment in which we compared persons

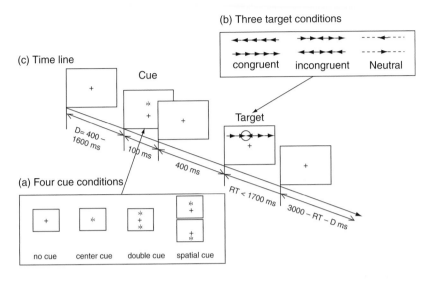

Figure 9.1 Schematic of the Attention Network Test (ANT) developed by Fan *et al.* (2002) to study individual differences in the three attentional networks : (a) illustrates the four cue conditions; (b) the three types of target; (c) the sequence of events; and (d) the substractions to indicate the efficiency of each network.

with two different alleles of these two genes while they performed the ANT. We found that these alleles produced different activation within the anterior cingulate, which is a major node of this network (Fan *et al.*, 2003). Subsequently a number of other dopamine and serotonin genes have been shown to be related to executive attention (Posner, Rothbart & Sheese, 2007).

Early childhood

Development of the network involved in orienting to visual objects has been traced to early infancy (Haith, Hazan, & Goodman, 1988; Clohessy, Posner, & Rothbart, 2001). However, infants perform poorly with an ambiguity that introduces conflict between responses (Clohessy, Posner, & Rothbart, 2001). The ability to resolve conflict is an important part of the executive attention network and this does not seem to be available until about two years of age.

Developmental changes in the control of cognition by executive attention were found during the third year of life using a conflict task (Gerardi-Caulton, 2000). Because children of this age do not read, location and identity rather than word meaning and ink color served as the dimensions of conflict (the spatial conflict task). Children sat in front of two response keys, one located to the child's left and one to the right. Each key displayed a picture, and on every trial, a picture identical to one of the pair appeared on either the left or right side of the screen. Children were rewarded for responding to the identity of the stimulus, regardless of its spatial compatibility with the matching response key (Gerardi-Caulton, 2000). Reduced accuracy and slowed reaction times for spatially incompatible relative to spatially compatible trials reflect the effort required to resist the prepotent response and resolve conflict between these two competing dimensions. Performance on this task produced a clear interference effect in adults and activated the anterior cingulate (Fan, Flombaum et al., 2003). Children 24 months of age tended to fix on a single response, while 36-month-old children performed at high accuracy levels, but like adults responded more slowly and with reduced accuracy to incompatible trials.

The importance of being able to study the emergence of executive attention is enhanced because cognitive measures of conflict resolution in these laboratory tasks have been linked to aspects of children's self control in naturalistic settings. Children relatively less affected by spatial conflict also received higher parental ratings of temperamental effortful control and higher scores on laboratory measures of inhibitory control (Gerardi-Caulton, 2000).

Questionnaires have shown the effortful control factor, defined in terms of scales measuring attentional focusing, inhibitory control, low intensity pleasure, and perceptual sensitivity (Rothbart, Ahadi, & Hershey, 1994), to be inversely related to temperamental negative affect. This relation is in keeping with the notion that attentional skill may help attenuate negative affect, while also serving to constrain impulsive approach tendencies.

Empathy is also strongly related to effortful control, with children high in effortful control showing greater empathy (Rothbart et al., 1994). To display empathy towards others requires that we interpret their signals of distress or pleasure. Imaging work in normals shows that sad faces activate the amygdala. As sadness increases, this activation is accompanied by activity in the anterior cingulate as part of the attention network (Blair, Morris, Frith, Perrett, & Dolan, 1999). It seems likely that the cingulate activity represents the basis for our attention to the distress of others.

These studies suggest two routes to successful socialization. A strongly reactive amygdala in more fearful children would provide the signals of distress that would easily allow empathic feelings toward others. These children are relatively easy to socialize. In the absence of this form of control, the development of the cingulate would allow appropriate attention to the signals provided by amygdala activity. Consistent with its influence on empathy, effortful control also appears to play a role in the development of conscience. The internalization of moral principles appears to be facilitated in fearful preschool-aged children, especially when their mothers use gentle discipline (Kochanska, 1995). In addition, internalized control is facilitated in children high in effortful control (Kochanska, Murray, Jacques, Koenig, & Vandegeest, 1996). Two separable control systems, one reactive (fear) and one self-regulative (effortful control) appear to regulate the development of conscience. In support of the link between effortful control and social behavior, Ellis, Rothbart, & Posner (2004) found that, for adolescents, effortful control and poor ability to control conflict as measured by the ANT, separately predicted antisocial behavior.

Individual differences in effortful control are also related to some aspects of metacognitive knowledge, such as theory of mind (i.e., knowing that people's behavior is guided by their beliefs, desires, and other mental states) (Carlson & Moses, 2001). Moreover, tasks that require the inhibition of a prepotent response are correlated with theory of mind tasks even when other factors, such as age, intelligence, and working memory are factored out (Carlson & Moses, 2001). Inhibitory control and theory of mind share a similar developmental time course, with advances in both areas between the ages of 2 and 5.

Preschool

We have traced the development of executive attention into the preschool period (Rueda, Fan, McCandliss, Halparin, Gruber, Pappert, & Posner, 2004) by using a version of the ANT adapted for children (see Table 9.2). In some respects, results are remarkably similar to those found for adults using the version of the task shown in Figure 9.1. The reaction times for the children are much longer, but they show similar independence between the three networks. Children have much larger scores for alerting and conflict, suggesting that they have trouble in maintaining the alert state when not warned of the new target, and in resolving conflict. Rather surprisingly, as measured by the ANT, the ability to resolve conflict in the flanker task remains about the same from age seven to adulthood (see Table 9.2).

Table 9.2 *Development of efficiency of the attentional networks. Study 1 shows development from 6 to 10 years of age as measured by the child version of the ANT. Study 2 compares 10-year-old children with adults using both the adult and child versions of the ANT.*

Child ANT						
		Attentional Networks Subtractions				
Study	Age	Alerting	Orienting	Conflict	Conflict for errors	Overall RT	Overall error rates
1	6	79 (75)	58 (76)	115 (80)	15.6	931 (42)	15.8
	7	100 (75)	62 (67)	63 (83)	0.7	833 (125)	5.7
	8	73 (67)	63 (66)	71 (77)	− 0.3	806 (102)	4.9
	9	79 (47)	42 (48)	67 (38)	1.6	734 (68)	2.7
2	10	41 (47)	46 (44)	69 (44)	2.1	640 (71)	2.2
	adults	30 (32)	32 (30)	61 (26)	1.6	483 (36)	1.2
Adult ANT							
2	10	78 (61)	60 (56)	156 (76)	3.9	710 (90)	2.8
	adults	40 (34)	52 (35)	131 (62)	4.7	532 (54)	2

There is considerable evidence that the executive attention network is of great importance in the acquisition of school subjects such as literacy (McCandliss, Sandak, Beck, & Perfetti, 2003) and in a wide variety of other subjects that draw upon general intelligence (Duncan *et al.*, 2000). It has been widely believed by psychologists that training always involves specific domains, and that more general training of the mind, for example, by formal disciplines like mathematics or Latin, did not generalize outside of the specific domain trained (Thorndike, 1899; Simon, 1969). However, attention may be an exception. It is both a domain that involves specific brain mechanisms, as we have seen, but whose function is to influence the operation of other brain networks (Posner & Petersen, 1990; Posner & Raichle, 1994). Moreover, anatomically the network involving resolution of conflict overlaps brain areas related to general intelligence (Duncan *et al.*, 2000). Training of attention either explicitly or implicitly is also often a part of the school curriculum (Mills & Mills, 2000), but little research is available to determine exactly how and when attention training can best be done.

A central aspect of the executive attention network is the ability to deal with conflict. We used this feature to design a set of training exercises that were adapted from efforts to send macaque monkeys into outer space (Rumbaugh & Washburn, 1995). These exercises resulted in monkeys' ability to resolve conflict in a Stroop-like task (Washburn, 1994).

Our exercises began with training the child to control the movement of a cat by using a joystick as well as prediction of where an object would move, given its initial trajectory (see Figure 9.2). Other exercises emphasized the use of working memory to retain information for a matching to sample task and the resolution of conflict (see Figure 9.3).

We have tested the efficacy of a very brief five days of attention training with groups of four-year-old children. The children were brought to the laboratory for seven days for sessions lasting about forty minutes. These sessions were conducted over a two-to three-week period. The first and last days were used to assess the effects of the training by use of the ANT, a general test of intelligence (the K-BIT, Kaufman & Kaufman, 1990) and a temperament scale (the Children Behavior Questionnaire or CBQ). During the administration of the ANT, we recorded 128 channels of EEG in order to observe the amplitude and time course of activation of brain areas associated with executive attention in adult studies (Rueda, Fan, & Posner, 2003).

During our first experiment, we compared twelve children who underwent our training procedure with twelve who were randomly selected and took no training, but came in twice for assessment. In our second experiment, we again used four-year-olds, but the control group came in seven times and saw videos which required an occasional response on their part to keep them playing. All of the children seemed to enjoy the experience (see Figure 9.4) and their caregivers were quite supportive of the effort.

In this chapter we illustrate the training exercises in Figures 9.2–9.4 and present a brief overview of our initial results. Of course, five days is a minimal amount of training to influence the development of networks that develop for many years. Nonetheless, we found a general improvement in intelligence in the experimental group as measured by the K-BIT. This is due to improvement of the experimental group in performance on the non-verbal portion of the IQ test. We also discovered that the Reaction Time (RT) measures registered with the ANT were highly unstable and of low reliability in children of the age we were testing; thus we were not able to obtain significant improvement in the measures of the various networks, although overall reaction time did improve. We did find the trained children had lower conflict scores (more efficient executive attention) than the controls. We did not observe changes in temperament over the course of the training. Our preliminary analysis of the brain networks using EEG recording suggested that the component most closely related to the anterior cingulate in prior studies could be seen in the

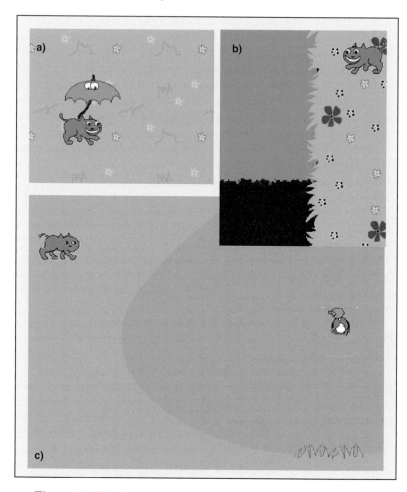

Figure 9.2 Tracking excercises. (a) The child's task is to move the cat under a moving umbrella to avoid the rain, once the umbrella is caught, the child has to keep the cat under it as the umbrella continues moving around, (b) The child moves the cat to the grass to avoid the mud. Over trials, the amount of grass is reduced and the mud increased until considerable concentration is required of the child to move the cat to a grassy section, (c) The child moves the cat to intercept the duck as it exits the pond. As the duck always swims in a straight line, in this exercise, the child can learn to predict where it will come out of the pond.

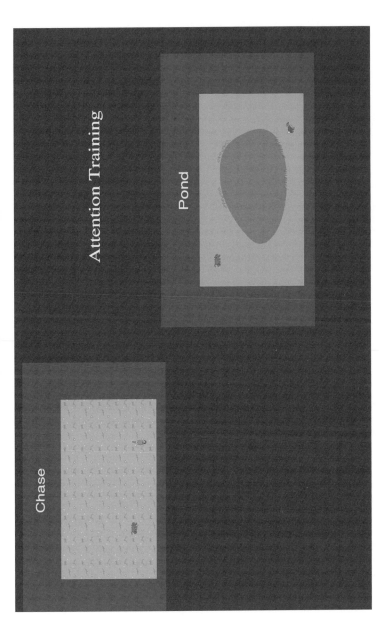

Figure 9.3 Visual attention and conflict resolution exercises. (a) Matching-to-sample exercise. The child must select the picture on the brown board that matches the sample on the upper left corner. Matching to sample difficulty is increased over the trials by making the competing pictures more similar. At advanced levels, the sample picture is removed from the screen and the child has to memorize it in order to select the correct matching picture; (b) Conflict resolution exercise: The child has to select the group with the most numbers on it. In congruent trials, like the one illustrated, the more numerous group is made up of numbers larger in value. In incongruent trials, the more numerous group is made of numbers smaller in value. (c) Illustration of the visual feedback for completing a set of trials of equal difficulty.

Figure 9.4 Illustrates the high level of concentration of a four-year-old child during attention training.

four-year-olds only after training. Because of the variability of RT in the four-year-old children, we replicated our study with six-year-olds. The results support the ability of the training program to change the executive attention network (Rueda, Rothbart, McCandliss, Saccamanno & Posner, 2005; Posner & Rothbart, 2007).

As the number of children who undergo our training increases, we can examine aspects of their temperament and genotype to help us understand who might benefit from attention training. To this end we are currently genotyping all of the children in an effort to examine the candidate genes found previously to be related to the efficacy of the executive attention networks (Rueda et al, 2005). We are also beginning to examine the precursors of executive attention in even younger children, with the goal of determining whether there is a sensitive period during which interventions might prove most effective.

There is already some evidence in the literature with older children who suffer from attention deficit hyperactivity disorder (ADHD) that using attention training methods can produce improvement in the ability to concentrate and in general intelligence (Kerns, Esso, & Thompson,

2000; Klingberg, Forssberg, & Westerberg, 2002; Shalev, Tsal, & Mevorach 2002). As a result, we are also working with other groups to carry out these exercises in children with learning related problems such as ADHD and autism. These projects will test whether the programs are efficacious with children who have special difficulties with attention as part of their disorder. We hope also to have some preschools adopt attention training as a specific part of their preschool curriculum. This would allow training over more extensive time periods, and testing of other forms of training such as could occur in social groups (Mills & Mills, 2000, see also van Geert & Steenbeek, this volume).

While we do not yet know whether our specific program is optimal, we believe that the evidence we have obtained for the development of specific brain networks during early childhood provides a strong rationale for sustained efforts to see if we can improve the attentional abilities of children. In addition, it would be possible to determine how well such methods might generalize to the learning of the wide variety of skills that must be acquired during school.

References

Andersen, R. A. (1989). Visual eye movement functions of the posterior parietal cortex. *Annual Review of Neuroscience*, 12, 377–403.

Beauregard, M., Levesque, J., and Bourgouin, P. (2001). Neural correlates of conscious self-regulation of emotion. *Journal of Neuroscience*, 21, RC 165.

Blair, R. J. R., Morris, J. S., Frith, C. D., Perrett, D. I., and Dolan, R. J. (1999). Dissociable neural responses to facial expression of sadness and anger. *Brain*, 1222, 883–893.

Botvinick, M. M., Braver, T. S., Barch, D. M., Carter, C. S., and Cohen, J. D. (2001). Conflict monitoring and cognitive control. *Psychological Review*, 108, 624–652.

Bush, G., Luu, P., and Posner, M. I. (2000). Cognitive and emotional influences in the anterior cingulate cortex. *Trends in Cognitive Science*, 4/6, 215–222.

Carlson, S. T. and Moses, L. J. (2001). Individual differences in inhibitory control in children's theory of mind. *Child Development*, 72, 1032–1053.

Clohessy, A. B., Posner, M. I., and Rothbart, M. K. (2001). Development of the functional visual field. *Acta Psychologica*, 106, 51–68.

Corbetta, M. and Shulman, G. L. (2002). Control of goal-directed and stimulus-driven attention in the brain. *Nature Neuroscience Reviews*, 3, 201–215.

Driver, J., Eimer, M., and Macaluso, E. (2004). Neurobiology of human spatial attention: Modulation, generation, and integration. In N. Kanwisher and J. Duncan (eds.), *Attention and Performance XX: Functional Brain Imaging of Visual Cognition* (pp. 267–300). Oxford: Oxford University Press.

Duncan, J., Seitz, R. J., Kolodny, J., Bor, D., Herzog, H., Ahmed, A., Newell, F. N., and Emslie, H. (2000). A neural basis for general intelligence. *Science*, 289, 457–460.

Ellis, L. K., Rothbart, M. K., and Posner, M. I. (2004). Individual differences in executive attention predict self-regulation and adolescent psychosocial behaviors. *Ann. NY Acad. Sci.* 1–21, 331–340.

Fan, J., Flombaum, J. I., McCandliss, B. D., Thomas, K. M., and Posner, M. I. (2003). Cognitive and brain mechanisms of conflict. *Neuroimage*, 18, 42–57.

Fan, J., Fossella, J. A., Summer T., and Posner, M. I. (2003). Mapping the genetic variation of executive attention onto brain activity. *Proceedings of the National Academy of Sciences, USA*, 100, 7406–7411.

Fan, J., McCandliss, B. D., Sommer, T., Raz, M., and Posner, M. I. (2002). Testing the efficiency and independence of attentional networks. *Journal of Cognitive Neuroscience*, 14(3), 340–347.

Fan, J., Wu, Y., Fossella, J., and Posner, M. I. (2001). Assessing the heritability of attentional networks. *BioMed Central Neuroscience*, 2, 14.

Fossella, J., Sommer, T., Fan, J., Wu, Y., Swanson, J. M., Pfaff, D. W., and Posner, M. I. (2002). Assessing the molecular genetics of attention networks. *BMC Neuroscience*, 3, 14.

Gerardi-Caulton, G. (2000). Sensitivity to spatial conflict and the development of self-regulation in children 24–36 months of age. *Developmental Science*, 3/4, 397–404.

Haith, M. M., Hazan, C., and Goodman, G. S. (1988). Expectation and anticipation of dynamic visual events by 3.5 month-old babies. *Child Development*, 59, 467–479.

Karnath, H-O., Ferber, S., and Himmelbach, M. (2001). Spatial awareness is a function of the temporal not the posterior parietal lobe. *Nature*, 411, 95–953.

Kaufman, A. S. and Kaufman, N. L. (1990). *Kaufman Brief Intelligence Test – Manual Circle Pines*, MN: American Guidance Service.

Kerns, K. A., Esso, K., and Thompson, J. (1999). Investigation of a direct intervention for improving attention in young children with ADHD. *Developmental Neuropsychology*, 16, 273–295.

Klingberg, T., Forssberg, H., and Westerberg, H. (2002). Training of working memory in children with ADHD. *Journal of Clinical and Experimental Neuropsychology*, 24, 781–791.

Kochanska, G. (1995). Children's temperament, mothers' discipline, and security of attachment: Multiple pathways to emerging internalization. *Child Development*, 66, 597–615.

Kochanska, G., Murray, K., Jacques, T. Y., Koenig, A. L., and Vandegeest, K. A. (1996). Inhibitory control in young children and its role in emerging internationalization. *Child Development*, 67, 490–507.

MacDonald, A. W., Cohen, J. D., Stenger, V. A., and Carter, C. S. (2000). Dissociating the role of the dorsolateral prefrontal and anterior cingulate cortex in cognitive control. *Science*, 288, 1835–1838.

Marrocco, R. T. and Davidson, M. C. (1998). Neurochemistry of attention. In R. Parasuraman (ed.), *The Attention Brain* (pp. 35–50). Cambridge, MA:MIT Press.

Mills, D. and Mills, C. (2000). *Hungarian Kindergarten Curriculum Translation*. London Mills Production Limited.

Ochsner, K. N., Kossyln, S. M., Cosgrove, G. R., Cassem, E. H., Price, B. H., Nierenberg, A. A., and Rauch, S. L. (2001). Deficits in visual cognition and attention following bilateral anterior cingulotomy. *Neuropsychologia*, 39, 219–230.

Posner, M. I. (1980). Orienting of attention. The 7th Sir F. C. Bartlett Lecture. *Quarterly Journal of Experimental Psychology*, 32, 3–25.

Posner, M. I. and Petersen, S. E. (1990). The attention system of the human brain. *Annual Review of Neuroscience*, 13, 25–42.

Posner, M. I. and Raichle, M. E. (1994). *Images of Mind*. Scientific American Books.

Posner, M. I. and Rothbart, M. K. (2007). *Educating the Human Brain*. Washington DC: APA.

Posner, M. I., Rothbart, M. K. and Sheese, B. E. (2007). Attention genes. *Developmental Science*, 10, 24–29.

Ramón y Cajal, S. (1937). *Recollection of My Life*. Philadelphia: American Philosophical Society.

Rothbart, M. K., Ahadi, S. A., and Hershey, K. (1994). Temperament and social behavior in children. *Merrill-Palmer Quarterly*, 40, 21–39.

Rueda, M. R., Fan, J., McCandliss, B., Halparin, J. D., Gruber, D. B., Pappert, L., and Posner, M. I. (2004). Development of attentional networks in childhood. *Neuropsychologia*, 42, 1028–1040.

Rueda, M. R., Fan, J., and Posner, M. I. (2003). Development of the time course for resolving conflict. Poster presented at the *Cognitive Neuroscience Society*.

Rueda, M. R., Rothbart, M. K., McCandliss, B., Saccamanno, L. and Posner, M. I. (2005). Training, maturation and genetic influences on the development of executive attention. *Proc. U.S. National Acad. of Sciences*, 102, 14931–14936.

Rumbaugh, D. M. and Washburn, D. A. (1995). Attention and memory in relation to learning: A comparative adaptation perspective. In G. R. Lyon, and Krasengor, N. A. (eds.), *Attention, Memory and Executive Function* (pp. 199–219). Baltimore, MD: Brookes Publishing Co.

Semrud-Clikeman, M., Nielsen, K. H., and Clinton, A. (1999). An intervention approach for children with teacher and parent-identified attentional difficulties. *Journal of Learning Disabilities*, 32, 581–589.

Shalev, L., Tsal, Y., and Mevorach, C. (2003). Progressive attentional training program: Effective direct intervention for children with ADHD. *Proceedings of the Cognitive Neuroscience Society*, New York, pp. 55–56.

Simon, H. A. (1969). *The Sciences of the Artificial*. Cambridge, MA: MIT Press.

Thorndike, E. L. (1903). *Educational Psychology*. New York: Teachers College.

van Veen, V. and Carter, C. S. (2002). The timing of action-monitoring processes in the anterior cingulate cortex. *Journal of Cognitive Neuroscience*, 14, 593–602.

Venter, J. C., Adams, M. D., Myers, E. W., Li, P. W., Mural, R. J., *et al.*, (2001). The sequence of the human genome. *Science*, 291, 1304–1335.

Washburn, D. A. (1994). Stroop-like effects for monkeys and humans: Processing speed or strength of association? *Journal of Psychological Science*, 5(6), 375–379.

10 Developing the brain: A functional imaging approach to learning and educational sciences

Hideaki Koizumi

Overview

There is a great difference between mere learning and true education. Mere learning involves simple adaptation to environmental cues, which has a proto- type in the imprinting mechanisms of birds. The second is found only in humans, where genetic and epigenetic processes interact to add and control new stimuli and information. Koizumi seeks to use brain imaging techniques to build knowledge of brain functioning so as to improve true education about important human issues, such as hatred and love as well as physics and biology. A technique pioneered by Koizumi is optical topography, a non-invasive brain imaging technique that uses near-infrared technology to assess brain activation in infants and children, as well as adults, the elderly, and brain-damaged patients. One topic that it has illuminated is the plasticity of infants' brains, including the ability to differentiate language from other sounds, and maternal speech from other language. This technology is promising for educational pur- poses because it does not require that children remain completely still for imaging and can be used in relatively natural settings, in contrast to other brain-imaging techniques.

The Editors

In the twentieth century, the modern methodology of reductionism that was initially advocated by Descartes in the seventeenth century has led to remarkable success, especially in science and technology. In the twenty-first century, however, I think that syntheses of the minutely differentiated disciplines produced by the now long reign of reductionism will become very important. The latter half of the twentieth century saw some initial steps in this direction, with multi-disciplinarity as the catch- cry for locating people from various fields under one roof. Yet experience has shown that this doesn't necessarily produce bridge-building (Bruer, this volume) and fusion leading to integration (Rothschild, 1996; Koizumi, 1999a). Integration requires dynamic processes. I call the con- cept and operation of such dynamic processes "trans-disciplinarity" (Koizumi, 1995, 1996a, 1999a, 2000a, 2001). This concept may be

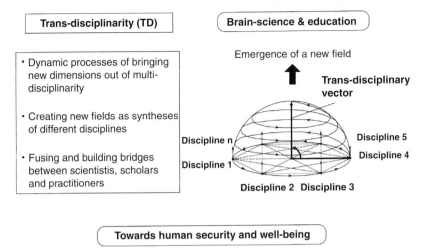

Figure 10.1 Trans-disciplinary: Synthesis over reductionism.

abbreviated as TD. In the TD context, integration is the process of bringing new dimensions out of multi-disciplinary collaboration by dynamically fusing and building bridges between different disciplines. The concept is summarized and depicted in Figure 10.1.

The depiction is based on an analogy with the coupling of angular momenta in the spin states of quantum mechanics. Japan's "Developing the Brain" and "Brain-Science & Education" programs constitute a representative embryonic trans-disciplinary field. This novel academic field has been providing sites for the generation of coherence between the various relevant disciplines in a set of national programs which started in 2000 (Koizumi, 1995, 1996b, 2000b, 2000c, 2003b, 2004b).

The bases of learning and education

The universe and life

When we consider the Earth's biosphere, we might regard it as being driven by the great thermal engine formed between the Sun and the wider universe. The biosphere is bathed in relatively high-energy and low-entropy photons from the Sun, and in turn emits relatively low-energy and high-entropy photons into space. Among other things, this great thermal engine drives global water circulation and life cycles within the biosphere. In this context, the definition of life as a self-reproducing system that uses energy to produce negentropy is particularly resonant.

The Big Bang is thought to have happened about 13,500 million years ago. We cannot know about anything before this; here, we have one of the basic limitations of science. Isotopic analysis of meteorites indicates that the solar system was born about 4,600 million years ago. On the basis of fossil analysis, life is thought to have appeared about 3,800 million years ago. Since then, information adapting life to the environment has been accumulating in genes over very many generations. The central nervous system appeared about 300 million years ago, and has evolved remarkably since then (Sagan, 1977; Britten *et al.*, 1969). The revolutionary feature of a central nervous system in terms of information processing for adaptation is that learning, and thus adaptation, can take place within a generation. The relation between genetic and epi-genetic processes is the key to a more scientific view of education (Koizumi, 1996b).

Biological definitions of learning and education

From the psychological point of view, imprinting is the archetypal example of learning. In this phenomenon, a newly hatched bird usually takes the first moving object it sees to be its "mother." Imprinting has to take place within a critical period up to 24 hours after birth (Hess, 1959).

In the case of wild geese among other species, further learned behavior includes migration; the bird does this by following its parents. An artificially incubated bird, however, won't normally have a way of learning how to migrate. In a famous work, Lishman succeeded in imprinting a light aircraft on artificially incubated geese and then guiding them from Northern Canada to the United States (Lishman, 1997). Once the birds have been taught, they are able to migrate independently in the next year. The discovery that migration is a learned behavior was important in terms of our knowledge of learning and education.

Although the difference in base arrangement between the DNA of humans and of chimpanzees is only about 1 percent, researchers studying primates have found that chimpanzees learn by imitation, but never educate each other (Goodall, 2001; Matsuzawa, 2003).

Several years ago, I noticed that Immanuel Kant, the great philosopher, mentioned an interesting experiment in his "Lecture Note on Pedagogy," published after his death (Kant, 1803). He put a sparrow's egg among several canary eggs in a canary nest. Kant found that he got a singing sparrow, and noted that the father-birds appeared to be actively instructing the offspring. This experiment is very similar to the "farm-out experiments" of ornithology, the first of which was conducted in the 1960s. More recently, ornithologists have confirmed that the father-bird has the role of teaching singing to his children.

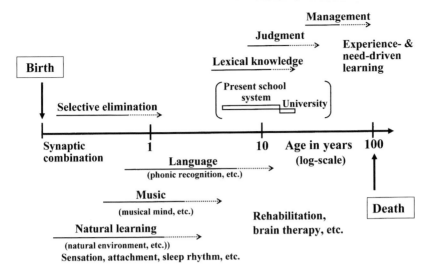

Source: Koizumi H., *Seizon and Life Sci.* (1998)

Figure 10.2 Learning and education over a lifetime. Suggestions for a curriculum based on developmental stages.

The viewpoint of biology makes new definitions of learning and education possible (see Fischer, this volume); learning is the process of making neuronal connections in response to external environmental stimuli, while education is the process of controlling or adding stimuli, and of inspiring the will to learn. These concepts are comprehensive, and cover the whole human life span (Koizumi, 2000c, 2004b).

Figure 10.2 shows learning and brain development over a life span. The time scale is logarithmic. The figure includes a few tentative suggestions for a curriculum based on critical and sensitive periods (Koizumi, 1999a).

Synaptogenesis and elimination

As an extension of the pioneering studies of the columnar structures in the primary visual cortex by the Nobel laureates Hubel and Wiesel, many researchers in the 1970s studied the critical period for the formation of these structures (Stryker *et al.*, 1978). If a kitten is raised in an environment where the only external visual stimulus is provided by vertical stripes, it becomes incapable of seeing horizontal lines, and remains so throughout its life. If stimuli from the environment do not include horizontal lines, the columns responsible for horizontal lines disappear.

Therefore, even formation of the visual system in the brain is attributable to a learning process which has a critical period (Singer, this volume).

Similar things happen with ocular dominance columns in the human visual cortex. A crucial clinical implication of the knowledge of column development is that eyesight becomes poor if one eye is covered by a patch during infancy. Now, ophthalmologists strongly recommend that infants in the first 18 months of life should never wear eye-patches.

Signals enter the body of a neuron from many dendrites, while output signals leave on the axon. A large excess of neurons is prepared by genetic information and then eliminated during the fetal stage. Huge numbers of synapses are prepared during the neonatal stage and then eliminated over most of the childhood years. In the case of the human primary visual area, the number of synapses peaks at around eight months after birth (Huttenlocher, 1990). This process of neuronal selection in individuals leads to environmental adaptation, and is why a cat raised in a visual environment of vertical stripes ends up incapable of seeing horizontal lines.

Myelination, the process whereby a sheath of myelin forms around the axons, is another factor we have to consider. This process provides a roughly 100-fold improvement in signal transmission speeds. The order of myelination is programmed by genes. Flechsig discovered this around 100 years ago and created an image of the brain depicting this order (Flechsig, 1898). Some areas are already myelinated in the prenatal stage. Myelination continues in other areas, proceeding up to around 20 years of age in the area for prefrontal association. This developmental order of functional areas could be applicable to the optimization of curricula (Koizumi, 1999).

Importance of noninvasive brain-function measurement

Completely noninvasive brain-function imaging methods are essential in applying the concept of "Brain-Science & Education" to practical problems. We currently have three noninvasive methods for imaging higher-order brain functions: functional magnetic resonance imaging (fMRI) (Ogawa *et al.*, 1992; Yamamoto, E. *et al.*, 1992), magneto-encephalography (MEG) (Brenner *et al.*, 1978) and optical topography (OT) (Maki *et al.*, 1995; Yamashita *et al.*, 1996; Koizumi *et al.*, 1999). Since each method has both merits and limitations, we sometimes use all three methods complementarily.

The principle of optical topography

In optical topography, we use infrared light to obtain images of higher-order brain functions. We published the world's first paper on optical topography in 1995 and have been developing the method since then

(Maki *et al.*, 1995; Koizumi *et al.*, 1999b, 2003a; Kennan *et al.*, 2002; Taga *et al.*, 2003). A matrix of flexible optical fibers with a diameter of 1 mm are placed between hair roots on the scalp. Near-infrared light enters the brain and is affected by the changes in concentration of oxy-, deoxy-, and all-hemoglobin levels which are induced by neuronal activity. Signals from photo detectors are then analyzed to map these changes. The attraction of this method (NIRS, Near-Infrared Spectroscopy) is that it can be used to test subjects under natural conditions (Petitto, this volume).

The safety of brain-function analysis is very important, since we want tests that are applicable to all human subjects, and particularly to babies and children. The chemical bonding energies of the molecules that form human tissue are in the several-electron-volt range. Therefore, if we use photons at less than one electron volt, the method should, in principle, be safe except for possible thermal effects. Optical topography is completely safe since the photon energies are within this range and the thermal effects have been shown to be negligible (Ito *et al.*, 2000). Functional MRI is also safe, at least from the viewpoint of photon energy. In this case, however, we need to be careful about the rapidly changing gradient magnetic fields as well as the strength of the static field.

Imaging of brain function in neonates and infants

Optical topography can give us images of brain activity during specific activities. In the act of writing, for example, activation is seen in both Broca's and Wernicke's areas (Figure 10.3) (Yamamoto *et al.*, 1999). Broca's area, on the left frontal lobe, is for word generation, while Wernicke's area, on the left temporal lobe, is for word comprehension.

We have also found examples of the astonishing plasticity of the infant brain. In perhaps the most remarkable of these, a one-year-old baby only had a small part of the full cerebral cortex for that age because of an accident in the fetal stage. Large hospitals had diagnosed her as blind and deaf based on MRI data alone, and conducted no further examinations. Her parents, however, thought that she could see to some extent. At their request, we used optical topography to test her, with the aid of medical doctors. The results showed that the residual part of the cerebral cortex was in fact being activated by visual stimuli (Kogure *et al.*, 1997).

We have used optical topography to study functional recovery in early infant brains, and again found incredible plasticity: e.g., motion despite an almost completely defective internal capsule, speech despite severe left-hemispheric damage, and complex motion despite an almost complete lack of a cerebellum. We arrived at the concept of "Developing the Brain" through these and other observations of infant-brain plasticity.

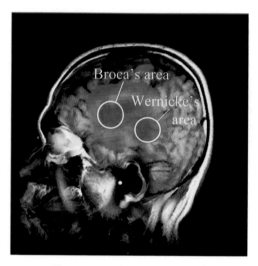

**Functional image
through optical topography**

**Anatomical image
through MRI**

Broca's area on left
frontal lobe:
word generation

Wernicke's area on left
temporal lobe:
semantic understanding

In collaboration with Iwata,
M., et al., Tokyo Women's
Medical University

Figure 10.3 The activation of language areas.

This work brought us to see that the process of developing the brain differs from that of rehabilitation, which deals with the recovery of lost functions (Koizumi, 2000c).

Optical topography can be used to safely observe the brain activity of neonates. Of course, this is difficult with fMRI or MEG because babies don't like to stay still during measurement. In France, we collaborated with Jacques Mehler's group to test neonates within five days of birth, having obtained prior approval from the French National Ethics Committee. The mother tongue in these cases was, of course, French. The neonates were exposed to French being read by a reporter. We found that the areas around the acoustic cortex were more strongly activated by French speech than by other sounds.

More precise tests were performed in Italy by a group that included many of the same workers. The results were published recently (Pena *et al.*, 2003). Subjects were again neonates within five days of birth, but the mother tongue in this case was Italian (Figure 10.4). Hearing Italian speech produced stronger activation than hearing the same speech in reverse or silence. The tape in reverse of course contains the same sound components, i.e., frequency and power spectra, but no identifiable words or language. We also found that, even in neonates, left-hemispheric laterality of function is demonstrated in response to speech (see also Petitto, this volume).

The neonates might be responding to the rhythms and intonations of the mother tongue. Furthermore, either of two hypotheses is capable of explaining these results. One is that neonates might learn to identify the mother

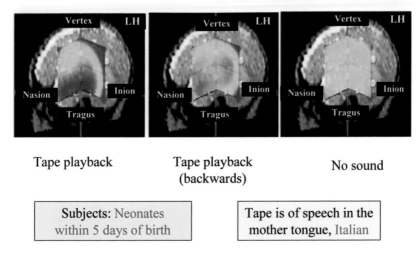

Tape playback	Tape playback (backwards)	No sound

Subjects: Neonates within 5 days of birth	**Tape is of speech in the mother tongue,** Italian

In collaboration with J. Mehler's group, International School for Advanced Studies (Italy), *Proc. Natl. Acad. Sci. USA* (2003)

Figure 10.4 How hearing the mother tongue affects the brain activity of a neonate.

tongue during the prenatal stage in their mothers' wombs. Experiments with dynamic three-dimensional ultrasonic imaging have shown that a fetus can respond to sounds passing through the mother's body. The other hypothesis is that neonates might have an innate ability to specifically respond to natural language. We are planning to continue tests of this kind, with our next experiment looking at the mother tongue vs. foreign languages. This should indicate the correctness of a single hypothesis.

Emotion and intelligence

As well as medical applications and answering questions of development and learning, "Brain-science and education" could be important in solving social problems ranging from learning disabilities to criminality, child abuse, and so on. Furthermore, a contribution to world peace might even be possible.

How the human brain encapsulates evolutionary history

The brain evolved as new layers formed around the brain stem. The brain stem maintains life, the limbic system gives us the drive to live, and the neocortex gives us control for a better life. Reason and knowledge are related to the neocortex, while basic emotions are related to the limbic system. Our life and society are built on the delicate balance between the limbic system and neocortex.

The evolutionary offspring of reptiles are separated into two branches. One branch reaches humans via the therapsids (repto-mammals), much later the monkeys, and eventually an ape like a proto-chimpanzee. The other branch reaches the birds via the dinosaurs. The human limbic system and neocortex are markedly more evolved than those of repto-mammals. Even in comparison with the chimpanzee, however, the human prefrontal cortex is twice as large, despite the mere 1 percent difference in the arrangement of DNA bases. The prefrontal cortex might generate deep emotions, like love and hatred.

How to cut chains of hatred

The present world suffers from chains of hatred. One of the most serious problems is how to cut these chains. On this point, I would like to introduce a message from Tokikuni Urushima, the father of Honen. He was assassinated in 1141, in front of the then 9-year-old Honen, in a night attack by an enemy. Just before he died, he said these words to his son. "I am suffering from severe injuries but persisting with my life. Anyone else placed in the same situation would do the same thing. Engage in self-reflection and realize that you should never hate your enemy. If you kill your enemies, their families will want to kill you. This chain of hatred will then never be diminished. Leave home immediately, and look for the ultimate solution in yourself." Long years passed before Honen was released from his anguish. For him, the solution was to continually proclaim the eternal power and existence of Amitabha, the bodhisattva of compassion.

The father of Honen deeply considered the standpoint of the other. This is closely related to "theories of mind." In this sense, a theory of matter is an ability to predict the path of a flying ball, for example, through neuronal processing, while a "theory of mind" is an ability to comprehend the minds of other people and predict their thoughts and responses. This ability is fostered through sufficient communications while children are around three to four years old. Since the lack of a "theory of mind" leads to an inability to understand the standpoints of others, this lack is responsible for various social problems.

Longitudinal study on the development of the human prefrontal cortex

We started to study the development of a "theory of mind" in the wider field of "Brain-science and education" by measuring the prefrontal areas

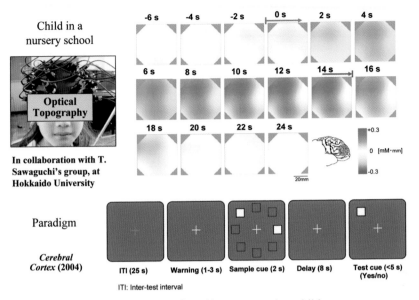

Figure 10.5 Activation of working memory in a child.

of children three to five years old. Figure 10.5 shows an example of a test of working-memory development. Optical topography readily provides images of working-memory activation, even in small children (Tsujimoto *et al.*, 2004).

Ethical issues raised by novel brain technologies

Brain-based direct communication

Optical topography provides us with a novel form of communication based on the direct observation of brain activity. We tested a completely locked-in patient suffering from amyotrophic lateral sclerosis (ALS). Her family had been unable to communicate with the patient for more than two years. They thought that the patient might no longer have consciousness, since she had been in a vegetative condition for a long time. We tested such brain functions as the imagination of motion, listening to speech, word generation (imagined), listening to music, and working-memory tasks. Optical topography demonstrated activity in every case. We were able to prove that the patient clearly had consciousness. Therefore, we asked her to imagine grasping with the right-hand to say "yes" and to imagine nothing to say "no." We observed clear activation of the contra-lateral (left hemisphere) motor area only when her answer was "yes" (Haida *et al.*, 2000).

Neuro-ethics

The above result poses serious problems in ethics. Firstly, at least one human has been shown to have consciousness despite physically being in a vegetative state. Even medical doctors had thought that ALS patients who had been locked-in for long periods would lose brain activity through nonuse. The new finding demolishes the assumption of non-consciousness, forcing us to face the problems of whether or not such patients have human rights and, if they do, how to secure these rights. It also raises the new problems of whether or not and how to legally enforce the patient's will as measured by direct brain measurement.

Neuro-ethics will become an important field in the near future (see Vidal, this volume). Noninvasive brain-function imaging might be used to deprive people of privacy because of its potential for revealing the individual mind. For example, personal likes and dislikes could be checked by using fMRI to observe activation of the amygdala. Also, truth or falsity of statements might be confirmed by measuring the activation of memory systems. Therefore, a novel form of neuro-ethics will be necessary, along with committees for its administration. I am now working to establish a neuro-ethics research and ethics committee system on a national level.

Brain-science and education in the twenty-first century

Healthcare in support of brain functions

Here, we consider how future information technology will affect our lives. As the convenience of cars and elevators, for example, spoil our leg muscles, so information technology holds the possibility of spoiling our brains. As shown in Figure 10.6, our working memory is in the prefrontal cortex (area 46), and is strongly activated during mental arithmetic, but not in calculation with a calculator. Recently, neuroscience has shown that this working memory is important in the retrieval of things memorized. Spoiled working memory causes a serious form of forgetfulness, even in younger adults (20–30 years old). As the possibilities in information technology grow, we will need ways to keep our brains healthy. Adopting this point of view is also important in the prevention and intervention of senile dementia.

The "brain-science and education" program in Japan

In 2000, I coordinated a four-day trans-disciplinary forum on "Developing the brain: the science of learning and education" under

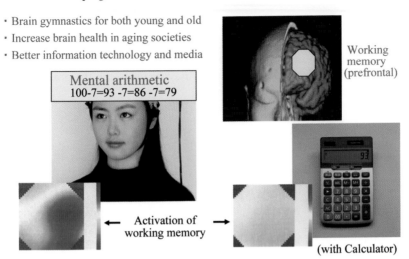

- Brain gymnastics for both young and old
- Increase brain health in aging societies
- Better information technology and media

Mental arithmetic
100-7=93 -7=86 -7=79

Working
memory
(prefrontal)

← Activation of →
working memory

(with Calculator)

Figure 10.6 Activation of the prefrontal cortex during mental arithmetic.

the sponsorship of the Japan Science and Technology Corporation and the Science and Technology Agency of Japan. This forum was held at the end of the twentieth century as the culmination of several years of work in this field (from 1995) and as part of a broader effort to forecast the developments and effects of science and technology in the early twenty-first century. As a consequence of this forum, the "Brain-science and education" program was established as a national program in 2001. This was the earliest flagship initiative of the new Ministry of Education, Culture, Sports, Science and Technology (MEXT), which was established by combining the former Ministry of Education with the Science and Technology Agency. I have been serving as the director of this program since it was set up. We are currently running twelve projects, selected from responses to a public announcement. The results to date have been very interesting.

Finally, I would like to mention the most basic reason why Brain-science and education is important in the twenty-first century. As the Curies stated at the end of their Nobel Prize lecture, "Science and technology are neutral, so whether they are applied to good or bad ends depends entirely upon humanity." I believe that education should take precedence over science and technology. Evidence-based work within the fields defined by "Developing the brain" and "Brain-science and education" should provide at least some keys to greater human security and well-being in the twenty-first century (Koizumi, 2004).

Acknowledgments

I would like to express my sincere gratitude to the Pontifical Academy of Sciences and the organizers, particularly Professors Antonio M. Battro, Kurt W. Fischer, and Pierre Léna for having given me the great opportunity of appearing at the symposium.

References

Brenner, D., Lipton, J., and Williamson, S. J. (1978). Somatically evoked magnetic fields of the human brain. *Science*, 199, 81–83.

Britten, R. J. and Davidson, E. H. (1969). Gene regulation for higher cells: A theory. *Science*, 165, 349–357.

Flechsig, P. (1898). Neue Untresuchungen uber die Markbildung in den menschlichen Grosshimlappen. *Neurol.* Centribit, 17, 977–996. ('A new understanding of myelination in the human cerebral cortex').

Goodall, J. (2001). Private communication.

Haida, M., Shinohara, Y., Ito, Y., Yamamoto, T., Kawaguchi, F., and Koizumi, H. (2000). Brain function of an ALS patient in complete locked-in state by using optical topography. *Search for Foundation of Science & Technology in the 21st Century: The Trans-disciplinary Symposium on the Frontier of Mind-Brain Science and Its Practical Applications* (Koizumi, H., ed.), 95–97, Hitachi Ltd., Tokyo.

Hess, E. H. (1959). Imprinting: An effect of early experience, imprinting determines later social behavior in animals. *Science*, 130, 133–141.

Huttenlocher, P. R. (1990). Morphometric study of human cerebral cortex development. *Neuropsychologia*, 28, 517–527.

Ito, Y., Kennan, R., Watanabe, E., and Koizumi, H. (2000). Assessment of heating effects in skin during continuous wave near-infrared spectroscopy. *Journal of Biomedical Optics*, 5, 383–390.

Kant, I. (1803). *Uber Pädagogik*, Herausgegeben von D. Friedrich Theodor Rink (Immanuel Kants Werke, Herausgegeben von Ernst Cassirer, *Band VIII* (1992)).

Kennan, R. P., Horovitz, S. G., Maki, A., Yamashita, Y., Koizumi, H., and Gore, J. C. (2002). Simultaneous recording of event-related auditory oddball response using transcranial near-infrared optical topography and surface EEG. *Neuroimage*, 16, 587–592.

Kogure, K., Yamashita, Y., Maki, A., Itagaki, H., Izumiyama, M., and Koizumi, H. (1997). Functional near-infrared spectrography (fNIR) in the neurology ward. *Journal of Cerebral Blood Flow and Metabolism*, 17(S1) S555.

Koizumi, H. ed. (1995). *Search for a Foundation of Science & Technology in the 21st Century: The Trans-disciplinary Symposium on the Frontier of Mind-Brain Science and Its Practical Applications*, Hitachi Ltd., Tokyo.

Koizumi, H. (1996a). A trans-disciplinary approach through analytical science towards global sustainability and human well-being, *The Trans-disciplinary Forum on Science and Technology for the Global Environment: Environmental Measurement and Analysis* (Koizumi, H., ed.), 3–10, Japan Science and Technology Co., Tokyo.

(1996b). The importance of considering the brain in environmental science, *The Trans-disciplinary Forum on Science and Technology for the Global Environment: Environmental Measurement and Analysis* (Koizumi, H., ed.), 128–132, Japan Science and Technology Co., Tokyo.

(1999a). A practical approach to trans-disciplinary studies for the 21st century. *Journal of Seizon and Life Science*, 9B, 5–24.

Koizumi, H., Yamashita, Y., Maki, A., Yamamoto, T., Ito, Y., Itagaki H., and Kennan, R. (1999b). Higher-order brain function analysis by trans-cranial dynamic NIRS imaging. *Journal of Biomedical Optics*, 4, front cover & 403–413.

Koizumi, H. (2000a). Trans-disciplinarity, *Search for Foundation of Science & Technology in the 21st Century: The Trans-disciplinary Symposium on the Frontier of Mind-Brain Science and Its Practical Applications, Part II* (Koizumi, H., ed.), 220–222, Hitachi Ltd., Tokyo.

(2000b). The concept of "Developing the Brain": A natural science for learning and education," *The Trans-disciplinary Symposium on the Frontier of Mind-Brain Science and Its Practical Applications, Part II* (H. Koizumi, ed.). 217–9, Hitachi Ltd., Tokyo.

(2000c). Developing the brain: a natural science for learning and education: *The Trans-disciplinary Forum on "Developing the Brain: The Science of Learning and Education* (Koizumi, H., ed.), Japan Science and Technology Co., Tokyo.

(2001). Trans-disciplinarity, *Neuro-endocrinology Letters*, 22, 219–221.

Koizumi, H., Yamamoto, T., Maki, A., Yamashita, Y., Sato, H., Kawaguchi, H., and Ichikawa, N. (2003a). Optical topography: Novel applications and practical problems. *Applied Optics*, 42, 3054–3062.

Koizumi, H. (2003b). The concept of developing the brain, a natural science for learning and education, *Learning Therapy* (Kawashima, R. and Koizumi, H., eds.), 1–14, Tohoku University Press, Sendai.

(2004a). Searching for a new science of humanity. *Trends in Science (Gakujyutsu-no-doko: The Journal of the Science Council of Japan)*, 2, 32–45, Japan Science Support Foundation, Tokyo. (in Japanese).

(2004b). The concept of "Developing the Brain": A new natural science for learning and education, *Brain & Development*, 26, 434–441.

Lishman, W. A., Teets, T. L., Duff, J., Sladen, W. J. L., Shire, G. G., Goolsby, K., Bezner Kerr, W. A., and Urbanek, R. P. (1997). A reintroduction technique for migratory birds: Leading Canada geese and isolation-reared sandhill cranes with ultralight aircraft. *Proc. North Am. Crane Workshop*, 7, 114–122.

Maki, A., Yamashita, Y., Ito, Y., Watanabe, E., Mayanagi, Y., and Koizumi, H. (1995). Spatial and temporal analysis of human motor activity using non-invasive NIR topography. *Medical Physics*, 22, 1997–2005.

Matsuzawa, T. (2003). Private communication.

Ogawa, S., Tank, D. W., Menon, R., Ellermann, J. M., Kim, S. G., Merkle, H., and Ugurbil, K. (1992). Intrinsic signal changes accompanying sensory stimulation: Functional brain mapping with magnetic resonance imaging,

Proceedings of the National Academy of Sciences of the United States of America, 89, 5951–5955.

Pena, M., Maki, A., Kovacic, D., Dehaene-Lambertz, G., Koizumi, H., Bouquet, F., and Mehler, J. (2003). Sounds and silence: An optical topography study of language recognition at birth. *Proceedings of the National Academy of Sciences of the United States of America*, 100, 11702–11705.

Rothschild, E. (1996). Environmental measurement, *The Trans-disciplinary Forum on Science and Technology for the Global Environment: Environmental Measurement and Analysis* (Koizumi, H., ed.). 11–21, Japan Science and Technology Co., Tokyo.

Sagan, C. (1977). *The dragons of eden: speculation on the evolution of human intelligence*, Random House: New York.

Striker, M. P., Sherk, H., Lenventhal. A. G. and Hirsch, H. V. B. (1978). Physiological consequences for the cat's visual cortex of effectively restricting early visual experience with oriented contours. *Journal of Neurophysiology*, 41, 896–909.

Taga, G., Asakawa, K., Maki, A., Konishi, Y., and Koizumi, H. (2003). Brain imaging in awake infants by near-infrared optical topography. *Proceedings of the National Academy of Sciences of the United State of America*, 100, 10722–10727.

Tsujimoto, S., Yamamoto, T., Kawaguchi, H., Koizumi, H., and Sawaguchi, T. (2004). Prefrontal cortical activation associated with visuospatial working memory in adults and preschool children: An event-related optical topography study. *Cerebral Cortex*, 14, 703–712.

Yamamoto, T., Yamashita, Y., Yoshizawa, H., Maki, A., Iwata, M., Watanabe, E., and Koizumi, H. (1999). Non-invasive measurement of language function by using optical topography. *SPIE (Journal of the International Society for Optical Engineering)*, 3597, 230–237.

Yamamoto, E., Takahashi, T., Takiguchi, K., Onodera, Y., Itagaki, H., and Koizumi, H. (1992). Noninvasive brain functional analysis by using ultrafast magnetic resonance imaging. *Imaging and Information Technology*, 24, front cover and 1466–1467.

Yamashita, Y., Maki, A., and Koizumi, H. (1996). Near-infrared topographic measurement system: Imaging of absorbers localized in a scattering medium. *Review of Scientific Instruments*, 67, 730–732.

Part III

Brain, language, and mathematics

11 A triptych of the reading brain: Evolution, development, pathology, and its intervention

Maryanne Wolf

Overview

The most remarkable property of the human brain is the capacity to develop new connections and establish new networks through the rearrangement of preexisting neuronal structures. To invent and assimilate new cognitive skills, like writing and reading, humans have used the cortical, subcortical, and cerebellar structures already produced by biological evolution, as Dehaene describes in his chapter. It took several millennia for our species to have reached the general literacy in the population, and today a child needs less than a decade of training to become fluent in reading. This remarkable neurological feat involves an impressive coordination of perceptual, attentional, motoric, linguistic, and cognitive components, all performing together at great speed. Any trouble within or among these complex components can produce disruptions or delays in the process of reading acquisition, as in developmental dyslexia. Wolf and her colleagues have created a successful intervention program with multiple parts (RAVE-O: Retrieval, Automaticity, Vocabulary, Engagement with language, Orthography) to improve reading fluency, with components based on research-based understanding of the delicate and complex processes of reading.

The Editors

The essence of intellectual change in recent human evolution lies not in the birth of new structures in our brain, but rather in the brain's extraordinary potential for the rearrangement of its existing neuronal pathways. Underlying the acquisition of each new skill learned by our species lies a capacity to rearrange and to forge whole new connections and circuits among structures originally designed for other things: the ability, for example, to see a visual pattern, to retrieve a word for a predator, to infer that a footprint augurs danger. The human brain's remarkable capacity to make novel connections within itself is the neurological basis for most of our species' cognitive leaps and inventions (see Dehaene and Singer, this volume).

Nowhere is this more in evidence than in the history of written language and in its development in the child. Reading or written language represents one of the major breakthroughs in the cognitive evolution of the species. Both its physiological structure and its development reflect and re-enact the brain's intrinsic capacity for rearrangement and for learning to use what is genetically given to go beyond it. The study of reading development and the factors that derail it offers cognitive neuro-scientists a superb example of how the brain learns an evolutionarily recent cognitive skill through the rearrangement of older neurological structures.

This chapter will describe a research program that uses evidence from reading's evolution, development, and pathology to construct a broad-ened conceptualization of both reading and reading breakdown in devel-opmental dyslexia. One of the most important implications of this triptych view of the reading process is a new, more comprehensive approach to the treatment of reading problems for children who struggle to learn to read. The final goal of this chapter is to show how an under-standing of reading's evolution, development, and pathology informs treatment and, at the same time, contributes to our understanding of how the brain learns.

A particular view of reading

No one was ever born to read. Human beings are genetically programmed to do a variety of functions, including learning to speak, using a highly sophisticated set of operations that contribute to the survival and flour-ishing of our species. But learning to read is not part of our genetic equipment. Rather, reading represents one of the marvels of the human brain's capacity to rearrange itself to learn something new. At its essence, reading is based on a rearrangement of existing neuronal circuitries in the cortical, subcortical, and cerebellar regions responsible for attentional, perceptual, linguistic, cognitive, and motoric operations. All of the latter processes were originally designed for functions other than reading. The human brain's ability to make new connections among these processes is the physiological basis of the reading act.

Thus, the architectural structure of reading is in Dehaene's terms, a pre-eminent example of "neuronal recycling" (see Dehaene's chapter in this volume). When human beings first began to represent an object using abstract visually-based signs, as in cave drawings, they were basically rewiring connections among existing neuronal circuits or pathways for visual and conceptual processes. As symbolic capacities increased (Deacon, 2001), human beings were learning to connect these same areas to areas responsible for linguistic processes as well. Based on this triune set of connections, a new ability emerged: the capacity to read and to transmit a written form of language that could be passed down generation after generation.

Insights from the evolution of writing

First logographic systems

The early history of the evolution of writing is set in exotic places like Sumeria, Wadi el Hol, and Crete. Full of lacunae and mystery, the story can be told from many perspectives. A "cognitive history" will be the subject of this brief section as we consider how each early type of writing demanded something a little different from our brain, beginning with tiny tokens enclosed in hard clay envelopes.

Used between 8000 BCE and 4000 BCE, the first tokens were tiny markings on pieces of clay found all over the near East. They were used as a kind of accounting system by our ancestors. Some researchers like Schmandt-Besserat (1996) consider them the first writing or, at a minimum, the precursor to writing. However they are conceptualized, tokens represent, along with cave drawings, the first known use of symbols. These symbols provided a permanent record for our ancestors – in this case, documenting the number of goods bought or sold. Most importantly, the invention of these symbols reflected the emergence of a new human cognitive ability: *symbolic representation* (see important work by Deacon, 2001, in this area).

The act of symbolization is the first of three epiphanies that mark the development of reading in early writing systems. The second epiphany involves the realization that a *system* of symbols can communicate across time and distance and can preserve the thoughts of a single person or a culture. Beginning with cuneiform and hieroglyphic systems, early writing systems reflect both these insights. The third epiphany is the most linguistically abstract and complex concept and is not universal among writing systems. This is the insight that each word in our oral language consists of a finite group of individual sounds (called phonemes by linguists) that can be represented by a finite group of individual letters (called graphemes). The alphabetic systems of the world are based on this principle, aptly called the *alphabetic principle*. It took approximately 2000 years of changes in writing between the earliest known cuneiform and hieroglyphic systems and the first widely accepted alphabetic-like system, created by the Ugarits in the latter half of the second millennium BCE.

The Sumerian cuneiform system is believed to be the first comprehensive writing system, created around 3100 BCE. This assumption, however, is under challenge by Egyptologists who recently found evidence of Egyptian hieroglyphic writing dated several centuries earlier. Regardless of which was technically first, both of these early systems demanded a very great deal from their novice and expert readers, particularly as each culture developed larger sets of symbols over time. From a cognitive viewpoint, both systems employed three major features: first, imagistic logographic symbols to convey a corpus of known concepts and words; second, a rebus principle that used the first sound of an older symbol to depict the sound of a new word (like a name); and third, a boustrephon (or plowing) directional style, whereby the reader scanned text first from left to right, then down a line and right to left. Depending on the edifice, an Egyptian or Sumerian reader might also be asked to read up or down a column as well. In other words, these early systems required a demanding variety of cognitive strategies and scanning styles, as well as a great deal of flexibility by the reader. Early reading was not for the faint of heart.

To be sure, the Sumerian instructional system sometimes took ten years for a novice reader to be properly trained. According to modern scholarship by Assyriologist Cohen (2003), the Sumerian pedagogical system contained remarkable insights into language. For example, the Sumerians taught their pupils through evolving lists of words, that were categorized ingeniously by any linguistic standard. There were groups of words that shared semantic or meaning-based features; others contained shared phonological or sound-based features; still others shared the same logographic root (comparable both to our morphological and orthographic principles). Later there were bi-lingual lists added. The upshot is that before linguistic classification was ever a thought, the Sumerians taught reading by teaching the various linguistic elements found in written words and by showing students explicitly the shared connections among words that could be classified together in particular ways. It is a stunning, humbling example to educators of the twentieth and twenty-first centuries, who often seem to be arrested in more unidimensional approaches to reading instruction (e.g., phonology-based phonics or semantic-based whole language). Over four millennia ago our Sumerian ancestors used variously classified lists to show their pupils the multidimensional nature of words. Similarly, after the Sumerian culture vanished, the widespread Akkadian writing system preserved many of the insights of the Sumerian system. And, by the end of this chapter, a very recent, innovative method of reading instruction will use a multidimensional approach to words that resembles many of the insights of the Sumerians.

The alphabet's emergence

The history of the Egyptian hieroglyph system has many mysteries, but one is particularly important for those who would understand the species' third epiphany and the birth of the alphabetic principle. Just as with the Sumerians, learning to read hieroglyphs was a cognitive feat. But unlike the Sumerians, the Egyptian system became considerably larger and more burdened over the course of time by the increasing layers of encrypted secret meanings placed within the hieroglyphs.

We do not know when or why, but a small subset of symbols appeared that was used to convey a very limited number of *sounds* in the oral language, possibly begun as an antidote to the burdens and hieroglyphs. One hypothesis is that Semitic scribes who worked in and out of Egypt used these signs to carry out instructions among workers who would never have been allowed to learn hieroglyphic writing. Whether this "proletariat shorthand" hypothesis is proven, a number of linguists believe that this tiny subset of sound-based symbols became the basis of what may be the first proto-Semitic alphabet-like script. Found recently in the desolate Wadi el Hol region in Egypt, this early script was used at the beginning of the second millennium (around 1800 BCE) and is thought to have influenced the much later development of the beautiful Ugarit script (1400 BCE). This latter form of Semitic writing is classified as an *abugida*, an alphabetic system that conveys all but vowel sounds. It was used for everything from courtly letters and poems to documents. Indeed some believe Ugarit was the first language of the Bible.

Linguists, Assyriologists, and classicists disagree stridently, however, about whether these earlier proto-Semitic systems qualify as the first alphabet. What is undisputed is that much later in the first millennium BCE, the Greeks "rearranged" what they knew about the neighboring Phoenician writing system and created an almost-but-not-quite-perfect alphabet, capable of depicting all the phonemes (consonants and vowels) in the Greek language. It was an extraordinary achievement. The Greeks analyzed all the phonemes in the Phoenician and the Greek oral language in order to construct an alphabet capable of conveying every sound in their language. They were the world's best if not first speech scientists!

From evolution to the development of reading in the child

What is often unrealized by the modern educator is that the prodigious feat by the Greeks requires many of the same basic cognitive insights that the child must achieve before he or she can learn to read. At a tacit level they must learn three similar concepts: first, symbolic representation; then the idea that a set or system of symbols convey words; and finally (the most difficult and abstract insight), that words are composed of discrete sounds and that letters map these sounds in writing. Children are given six to seven years to discover, understand, and prove their competence in mastering insights that took the species millennia to achieve!

Unappreciated by most people, these insights into reading never just happen in childhood. In fact, the acquisition and development of reading in the child represents the full sum of hundreds of words, thousands of concepts, and tens of thousands of percepts, all of which contribute to the development of a process that demands a great deal of the human brain. And none of this can be taken for granted. In a well-known study by Teale and Sulzby (1986), that compared the "literacy backgrounds" which children bring to Kindergarten, some children who came from less privileged backgrounds encountered the equivalent of 60 hours of "literacy" based materials in their first five years. By contrast, children in most middle-class families received the equivalent of thousands of hours. An equally telling study by Hart and Risley (2003) showed that by three years of age, there is a *"30 million word gap"* in the number of words children from different socio-economic backgrounds are exposed to in their homes. In the view of reading espoused here, the precursors of reading have a life of their own that affects not only the acquisition of reading, but also its development over time. Why would this be so after the basic decoding principles of reading are acquired?

Picture what it takes for a child to read the tiny word "cat" (see fuller description in Wolf *et al.*, 2001), and also "catastrophe." A range of attentional, memory, visual perceptual, orthographic pattern recognition, auditory perceptual, phonological, semantic, retrieval, and comprehension processes are necessary for reading. Each of these sets of processes must function accurately and rapidly in time before they are then integrated within milliseconds to be able to read a single word. There are very different but related points to be made here. First, this view of cognitive and linguistic processes shows the importance of multiple linguistic processes, including semantic, syntactic, and comprehension processes, as well as the decoding-related processes. For children to develop into fluent, comprehending analyzers of text, they must be developing their knowledge of words at deep and more complex levels, as well as their decoding skills. The first years of cognitive and language development provide a foundation for the rest of their lives. It is not that children can't catch up, but the reality is that they often don't. Their invisible 30 million word gap and all that this implies chronically impedes their ability to get as much from text as they would otherwise.

The second point brings us back to the reading brain. All of these attentional, perceptual, cognitive, and linguistic processes rest on an intricate reorganization of regions in the developing brain. This does not happen because of some genetic program. It happens or fails to happen because of human work – on the part of society (i.e., the teacher) and the individual learner. Linguist Steven Pinker said it best: "Children are wired for sound, but print is an optional accessory that must be painstakingly bolted on."

The development of reading involves exactly that – the *painstaking bolting on* and *bolting together* of the processes. Many learners, replete with a rich history of precursors, are ready to learn almost, it would "seem," without effort. Other children, sometimes because of environmental reasons, and sometimes because of physiological differences in the brain regions subserving reading, have great difficulty acquiring reading. These large groups of children require systematic explicit instruction in the various processes that comprise the components of reading.

A major implication of this particular view of reading is that the multiple components involved in reading can lead to multiple possible sources of breakdown. And if that is the case, there should be subtypes of children with different causes of reading failure, a conclusion that runs counter to the conventional view of reading failure for the last thirty years. Based on groundbreaking research in psycholinguistics in the 1970s, the conventional view assumes that the primary source of reading failure lies in one-half of the processes underlying the child's ability to learn and apply the grapheme-phoneme correspondence rules: that is, the phonological processes. According to this more uni-dimensional view, a deficit in phonological processes impedes the child's ability to develop phoneme awareness, which impedes the ability to learn grapheme-phoneme correspondence rules, which then impedes learning to decode and comprehend. It is our position that the phonological explanation is necessary but insufficient.

An alternative view that emerged from work in the neurosciences on word-retrieval and naming speed processes in alexia, aphasia, and dyslexia suggests that there are other possible deficits in dyslexia, particularly involving the need for fast automatic processing that are independent of phonology and cannot be explained by phonological deficits.

Subtype classification: The double-deficit hypothesis

Originally conceived by Bowers and Wolf (1993), what has come to be called the Double Deficit Hypothesis (DDH) represents an effort to capture the heterogeneity found in dyslexic readers. Its emphasis is on the description of at least three major subtypes of children, characterized by the presence, absence, or combination of two core deficits in phonology and the processes underlying naming speed. There are now considerable data (Lovett, Steinback, & Frijters, 2000a; Manis, Doi, & Bhadha,

2000; Badian, 1996; and Ho, Chan, Tsang, & Lee, 2002) that there are (a) poor readers who have phonological deficits without problems in naming speed; (b) readers who have adequate phonological and word attack skills, but early naming-speed deficits and later reading fluency and comprehension deficits (Note: these children would be missed by most diagnostic batteries, because decoding is accurate); and (c) children with both areas of weaknesses or "double deficits." Children with both core deficits represent the most severely impaired subtype in all aspects of reading – particularly in reading fluency and comprehension – because there are less areas of compensation available.

Wolf and Bowers (1999, 2000) used the term the Double-Deficit Hypothesis as an acknowledged transitional vehicle to underscore the need to go beyond an emphasis too exclusively placed on phonological deficits. Unlike phonological deficits, naming-speed deficits can be caused by a variety of possible sources. This is because rapid naming, like the multi-component view of reading espoused here, is conceptualized as a set of perceptual, cognitive, motoric, and linguistic processes that require seriation, integration, and great rapidity within and across all these processes. These processes are seen as a subset of the same components and requirements for speed used in reading. Such a view explains the powerful ability of naming speed both to predict reading failure among many children and to differentiate these children from those without reading disabilities. Extensive data now replicate the existence of these subtypes in German, Dutch, Finnish, and Hebrew; preliminary data are also found for Chinese and Japanese.

The Double-Deficit Hypothesis, therefore, can be viewed as an effort to understand several major sources of reading failure. It is not meant to imply that there are only these types of deficit patterns. In every analysis by us and in other colleagues' reanalyses, there are small groups of children who cannot be characterized by either deficit, and yet still have severe reading disability (see Lovett, Steinbach, & Frijters, 2000). What the Double-Deficit Hypothesis was meant to underscore is the need to understand how independent these major types of deficits can be in our samples and in our classrooms, with all the implications this has for expanding the foci of existing interventions. The single most important implication is that most children with naming-speed deficits have fluency problems. Most existing programs for children with dyslexia focus largely on phonological skills with their necessary but insufficient emphases for these children. They need additional early and daily emphases on automaticity and fluency.

The ultimate importance of the Double-Deficit Hypothesis is that it underscores the need both to understand the role of rate of processing and fluency in reading development and to create fluency intervention that addresses these issues. Until recently, children with single, phonological deficits were adequately treated with current programs emphasizing phonological awareness and decoding. However, the other two subtypes with their explicit problems in naming speed and reading fluency were never sufficiently remediated. The final section of this chapter describes a componential reading intervention program that integrates phonological emphases with a new view of "fluency and comprehension."

Component-based view of fluency in reading intervention

Our view of fluency development incorporates key elements from past research by Hebb (1949), Geschwind (1965), Denckla and Rudel (1976), Laberge and Samuels (1974), Doehring (1976), and Perfetti (1985), and is discussed at length in Wolf and Katzir-Cohen (2001). First, within this view fluency demands the development of high-quality orthographic, phonological, semantic, and syntactic representational systems. Second, it requires rapid connections between and among these systems. And, third, it demands learning and practice to insure the rapid retrieval of information from each system. Most current perspectives on fluency incorporate very little from past research, with most definitions approaching fluency as basically an *outcome* of accuracy in processes like decoding. In two excellent recent reviews of the fluency literature, Meyer and Felton (1999) and Meyer (2002) summarize most consensual views of fluency as "the ability to read connected text rapidly, smoothly, effortlessly, and automatically with little conscious attention to the mechanics of reading such as decoding." Such a view of fluency reflects little of the teeming subprocesses that contribute to it!

We believe it is essential to define fluency in terms of its component processes and various levels of reading subskills: that is, from the level of letter, letter pattern, and word to the sentence and passage level. Together with Kame'enui, Simmons, Good, and Harn (2001), we suggest a figure-ground shift for the conceptualization of fluency – specifically, as a developmental process, as well as an outcome. Kame'enui and his colleagues conceptualized fluency in a more developmental manner as both the *development* of "proficiency" in underlying lower-level, component skills of reading (e.g., phoneme awareness), and also as the *outcome* of proficiency in higher-level processes and component skills (e.g., accuracy in comprehension).

Berninger and her colleagues (Berninger, Abbot, Billingsley, & Nagy 2001) take a still broader, systems approach to fluency with special importance given to the role of morphological knowledge about words in facilitating the development of orthographic rate and overall fluency.

In an effort to integrate historical and current research on fluency, Wolf and Katzir-Cohen (2001) put forth the following developmental definition:

In its beginnings, reading fluency is the product of the initial development of accuracy and the subsequent development of automaticity in underlying sub-lexical processes, lexical processes, and their integration in single-word reading and connected text. These include perceptual, phonological, orthographic, and morphological processes at the letter-, letter-pattern, and word-level; as well as semantic and syntactic processes at the word-level and connected-text level. After it is fully developed, reading fluency refers to a level of accuracy and rate, where decoding is relatively effortless; where oral reading is smooth and accurate with correct prosody; and where attention can be allocated to comprehension. (p. 219)

Such a developmental, more encompassing view of reading fluency has, we believe, profound implications for prevention, intervention, and assessment. For, within a developmental perspective, efforts to address fluency must start at the beginning of the reading acquisition process, not after reading is already acquired.

The importance of working preventatively before difficult fluency problems ever begin is an implicit theme of Lyon and Moats (1997), who articulated some of the major concerns in current reading intervention research:

Improvements in decoding and word-reading accuracy have been far easier to obtain than improvements in reading fluency and automaticity. This persistent finding indicated there is much we have to learn about the *development of compo-nential reading skills* and how such skills mediate reading rate and reading comprehension. (p. 570, our italics)

In this passage Lyon and Moats (1997) pinpointed not only the field's difficulty in ameliorating the problem of fluency, but also a potential method for solving it: that is, specifying the subcomponents involved in fluency over development.

As summarized briefly earlier, we believe some of the historical research – from Hebb to Perfetti – when complemented by current work (e.g., models of naming speed) provides a reasonable foundation for a first specification of the multiple processes and components involved. These include the following fluency-related processes: letter perception; orthographic representation; phonological representation; semantic representation; lexical access and retrieval; decoding and word-identification skills; morphological, syntactic, and prosodic knowledge; and finally, inference and comprehension skills. In other words, the difficult implication of past and present work on automaticity and efficiency is that reading fluency calls upon the explicit instruction of all the major processes and subskills involved in reading itself. It implies that for children with issues in fluency we must go below the surface of our theoretical definitions and specifications to apply what we know about the structure of reading fluency to what we teach.

Fluency intervention: RAVE-O

Funded by the National Institute of Child Health and Human Development, we designed and tested an experimental, multi-componential approach to fluency instruction. The program emerged as the result of a collaboration by Morris, Lovett, and Wolf to investigate a multi-dimensional view of reading disabilities and to evaluate the efficacy of different theory-based treatments for children with specific forms of dyslexia.

Described in detail elsewhere (Wolf, Miller, & Donnelly 2000; Wolf, O'Brien, & Adams 2003), the RAVE-O program (Retrieval, Automaticity, Vocabulary, Engagement with Language, and Orthography) has three large aims for each child: first, the development of accuracy and automaticity in letter pattern and word levels; second, increased rate in word attack, word identification and comprehension; and third, a transformed attitude toward words and language. Towards these ends, the program simultaneously addresses both the need for automaticity in phonological, orthographic, semantic, syntactic, and morphological systems and the importance of teaching *explicit connections* among these linguistic systems. This latter feature is based in part on research that stresses the explicit linkages or connections among the orthographic, semantic, and phonological processes (Adams, 1990; Foorman, 1994; Seidenberg & McClelland, 1989). Further, Berninger *et al.*, (2001), Adams (1990), and Moats (2000) stress the connections between morphosyntactic knowledge and these other processes.

The RAVE-O program is taught only in combination with a program that teaches systematic phonological analysis and blending (see Lovett *et al.*, 2000). Children are taught a group of *core words* each week that exemplify critical phonological, orthographic, and semantic principles. Syntactic and morphological principles are gradually added after initial work has begun in the program. Each core word is chosen on the basis of: (a) shared phonemes with the phonological-treatment program; (b) sequenced orthographic patterns; and (c) semantic richness (e.g., each core word has at least three different meanings). First, the multiple meanings of core words are introduced in varied semantic contexts. Second, children are taught to connect the phonemes in the core words with the trained orthographic patterns in RAVE-O. For example, children are taught individual phonemes in the phonological program (like "a," "t," and "m") and *orthographic chunks* with the same phonemes in RAVE-O (e.g., "at" and "am" along with their word families; see work of Goswami, 1999 and Goswami in this volume).

There is daily emphasis on practice and rapid recognition of the most frequent orthographic letter patterns in English. Computerized games (see Speed Wizards, Wolf, & Goodman, 1996) and a new set of manipulative materials (e.g., letter dice, sound sliders, cards, etc.) were designed to allow for maximal practice and to increase the speed of orthographic pattern recognition (i.e., onset and rime) in an engaging fashion.

There is a simultaneous emphasis on vocabulary and retrieval, based on earlier work in vocabulary development that suggests that one retrieves fastest what one knows best (see Beck, Perfetti, & McKeown, 1982; German, 1992; Kame'enui, Dixon, & Carnine, 1987; Wolf & Segal, 1999). Vocabulary growth is conceptualized as essential to both rapid retrieval (in oral *and* written language) and also to improved comprehension, an ultimate goal in the program. Retrieval skills are taught through a variety of ways including a set of metacognitive strategies.

A series of comprehension stories (e.g., *Minute Mysteries* and *Minute Adventures*) accompany each week of RAVE-O and directly address fluency and comprehension in several ways. The controlled vocabulary in the timed and untimed stories both incorporates the week's particular orthographic and morphological patterns, and also emphasizes the multiple meanings and syntactic uses of the week's core words. The stories provide a superb vehicle for repeated reading practice, which, in turn, helps fluency in connected text. Thus, the *Minute Stories* are multi-purpose vehicles for facilitating fluency in phonological, orthographic, syntactic and semantic systems at the same time that they build comprehension skills. Fluency is our best known bridge to comprehension. The end goal of RAVE-O, therefore, is not about how rapidly children read, but about how well they understand and enjoy what they read.

Connected to this ultimate goal in every daily lesson in RAVE-O is an additional system too little discussed by many researchers – that is, the affective-motivational one. The secret weapon of this program is the game-like *whimsy* in every aspect of the program's activities. We want children to want to read and to play with their oral and written language. We seek to empower what are often linguistically disenfranchised children.

Such a method of instruction demands a special involvement from teachers. Throughout the program, therefore, we strive in as many ways as we can to engage not only the learner, but also the teacher and the teacher's own love of language. Our goal throughout is a group of mutually engaged teachers and engaged learners.

The preliminary results from this study strongly support RAVE-O's potential for advancing children's reading performance at the letter, word, and text levels in several ways. In growth curve analyses our results indicate that children in the RAVE-O program make significant gains after 70 one-hour sessions in all word attack, word identification variables; in vocabulary; in fluency at the word and sentence level; and in a combined fluency and comprehension measure at the connected text level (the Gray Oral Reading Quotient measure).

Summary

The leitmotiv of this chapter is the evolutionarily powerful notion of the brain's ability to *rearrange* itself to learn new cognitive functions. We applied this concept in two ways. First, we presented a conceptualization of the reading brain, in which over the last 5000 years the human brain learned to call upon an array of regions originally devoted to other things: the perception of tiny, visual features; the hearing and segmenting of the smallest units of sounds in spoken language; the understanding of a symbol; the retrieving of words and their meaning(s); and the integration of all these regions in lightning, almost-automatic speeds. Second, we applied the concept of rearrangement to the design of intervention where we illustrated how a reconfiguration of new and old "best teaching practices" can address the continuum of processes underlying reading. The ability to integrate these processes in sufficiently rapid time to allow for accurate decoding and fluent comprehension is the overarching goal of the RAVE-O intervention program. Finally, we wish to end by suggesting that the RAVE-O program with its explicit attempts to depict the multi-dimensional nature of words is a new iteration of principles first employed by the Sumerians 5000 years ago.

References

Adams, M. J. (1990). *Beginning to Read: Thinking and Learning about Print.* Cambridge, MA: MIT Press.

Badian, N. (1996). *Dyslexia: does it exist? Dyslexia, garden-variety poor reading, and the Double-Deficit Hypothesis.* Paper presented at the Orton Dyslexia Society, Boston, MA.

Beck, I. L., Perfetti, C. A., and McKeown, M. G. (1982). Effects of long-term vocabulary instructions on lexical access and reading comprehension. *Journal of Educational Psychology,* 74, 506–521.

Berninger, V. W., Abbott, R. D., Billingsley, F., and Nagy, W. (2001). Processes underlying timing and fluency of reading: Efficiency, automaticity, coordination, and morphological awareness. In M.Wolf (ed.), *Time, Fluency, and Dyslexia*. Timonium, MD: York Press.

Bowers, P. G. and Wolf, M. (1993). Theoretical links among naming speed, precise timing mechanisms and orthographic skill in dyslexia. *Reading and Writing*, 5, 69–85.

Cohen, U. (2003). Personal correspondence.

Dehaene, S. (2003). *Pre-emption of human cortical circuits by numbers and language: The "neuronal" recycling hypothesis*. Paper presented at Pontifical Academy of Sciences meeting. Vatican City.

Deacon, T. (1997). *The Symbolic Species: The Co-evolution of Language and the Human Brain*. New York: W.W. Norton & Company.

Denckla, M. B. and Rudel, R. G. (1976). Naming of objects by dyslexic and other learning-disabled children. *Brain and Language*, 3, 1–15.

Doehring, D. G. (1976). *Acquisition of rapid reading responses*. Monograph of the Society for Research in Child Development. Vols. 165 (2).

Foorman, B. R. (1994). Phonological and orthographic processing: Separate but equal? In V. W. Berninger (ed.), *The Varieties of Orthographic Knowledge I: Theoretical and Developmental Issues* (pp. 319–355). Dordrecht, The Netherlands: Kluwer.

German, D. J. (1992). Word finding intervention for children and adolescents. *Topics in Learning Disorders*, 13, 33–50.

Geschwind, N. (1965). Disconnection syndrome in animals and man (Parts I, II). *Brain*, 88, 237–294, 585–644.

Goswami, U. (1999). Causal connections in beginning reading: the importance of rhyme. *Journal of Research in Reading*, 22, 217–240.

Hart, B. and Risley, T. R. (2003). The early catastrophe: The "30 million word gap." *American Educator*, 27(1), 4–9.

Hebb, D. O. (1949). *The Organization of Behaviour*. New York: John Wiley.

Ho Chan, D., Tsang, S.-M., and Lee, S.-H. (2002). The cognitive profile and multiple-deficit hypothesis in Chinese developmental psychology. *Developmental Psychology*, 38, 543–553.

Kame'enui, E. J., Simmons, D. C., Good, R. H., and Harn, B. A. (2001). The use of fluency-based measures in early identification and evaluation of intervention efficacy in schools. In M. Wolf (ed.), *Time, Fluency, and Dyslexia*. Timonium, MD: York Press.

Kame'enui, E. J., Dixon, R. C., and Carnine, D. W. (1987). Issues in the design of vocabulary instruction. In M. G. McKeown and M. E. Curtis (eds.), *The Nature of Vocabulary Acquisition* (pp. 129–145). Hillsdale, NJ: Erlbaum.

LaBerge, D. and Samuels, S. J. (1974). Toward a theory of automatic information processing in reading. *Cognitive Psychology*, 6, 293–323.

Lovett, M. W., Steinbach, K. A., and Frijters, J. C. (2000). Remediating the core deficits of developmental reading disability: A double-deficit perspective. *Journal of Learning Disabilities*, 33(4), 334–358.

Lyon, G. R. and Moats, L. C. (1997). Critical conceptual and methodological considerations in reading intervention research. *Journal of Learning Disabilities*, 30, 578–588.

Manis, F. R., Doi, L. M., and Bhadha, B. (2000). Naming speed, phonological awareness, and orthographic knowledge in second graders. *Journal of Learning Disabilities*, 33, 325–333.

Meyer, M. S. and Felton, R. H. (1999). Repeated reading to enhance fluency: Old approaches and new directions. *Annals of Dyslexia*, 49, 283–306.

Moats, L. (2000). *Speech to Print: Language Essentials for Teachers*. Baltimore: Paul H. Brookes Publishing Company.

Morris, R., Lovett, M., and Wolf, M. (1996). *Treatment of developmental reading disabilities*. NICHD grant proposal.

Perfetti, C. A. (1985). *Reading Ability*. New York: Oxford Press.

Schmandt-Besserat, D. (1992). *Before Writing: From Counting to Cuneiform*. College Station, TX: Texas University Press.

Seidenberg, M. and McCelland, J. (1989). A distributed developmental model of word recognition and naming. *Psychological Review*, 96, 35–49.

Teale, W. and Sulzby, E. (eds.). (1986). *Emergent Literacy: Writing and Reading*. Norwood, NJ: Ablex, Co.

Wolf, M., O'Brien, B., Adams, K., Joffe, T., Jeffrey, J., Lovett, M., and Morris, R. (2003). Working for time: Reflections on naming speed, reading fluency, and intervention. In B. Foorman (ed.)., *Preventing and Remediating Reading Difficulties: Bringing Science to Scale*. Timonium, MD: York Press.

Wolf, M. and Katzir-Cohen, T. (2001). Reading fluency and its intervention. Scientific Studies of Reading (*Special Issue on Fluency*. Editors: E. Kame'enui and D. Simmons), 5, 211–238.

Wolf, M., Miller, L., and Donnelly, K. (2000). Retrieval, Automaticity, Vocabulary Elaboration, Orthography (RAVE-O): A comprehensive fluency-based reading intervention program. *Journal of Learning Disabilities*, 33(4), 375–386.

Wolf, M. and Bowers, P. (2000). The question of naming-speed deficits in developmental reading disabilities: An introduction to the Double-Deficit Hypothesis. *Journal of Learning Disabilities*, 33, 322–324.

(1999). The "Double-Deficit Hypothesis" for the developmental dyslexias. *Journal of Educational Psychology*, 91(3), 1–24.

Wolf, M. and Segal, D. (1999). Retrieval-rate, accuracy and vocabulary elaboration (RAVE) in reading-impaired children: A pilot intervention program. *Dyslexia*, 5, 1–27.

Wolf, M. and Goodman, G. (1996). Speed Wizards: Computerized games for the teaching of reading fluency. Tufts University and Rochester Institute of Technology.

12   Reading and the brain: A cross-language approach

Usha Goswami

Overview

The learning of reading skills is causally related to some properties of the language itself. Transparent or consistent alphabetic languages, such as Spanish, map most easily from orthography to sounds, with one-to-one correspondence from letters to phonemes. Inconsistent orthographies, such as English, show instead a greater mismatch between orthography and phonology. A pre-reading child detects small units within syllables in his spoken vocabulary, units comprised of onset and rime. Analyzing speech into these components is central to phonological awareness, the ability to analyze speech into its component sounds. Reading in an alphabetic language requires relating letters to sound units that are smaller than onset and rime, units called phonemes. Goswami argues that children learn phonemes through mastering the orthography (letters in combination) of their language. To master the code relating written letters to spoken sounds, children need more time for languages with inconsistent orthography, even when they do not have dyslexia. Dyslexic children of all languages have greater trouble learning letter-sound relationships, typically because of poor representation of sounds, which can be investigated in both behavior and brain imaging. Electrical potentials from cortical activity evoked by sounds and other stimuli indicate that the auditory systems of dyslexic children seem to be more immature than those of normal children. This kind of research combining both behavior and brain activity to analyze reading is one of the areas that is most likely to produce important knowledge relevant for schooling in the near future.
The Editors

A plethora of studies in cognitive developmental psychology across many languages has shown a causal connection between a child's awareness of sounds within words – "phonological awareness" – and their reading and spelling development (see Goswami, 2003a, for overview and Wolf in this volume). Studies have also shown that there is a language-universal sequence in the development of phonological awareness. Children first seem to develop an awareness of syllables ("pop-si-cle"; "wig-wam"; "soap"). This is followed by the development of awareness of the intra-syllabic units of onset and rime (the onset corresponds to the initial consonant sounds in any syllable, the rime corresponds to the vowel and any following sounds, as in "s-eat", "sw-eet", "str-eet"[1]). Phonological sensitivity at the syllabic and onset-rime levels can be measured in pre-readers, and is an important predictor of literacy acquisition (e.g., Bradley & Bryant, 1983; Hoien, Lundberg, Stanovich, & Bjaalid, 1995; Siok & Fletcher, 2001).

Phonological awareness and learning to read across languages

Early phonological awareness is focused on "large" units like syllables and rimes. Syllable awareness is usually present by about age 3, and onset-rime awareness by about age 4 to 5. In all languages so far tested, awareness of syllables, onsets and rimes is present before reading is taught. Letters represent smaller sound units in words called phonemes. Phonemes are abstract units in the speech stream that are defined in terms of changes in meaning. The words "cot" and "cat" differ in terms of the medial phoneme, the words "cot" and "hot" differ in terms of the initial phoneme. Phoneme awareness develops as a consequence of learning to read and write. In fact, illiterate adults are not aware of phonemes. It seems that learning about letters *causes* a phoneme-based re-organization of the mental lexicon (see Goswami, 2002). This means that learning to read cannot be conceptualized as a process of orally segmenting the words in one's vocabulary into phonemes, and then matching letters to these phonemes. Rather, children learn about phonemes via letters.

Many studies have shown poor phoneme awareness in pre-readers. For example, the *tapping* task can be used to compare syllable and phoneme awareness in children. Children must tap out the number of sounds in words that have either one syllable or phoneme ("dog," "I"), two syllables or phonemes ("dinner", "my"), or three syllables or phonemes ("president," "book"). Liberman, Shankweiler, Fischer and Carter (1974) found that 46% of American 4-year-olds could segment words into syllables, whereas 0% of this age group could manage phonemes. American 5-year-olds scored 48% and 17% correct, respectively. Only American 6-year-olds, who had been learning to read for about a year, were successful in the phoneme task. A study with Italian children

---

[1] The linguistic term 'rime' is used because multi-syllabic words have more than one rime. Whereas "mountain" and "fountain" rhyme, each word has two rimes, "-ount" and "-ain." "Mountain" and "counting" do not rhyme, even though they share the initial rime "-ount."

showed a similar developmental pattern (Cossu, Shankweiler, Liberman, Katz, & Tola, 1988). Cossu *et al.* compared preschool Italian children (aged 4 and 5 years) with older children already at school (7- and 8-year-olds). Criterion at the syllable level was reached by 67% of the 4-year-olds, 80% of the 5-year-olds, and 100% of the school-age sample. Criterion in the phoneme task was reached by 13% of the 4-year-olds, 27% of the 5-year-olds and 97% of the school-age sample. The patterns of performance shown by American and Italian children were thus remarkably similar. The children showed good syllabic awareness prior to entering school, and poor phonemic awareness until reading was taught.

Similar patterns have been documented for other languages, and this is shown in Table 12.1. On the basis of research conducted so far, which has been limited to European languages and to Japanese and Chinese, the developmental sequence of phonological awareness appears to be language-universal. Syllables, onsets and rimes are represented prior to literacy. Phonemes are represented only as the alphabet is learned and literacy is taught. This process of learning about phonemes may be either facilitated or inhibited by the nature of the orthography that the child is learning to read. Children who are learning to read languages with transparent orthographies, where there is a 1:1 correspondence between letters and phonemes, typically represent phonemes fairly rapidly. Children who are learning to read languages with non-transparent orthographies, where a 1:1 correspondence between letters and phonemes is lacking, typically do not. Because phonemic development depends on literacy, there are systematic differences in the *rate* of phonemic development depending on the orthography that the child is learning to read.

The impact of orthography on phonological representation and reading strategies

This co-dependence of phonological representation and orthographic consistency has been described in terms of a mapping problem (Brown & Ellis, 1994; Goswami, Ziegler, Dalton, & Schneider, 2003). The child needs to understand how the alphabet codes sounds. The sounds that the pre-reading child is aware of are the "large" units of the syllable, onset and rime. The units in print are single letters. Single letters typically correspond to phonemes, and so there is a mis-match between the levels of phonology and orthography that need to be mapped for efficient reading.

For children learning to read consistent alphabetic orthographies with an open (consonant-vowel or CV) syllable structure, the mapping problem is least difficult. In such languages, like Italian and Spanish,

Table 12.1 *Data (% correct) from five studies comparing syllable and phoneme awareness in beginning readers of different European languages.*

Language	Syllable	Phoneme
Greek[1]	98	50
Turkish[2]	94	67
Norwegian[3]	83	56
German[4]	81	51
French[5]	73	32

Notes:
1 = Harris & Giannoulis, 1999;
2 = Durgunoglu & Oney, 1999;
3 = Hoien *et al.*, 1995;
4 = Wimmer *et al.*, 1991;
5 = Demont & Gombert, 1996.

onset-rime segmentation (available prior to literacy) is equivalent to phonemic segmentation (theoretically learned via literacy) for many words (e.g., "casa," "mama"). The typically-developing child who has organized her spoken vocabulary in terms of the intra-syllabic units of onset and rime is thus well-placed to acquire alphabetic literacy. She is learning an orthography where one letter consistently maps to one phoneme. Many of those phonemes are already represented in her spoken lexicon, because they *are* onsets and rimes (e.g., for a word like "casa," the onset- rimes are /k/ /a/ /z/ /a/ and so are the phonemes). Italian and Spanish children typically acquire reading very rapidly, and this is shown in Table 12.2.

Children learning to read consistent alphabetic orthographies with more complex syllable structures, such as German, face a more difficult mapping problem. In such languages, onset-rime segmentation (available prior to literacy) is not usually equivalent to phonemic segmentation (theoretically learned via literacy) for most words. This is because most words either have codas (consonant phonemes) after the vowel (e.g., Hand), or complex (consonant cluster) onsets (e.g., Pflaum [plum]). However, for languages like German one letter consistently maps to one phoneme. Hence letters are a consistent clue to phonemes. The German child is still at an advantage, and this is also clear from Table 12.2.

The children faced with the most serious mapping problem in initial reading are those who are learning to read orthographically inconsistent languages which also have complex syllabic structures. The best example

Table 12.2 *Data (% correct) from the COST A8 study of grapheme-phoneme recoding skills for monosyllables in 14 European languages (from Seymour, Aro & Erskine, 2003).*

Language	Familiar real words	Nonwords
Greek	98	97
Finnish	98	98
German	98	98
Austrian German	97	97
Italian	95	92
Spanish	95	93
Swedish	95	91
Dutch	95	90
Icelandic	94	91
Norwegian	92	93
French	79	88
Portuguese	73	76
Danish	71	63
Scottish English	34	41

is English. For English, onset-rime segmentation is rarely equivalent to phonemic segmentation. Furthermore, one letter does not consistently map to one phoneme for reading. Accordingly, phonemic awareness develops relatively slowly, and so does the use of grapheme-phoneme recoding strategies for reading single words. English children must also learn to exploit larger regularities in the spelling system, for example by using rhyme "analogies" to help them to build up a reading vocabulary ("light" – "fight," "beak" – "weak"), and they must learn some words as holistic patterns ("the," "choir," "people"). This need to develop multiple strategies for successful reading may be one reason why English-speaking children appear at the bottom of Table 12.2.

Implications for dyslexia

For reasons yet to be determined, dyslexic children (those who do not acquire reading easily despite having good vocabularies and normal IQ) find it difficult to represent mentally the sound patterns of the words in their language in a detailed and specific way. Their "phonological representations" of the words in their vocabulary are under-specified, or fuzzy, and this makes it difficult for them to develop an awareness of the internal sound structure of different words (Snowling, 2000). This in turn makes it difficult for them to learn letter-sound relationships. This is not because they find it difficult to learn letters, but because the sounds to which they need to match the letters are relatively poorly specified in the brain. Dyslexic children find it more difficult to decide whether words rhyme, to count the syllables in a word, to delete sounds from the beginnings of words ("star" to "tar"), and to make up "Spoonerisms" (Chuck Berry to Buck Cherry). They also find it very difficult to decode nonsense words like "dem" and "fip" (Goswami, 2003b for overview).

The primary deficit in developmental dyslexia in all languages appears to involve problems in phonological representation (the "phonological representations" hypothesis, see Goswami, 2000a, 2000b; Snowling, 2000 for overviews). This hypothesis is well-supported by many studies in developmental psychology, genetics, and brain imaging that will not be surveyed here. However, this "phonological deficit" affects reading in somewhat different ways depending on orthography. Literacy problems are greater for dyslexic children learning to read inconsistent orthographies (e.g., English) than consistent orthographies (e.g., Italian, German, Greek). According to the cognitive analysis developed in the earlier parts of this chapter, this is unsurprising.

Dyslexic children learning to read English are slow and inaccurate readers, and never develop full phonemic awareness. In contrast, dyslexic children learning to read German or Greek are very accurate readers, but they are extremely slow. For example, Porpodas (1999) found significant differences in phoneme awareness between Greek first graders with literacy difficulties and chronological-age-matched (CA) control children. The "at risk" children scored 88% correct in a phoneme segmentation task compared to 100% for the CA controls, and they scored 78% correct in a phoneme deletion task compared to 98% for the CA controls. They also decoded 93% of simple 2- and 3-syllable nonwords correctly, compared to 97% for the CA controls (a significant difference). A similar study of "at risk" German first graders was reported by Wimmer (1996). He examined the performance of a cohort of German dyslexic children on a phoneme reversal task in Grade 1, before they were diagnosed as dyslexic. The "at risk" children scored 22% correct in this task, compared to 69% correct for the control children. Forty-two percent of the dyslexic children could not attempt the task at all. Wimmer also found that 7 out of 12 German children who later became dyslexic read less than 60% of simple nonwords like "Mana" and "Aufo" accurately, compared to an average performance of 96% correct for beginning readers who did not subsequently become dyslexic. As reading was acquired, this accuracy deficit in nonword reading disappeared. When they were aged 10,

Wimmer (1993) gave the same children a timed nonword reading task based on "Italian" type nonwords with open syllables ("ketu," "heleki," "tarulo"). The dyslexic children scored 92% correct, and the CA matched control children 96% correct.

These performance levels are impressive when compared to English-speaking dyslexic children. For example, Bruck (1992) used a phoneme deletion task with nonword stimuli. She asked dyslexic children aged from 8 to 15 years to delete either the initial or the final sound in non-words like "snup" and "lusk." The dyslexic children performed correctly in 47% of trials compared to 77% of trials for CA matched children. A comprehensive review of nonword reading in developmental dyslexia in English was provided by Rack, Snowling, and Olson (1992). Error rates for dyslexic children were high, typically between 40% and 60%. Recall that the German dyslexic children studied by Wimmer (1993) showed an error rate of 8%. This cross-language difference is consistent with the view that grapheme-phoneme recoding skills take longer to develop in inconsistent orthographies, especially for dyslexic children.

Basic auditory processing deficits in dyslexia: The p-centres hypothesis

In seeking causes for the deficit in phonological representation in developmental dyslexia, one popular class of theories has suggested that there must be lower-level deficits in basic auditory processing (see McArthur & Bishop, 2001, for an overview). Speech is a very complex signal, and so it seems logical that there could be problems in processing auditory information in dyslexia that, in turn, lead to problems in representing it accurately. The speech signal requires spectral, temporal, and frequency-based analysis. Particular interest in dyslexia has focused on temporal aspects of signal processing (e.g., Tallal, 1980; Wright, Bowen, & Zecker, 2000). However, the majority of studies of temporal processing have focused on rapid transient information, information that is important for identifying phonemes in the speech signal. Yet developmentally, deficits in phonemic awareness *follow* earlier problems in the phonological representation of syllables and onset-rimes. Perhaps the phoneme level is the wrong place to look for a basic auditory processing deficit. Rather, it may be important to explore possible deficits in representing phonological information at earlier-developing phonological levels.

We have argued that one likely perceptual cause of the characteristic difficulties in phonological representation found in dyslexia is a deficit in the perceptual experience of rhythmic timing (Goswami et al., 2002).

Speech rhythm is one of the earliest cues used by infants to discriminate syllables. Rhythmic timing is partly dependent on "P-centre" processing. P-centres or "perceptual centres" are syllable-internal events that determine speech rhythm. Adults hear alternating syllables like "ba" and "la" as non-rhythmic in timing when syllable onset-onset times are isochronous. This is because rhythmic timing depends on the P-centres being isochronous rather than the syllable onsets. P-centres (sometimes called stress beats) are principally determined by the acoustic structure of amplitude modulation at relatively low rates in the signal. The change in amplitude at syllable onset at these lower rates (the amplitude rise time) is particularly important. The structure of amplitude modulation at syllable onset is largely determined by the rise time of the vowel. For example, in "ba" the plosive onset means that the vowel occurs relatively early in the syllable. In "la," the sonorant onset means that the vowel occurs relatively late in the syllable. Hence to produce "la" and "ba" alternately with a regular rhythm, the speaker must begin saying "la" relatively early compared to "ba."

As P-centres depend on the rise time of the vowel, they may be important cues for representing onset-rime segments in syllables. They may thus have important links to the development of phonological awareness and literacy. Goswami et al. (2002) measured the psychometric functions for amplitude rise time detection in dyslexic and matched control children, and in precocious readers and their matched controls. Rise time detection was measured via a "beat" detection task, based on a rate of amplitude modulation change detection procedure. The task was based on a sinusoid that was modulated in amplitude to a depth of 50%. Within this, the rate of amplitude change only was varied by varying the rise time of the modulation, while the overall rate of modulation was held constant at 0.7 Hz (see Figure 12.1). Very slow rise times ($> 250 \, ms$) give the percept of a continuous sound that varies in loudness. When the rise time is sufficiently shortened, however (e.g., to 120 ms), the percept changes to that of a continuous sound with a loud "beat" occurring rhythmically at the same rate as the modulation (Bregman, 1993; this beat corresponds to the P-centres of the rhythmic sequence). The children had to decide whether they could hear a beat or not as rise times were varied.

As rise time was varied, the dyslexic children indeed showed an insensitivity to the amplitude modulation-related experiences of beat perception. The psychometric functions for the dyslexic children showed much flatter slopes than those of IQ-matched CA controls (mean slope = -0.03 for dyslexics [s.d. $= 0.04$] and -0.12 for controls [s.d. $= 0.08$], $p < 0.000$), see Figure 12.2. A younger reading age match control group

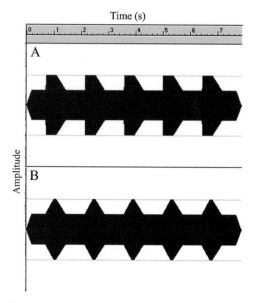

Figure 12.1 Schematic depiction of the stimuli used varying in rise time. Panel (A) depicts a 15 ms rise time, panel (B) depicts a 300 ms rise time. The 15 ms rise time yields a percept of a sharp beat overlaying a second carrier sound, the 300 ms rise time yields the percept of a single sound waxing and waning in loudness.

showed intermediate slopes (mean slope $= -0.06$, s.d. $= 0.05$, dyslexics versus reading level controls, $p < .06$). Detection of beats in amplitude-modulated (AM) signals was thus poorer in the dyslexic children than in their peers, and varied with reading level. Exceptional child readers and IQ-matched controls were also given the rate of amplitude change task. The exceptional readers were significantly better at the beat detection task, with significantly sharper psychometric functions (young early readers, mean slope $= -0.14$ [s.d. 0.06], matched controls $= -0.10$ [s.d. 0.04], $p < .04$). Beat detection was also a strong predictor of progress in reading and spelling across the dyslexics and their controls, accounting for 25% of the variance in both skills after controlling for age, nonverbal IQ and vocabulary (p's $< .0001$). As discussed previously, the detection of beats in AM sequences such as those employed in our work corresponds theoretically to the detection of "perceptual centres," or P-centres, in acoustic signals, which are important for rhythmic processing. This suggests interesting links with the work of Petitto and colleagues (this volume). Via an exploration of manual babbling in deaf babies, they argue that the heart of the human language capacity is a sensitivity to specific rhythmic patterns at the syllable rate. The beat detection task is essentially measuring children's sensitivity to such rhythmic patterns in the auditory modality.

The neural representation of rise time

Most recently, we have begun to investigate the neural profile for rise time processing in our dyslexic and typically-progressing children (Thomson, Baldeweg, & Goswami, 2004). The same dyslexic and control children who were studied in 2002 returned to the laboratory to participate in a neuroimaging study of rise time processing based on evoked response potentials (ERPs). ERPs enable the timing of neural events to be studied. Sensitive electrodes are placed on the skin of the child's scalp, and recordings of brain activity are taken. Systematic deflections in electrical activity occur to precede, accompany or follow experimenter-determined events. The most usual outcome measures are (i) the latency of the potentials, (ii) the amplitude (magnitude) of the various positive and negative changes in neural response, and (iii) the distribution of the activity. The different potentials (characterized in countless ERP studies) are called N100, P200, N400 and so on, denoting Negative peak at 100 ms, Positive peak at 200 ms and so on.

For our purposes, we were particularly interested in the N100 response to different rise times. We were also interested in possible mis-match negativity (MMN) responses to changes in rise time. The N100 is an early auditory component signifying the *detection* of auditory events. The MMN is a pre-attentive measure of the automatic detection of auditory *change*. The MMN is thought to be based on the brain's comparison of incoming events with an echoic trace of previous events. Our children listened to rise times of either 15 ms or 90 ms through headphones as they watched a silent video. On 90% of occasions, the 15 ms rise time was heard, and on 5% of occasions the 90 ms rise time (or vice versa, this is called an "oddball" paradigm. The stimulus heard on 5% of occasions is the oddball). On the other 5% of occasions, there was a change in the pitch of the stimulus. It is already known that dyslexic children show an MMN response to pitch changes (see Baldeweg *et al.*, 1999). The pitch oddball was included as a control measure, to check that MMN responses were occurring in our sample.

Given our hypothesis about impaired P-centre processing in dyslexia, our interest focused on the children's N100 response to the two rise times, and their MMN responses to the rise time oddballs. At the time

a) Dyslexic group

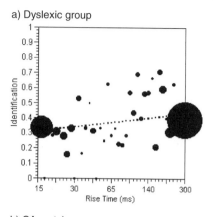

b) CA match group

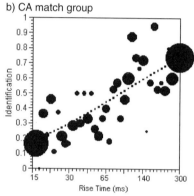

c) RL match group

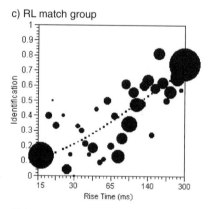

Figure 12.2 Psychometric functions for identification of the stimulus as one sound (proportion) from (a) the dyslexic group, (b) the CA control group, and (c) the RL control group in the beat detection task. The size of the bubbles reflects the number of responses. The dyslexic children show significantly flatter functions, indicating reduced sensitivity to the rise time of the amplitude modulation.

of writing, only fourteen children have been tested (four dyslexic, six younger reading level or RL controls, four CA controls; a nose reference was used). However, very clear patterns of N100 responding have been found. Previous literature has highlighted the greater consistency of temporal N100 deflections in pre-adolescent children (see Bruneau *et al.*, 1997). For the 15 ms rise time stimuli, all groups showed a clear N100 at the temporal electrode sites. The amplitude of this response was much larger in the younger typically-developing children (the RL controls, response about −3.5 microvolts) than in the CA controls (the children age-matched to the dyslexics, −1.5 microvolts). The amplitude of the N100 in the dyslexics was almost exactly the same as that of the younger RL control children. A similar pattern was found for the 90 ms rise time stimuli, although here all amplitudes were reduced. Again, however, the N100 response of the younger RL children was about twice as large as that of the older CA children. The dyslexic children's N100 amplitudes corresponded to those of the younger RL controls.

These findings suggest that the auditory systems of the dyslexic children are immature rather than deviant. The dyslexic children's brains are responding in the same way to amplitude rise time as the brains of younger, normally-developing children. The dyslexic children's neural responses are those appropriate for their reading level rather than for their age. In our data, the amplitude of the N100 was also significantly correlated with behavioral performance on a rise time discrimination task, as would be expected (e.g., $r = 0.60$, temporal electrode T5; $r = 0.69$, temporal electrode LM, p's$< .01$; the temporal regions of the brain are those specialized for language processing). These patterns are at least suggestive of the possibility that reading in the dyslexic children has developed to the extent that would be expected given their auditory processing abilities (and accordingly, the development of their phonological systems). However, as the data are purely correlational, reading development itself could improve rise time processing in children. Longitudinal data is required to distinguish between these two possibilities.

Conclusions

Phonological awareness and literacy acquisition are causally linked. Children with well-specified phonological representations of words in their mental lexicons become better readers. One important factor in the development of well-specified phonological representations is the perception of supra-syllabic aspects of the speech stream such as speech rhythm. For example, information about the perceptual centres of syllables relevant to their segmentation into onset-rime units is theoretically important. Dyslexic children have a deficit, probably neural in origin, in the perception of amplitude rise times, which would interfere with P-centre detection. This deficit theoretically interferes with the development of phonological awareness at the syllable, onset and rime levels prior to literacy acquisition, and probably also interferes with the representation of phonemic information once literacy is taught.

Importantly, orthographic consistency facilitates the development of phoneme awareness for both typically-developing and dyslexic children. Dyslexic children learning consistent orthographies can use letter-sound correspondences as an aid to representing phonology at both the onset-rime and phoneme levels. They can compensate to some extent for their neural difficulties with phonological representation by using letter knowledge. Dyslexic children learning to read less consistent orthographies, such as English, are not afforded this bootstrapping process. English dyslexic children show a persisting deficit at the phoneme level, which continues into adulthood. These persisting deficits appear to be due, in part, to the inconsistent nature of the orthography that they need to learn to read.

According to this cross-linguistic analysis, a deficit in phonemic awareness is not really a *cause* of dyslexic children's reading problems. Rather, the reading problem arises from a pre-existing problem with phonological representation, which impedes learning about letters and learning about phonemes. This learning problem can be ameliorated to some extent by learning to read a consistent orthography. A future challenge is to examine neural responses to auditory cues like rise time cross-linguistically, in order to characterize more specifically the relationship between rhythmic processing, phonological representation, and literacy.

References

Baldeweg, T., Richardson, A., Watkins, S., Foale, C., and Gruzelier, J. (1999). *Ann. Neurology*, 45 (4), 495–503.

Bradley, L. and Bryant, P. E. (1983). Categorising sounds and learning to read: A causal connection. *Nature*, 310, 419–421.

Bregman, A. S. (1993). Auditory scene analysis: hearing in complex environments. In McAdams, S. and Bigand, E. (eds.), *Thinking in Sound: The Cognitive Psychology of Human Audition*, (pp. 10–36). Oxford: Oxford University Press.

Brown, G. D. A. and Ellis, N. C. (1994). Issues in spelling research. In G. D. A. Brown and N. C. Ellis (eds.), *Handbook of Spelling: Theory, Process and Intervention* (pp. 3–25). Chichester: Wiley.

Bruck, M. (1992). Persistence of dyslexics' phonological awareness deficits. *Developmental Psychology*, 28, 874–886.

Bruneau, N., Roux, S., Guérin, P., Barthélémy, C., and Lelord, G. (1997). Temporal prominence of auditory evoked potentials (N1 wave) in 4- 8-year-old children. *Psychophysiology*, 34, 32–38.

Cossu, G., Shankweiler, D., Liberman, I. Y., Katz, L., and Tola, G. (1988). Awareness of phonological segments and reading ability in Italian children. *Applied Psycholinguistics*, 9, 1–16.

Goswami, U. (2000a). Phonological representations, reading development and dyslexia: Towards a cross-linguistic theoretical framework. *Dyslexia*, 6, 133–151.

(2000b). The potential of a neuro-constructivist framework for developmental dyslexia: The abnormal development of phonological representations? *Developmental Science*, 3, 27–29.

(2002). In the beginning was the rhyme? A reflection on Hulme, Hatcher, Nation, Brown, Adams & Stuart, 2002. *Journal of Experimental Child Psychology*, 82, 47–57.

(2003a). Phonology, learning to read and dyslexia: A cross-linguistic analysis. In V. Csepe (ed.), *Dyslexia: Different Brain, Different Behaviour*, (pp. 1–40). NL: Kluwer Academic.

(2003b). Why theories about developmental dyslexia require developmental designs. *Trends in Cognitive Sciences*, 7, 534–540.

Goswami, U., Thomson, J., Richardson, U., Stainthorp, R., Hughes, D., Rosen, S., and Scott, S. K. (2002). Amplitude envelope onsets and developmental dyslexia: A new hypothesis. *Proceedings of the National Academy of Sciences*, 99 (16), 10911–10916.

Goswami, U., Ziegler, J., Dalton, L., and Schneider, W. (2003). Nonword reading across orthographies: How flexible is the choice of reading units? *Applied Psycholinguistics*, 24, 235–247.

Hoien, T., Lundberg, L., Stanovich, K. E., and Bjaalid, I. K. (1995). Components of phonological awareness. *Reading & Writing*, 7, 171–188.

Liberman, I. Y., Shankweiler, D., Fischer, F. W., and Carter, B. (1974). Explicit syllable and phoneme segmentation in the young child. *Journal of Experimental Child Psychology*, 18, 201–212.

McArthur, G. M. and Bishop, D. V. M. (2001). Auditory perceptual processing in people with reading and oral language impairments: Current issues and recommendations. *Dyslexia*, 7, 150–170.

Porpodas, C. D. (1999). Patterns of phonological and memory processing in beginning readers and spellers of Greek. *Journal of Learning Disabilities*, 32, 406–416.

Rack, J. P., Snowling, M. J., and Olson, R. (1992). The nonword reading deficit in developmental dyslexia: A review. *Reading Research Quarterly*, 27, 29–53.

Siok, W. T. and Fletcher, P. (2001). The role of phonological awareness and visual-orthographic skills in Chinese reading acquisition. *Developmental Psychology*, 37, 886–899.

Snowling, M. J. (2000). *Dyslexia*. 2nd edition. Oxford: Blackwells.

Tallal, P. (1980). Auditory temporal perception, phonics and reading disabilities in children. *Brain & Language*, 9, 182–198.

Thomson, J., Baldeweg, T., and Goswami, U. (2004). *Amplitude envelope onsets and dyslexia: a behavioural and electrophysiological study*. Poster presented at the Annual Conference of the Society for the Scientific Study of Reading, Amsterdam, June 2004.

Wimmer, H. (1993). Characteristics of developmental dyslexia in a regular writing system. *Applied Psycholinguistics*, 14, 1–33.

(1996). The early manifestation of developmental dyslexia: Evidence from German children. *Reading & Writing*, 8, 171–188.

Wright, B. A., Bowen, R. W., and Zecker, S. G. (2000). Nonlinguistic perceptual deficits associated with reading and language disorders. *Current Opinions in Neurobiology*, 10, 482–486.

13 Cortical images of early language and phonetic development using near infrared spectroscopy

Laura-Ann Petitto

Overview

Educational neuroscience provides powerful tools and new knowledge to help researchers and educators to build on cognitive neuroscience to open new perspectives for education and for remediation of young children at risk. A promising new tool is Near-Infrared Spectroscopy (NIRS), which can be used with very young children to explore many cognitive capacities and performances. In particular, NIRS gives solid evidence for the existence of language-specific neural networks in infants well before they can speak. For linguistic stimuli, the networks include the left superior temporal gyrus and Broca's area, areas that are strongly involved in language in older children and adults. Brain imaging research can provide new arguments and tests for a model of language acquisition based on the early endowment of specific linguistic areas. Educational neuroscience research can address many other educationally relevant questions in a similar way.

The Editors

Revolutions can start in unlikely places. Beginning around twenty years ago, researchers in hospital sub-basements began using new brain imaging technology to look inside the skulls of volunteers while they were alive and performing a variety of cognitive tasks. This exciting imaging technology, designed to detect brain areas that drank up more oxygen than others during specific cognitive tasks, was used to discover how the brain was organized and which systems of neural areas made possible the spectacular mental functions that we humans enjoy. Alongside these cognitive neuroscience studies of adults, researchers in the disciplines of cognitive science, cognitive psychology, social psychology, and others, were making fundamental advances regarding our perceptual, cognitive, and social worlds.

Using elegant behavioral experimentation, other researchers in the fields of child development and child language began the careful study of children. They examined both the learned and unlearned capacities that infants bring to bear when they hear sounds, babble, understand, and produce language, discover concepts of numbers and math, perceive faces and objects in their world, learn and grow, as well as how these capacities interact with crucial features in the environment en route to becoming healthy adults. Following quickly was the use of new brain imaging technology with children to identify the neural pathways that contribute to the child's mastery of such content, with a new thrust toward studying the *time course* and *sequence* when the child is most likely to develop and grow in these capacities. These research findings suggested optimal points of entry for teaching, motivating, and learning specific content at specific ages across development. Furthermore, new research findings emerging from scientists, medical and clinical practitioners, and educators confirmed that the growing child's social context was vital: families, communities, and schools have the potential to positively influence children's development through systematic and well-timed interventions.

Soon, a collection of people from a variety of disciplines were making extraordinary discoveries about how children grow, acquire language, think, reason, learn a variety of skills and knowledge (including reading, math, and science), and how they conceptualize their social, emotional, and moral world. Hence, the revolution in education was born!

Researchers and educators alike began to converge on educationally important basic mechanisms in learning across diverse content areas that dynamically interact and change over time. Indeed, these extraordinary discoveries about the child's developing brain and environment have yielded a revolution within education of the magnitude seen only once before in the last century when Piaget's stages of child development swept the world and served as the Holy Grail upon which school programs were based. Recently, this exciting new union among researchers, educators, and practitioners has been called *Educational Neuroscience* (e.g., Petitto & Dunbar, in press). Educational Neuroscience brings together individuals from diverse backgrounds, including cognitive brain scientists, learning scientists, medical and clinical practitioners, and those in educational policy and teaching, who are joined in their mutual commitment to solve prevailing problems in the lives of developing children, understand the human learning capabilities over the life span (both in brain and in behavior), and ground educational change in the highly principled application of research that employs both behavioral as well as a multitude of modern methodologies, including brain imaging (e.g., Petitto & Dunbar).

The biggest dangers will be to avoid the reductionist expectation (Mittelstrass, this volume) that each aspect of mental life can and must be identified by specific neural activity before going forward with educational policy building, and we must forever remain aware that the developing brains of children are directly impacted by the situations and contexts that they find themselves in; biology and environment must work hand in hand (Singer, this volume). With these factors in mind, however, the unique interdisciplinary field of Educational Neuroscience has already yielded remarkable advances in our understanding of optimal ways to educate young children in a variety of content areas (e.g., language and bilingualism, reading, math, science) and it has already provided important insights into particular developmental disorders. For example, there has already been a whole host of more appropriate assessment tools, treatment, and educational intervention for children with, for example, attention deficit and hyperactivity disorders, Asperger's syndrome, and autism. This is also true for children with atypical language development such as dyslexia and specific language impairment.

Identification of "sensitive periods" in development has yielded insights into when learning of key content is especially optimal (for a critical view see Bruer, this volume). For example, new insights have come regarding when in the curricula to introduce foreign languages, whether phonetic vs. whole-word reading instruction methods are most optimal, how phonological awareness teaching activities can improve good and atypical readers (e.g., dyslexics, Shaywitz *et al.*, 1998), and the developmental sequence underlying the learning of math and science; all of which have already begun to impact educational curricula. (For excellent discussions of such advances see Byrnes & Fox, 1998; Geake, 2003, 2004; Geake & Cooper, 2003; Goswami, 2004; O'Boyle & Gill, 1998.)

Below, I provide one example of a new Educational Neuroscience research finding. It is an "Educational Neuroscience" finding specifically because it unites (i) cognitive neuroscience imaging findings about the brain, (ii) established behavioral methods and content (here, from child language), and (iii) a principled application to national educational priorities (here, the early identification and remediation of young children at risk for language disorders). Crucially, the Educational Neuroscience finding at hand can advance both the said field (child language) as well as the greater field of education *in ways that could not have been done previously simply by using behavioral or observational methods alone.*

Our specific example will ask how do young infants discover the finite set of phonetic units that will form the basis of their entire language from the constantly varying linguistic and perceptual stream around them? Traditional attempts to answer this question have largely used behavioral methods with young infants *to infer* whether specific-linguistic versus general-perceptual mechanisms underlie this capacity. Here we show how a new brain imaging technology can shed new light on resolving this decades-old question in child language, while providing a new tool that can aid the early identification and education of young babies at risk for language disorders even before they utter their first words.

Out of the chaos of sights and sounds in our world, all human babies discover the finite set of phonetic units that form the basis of their entire native language by approximately age 10 months. For four decades, heated scientific debate has centered on how this is possible – how do infants come to have this remarkable capacity? Some have argued that this capacity reflects the neural superiority of our species to process specific properties of natural *language*, while others have argued that this capacity is built up from mechanisms of general *perception*.

The question of how young infants discover the phonetic building blocks of their language from the constantly varying stream of sounds and sights around them has been the looming question in early child language acquisition since the 1960s. Decades of research showed that young babies (under age 6 months) demonstrate an initial capacity to discriminate all of the world's languages' phonetic contrasts, including both native and non-native (foreign language) oral phonetic contrasts, without ever having heard them before. But, by 10–12 months of age, babies perform like adults and discriminate only their native phonetic contrasts – as if their initial open capacity had, over development, set on (or deduced or neurologically tuned to) the specific language contrasts present in their environment (for a review see Jusczyk, 1997; also Eimas, 1975; Eimas, Siqueland, Jusczyk, & Vigorito, 1971; Kuhl, 1979; Polka & Werker, 1994; Stager & Werker, 1997; Werker, Cohen, Lloyd, Casasola, & Stager, 1998; Werker & Lalonde, 1988; Werker & Stager, 2000; Werker & Tees, 1983, 1999). Thus, human infants were thought to be innately endowed with a specialized *language* mechanism for segmenting and processing phonetic units *per se*.

The claim for a specialized language mechanism in young infants has been challenged by several lines of research, however. It has been weakened by research showing that certain non-human animals also exhibit categorical discrimination for human speech sounds (Kluender, Diehl, & Killeen, 1987; Kuhl, 1981; Kuhl & Miller, 1975, 1978; Kuhl & Padden, 1982, 1983; Morse & Snowdon, 1975; Waters & Wilson, 1976), and by research demonstrating categorical discrimination in infants for some non-speech sounds (Jusczyk *et al.*, 1977). It has also been shown that both human infants and cotton-top tamarin monkeys can discriminate sentences from unfamiliar languages such as Dutch and Japanese when sentences are played forwards but not backwards (Ramus, Hauser, Miller, Morris, & Mehler, 2000). Additionally, it has been shown that both human infants and cotton-top tamarins can discriminate between syllables that differed only in the frequency with which they occurred in streams of input speech (Hauser, Newport, & Aslin, 2001; Saffran, Aslin, & Newport, 1996). Based on these findings, many researchers have rejected the view that infants have specialized mechanisms for linguistic/phonetic processing. Instead, it has been suggested that speech/language perception in young infants can be best explained by general *auditory* (perceptual) mechanisms also present in other species (Aslin, 1987; Jusczyk, 1985).

One intriguing reason for the remarkable perseverance of this debate is due to the fact that the empirical question – in both its previous and its present guise – has been *a priori* largely unanswerable. Specifically, all research to date has used speech and sound to test whether speech and sound are key to this categorization capacity. As a result, the specific (phonetic/language) versus general (auditory/perceptual) distinction for the processes driving language perception have not been able to be teased apart experimentally, leaving contemporary science unable to adjudicate between the phonetic representation hypothesis and the general auditory (general perceptual) representation hypothesis. Recent evidence from Baker, Sootsman, Golinkoff, and Petitto (2003), Baker, Idsardi, Golinkoff, and Petitto (2005), Baker, Golinkoff, and Petitto (in press), and Baker, Groh, Cohen, and Petitto (submitted) has shed new light on this debate by providing behavioral evidence that these early phonetic processing abilities are specific to language rather than general-auditory/ perceptual. Moreover, they are specific to humans, as they are not observed in non-human primates such as the monkeys that Petitto and colleagues also studied in comparison to the infants (Baker, Groh, Cohen, & Petitto, submitted). Using Petitto's Infant Habituation Laboratory, Petitto and colleagues showed that hearing, speech-exposed 4-month-old infants were able to discriminate American Sign Language (ASL) phonetic handshapes by category membership. That is, they treated them like true linguistic/phonetic units in the same way that young hearing infants, for example, exposed to English can nonetheless discriminate phonetic units in Hindi (even though the infants have never before encountered them; Stager & Werker, 1997; Werker *et al.*, 1998; Werker & Stager, 2000; and other classic studies: for a review see Jusczyk, 1997). Crucially, these infants did not discriminate the handshapes at 14 months, just as in speech perception results. The monkeys never showed the ability to discriminate phonetic sign-handshape units, and performed similarly to the non-categorizing 14-month-olds. Thus, based on these *behavioral* studies, early phonetic processing and the development of phonetic categories may be "linguistic-specific" and not a result of general perceptual processing.

New contributions from NIRS neuroimaging

While our behavioral studies of phonetic discrimination provided tantalizing clues as to how the young baby may analyze the input stream, one important piece of the puzzle is missing: whether the *brains* of young children actually recruit classically-understood, specifically *linguistic sites* and *linguistic neural networks* to perform these phonetic discriminations or other areas associated with the general perception of stimuli (either visual or auditory)? If the former, what is the developmental time course of these neural areas underlying language processing? Knowing this important information constitutes a crucial "missing piece" of this prevailing puzzle and it would indeed fundamentally advance our knowledge of this vital issue in human development in a manner not previously possible.

To answer this question, we built on previous behavioral experiments with a series of new related experiments utilizing state-of-the-art optical neuroimaging technology, *Near-Infrared Spectroscopy* (NIRS), to probe the neural correlates of young infants' developing phonetic processing capabilities. NIRS is non-invasive optical technology that, like fMRI, measures cerebral hemodynamic activity in the brain and thus permits one to "see" inside the brains of children and adults while they are processing specific aspects of a task. Unlike fMRI, NIRS is highly portable, child-friendly, tolerates more movement than fMRI, and can be used with alert (vocalizing and/or talking) participants.

Only three studies had used the NIRS technology to study human infants' cognition, specifically, object permanence (Baird *et al.*, 2002) and emotions (Sakatani, Chen, Lichty, Zuo, & Wang, 1999; Zaramella *et al.*, 2001) – all with great success. Moreover, one study had looked at the processing of language in young infants (Peña *et al.*, 2003), though they used very gross comparisons of whether activation occurred in the right or the left hemisphere. With the exception of the present research, no study had looked at the *focal* activation of language development in children, analyzing *within-hemisphere* differences in infants.

In our NIRS studies of infant neural processing of language and perceptual stimuli, we used standardized behavioral tasks (including general visual perception and language processing), which were conducted with infants while in our Habituation Laboratory (classic infant looking/discrimination paradigm). At the same time, the infants were also undergoing NIRS brain recordings to test specific within-hemisphere neuroanatomical hypotheses about focal neural tissue (and networks of

(a)

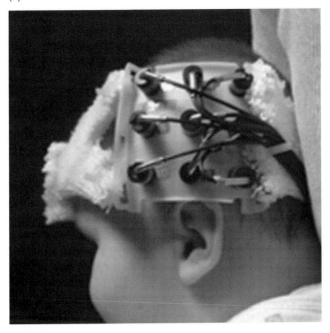

Photo 13A Typical temporal placement (Infant).

neural tissue) regarding their general perceptual versus linguistic processing functions. A silicon probe set (or probe holder) contained the optical
fibers, and the probes were held in place on the participant's head by a
soft terrycloth runner's headband (see Photo 13A). Several pilot studies
were conducted with infants and adults of which only a subset with the
infants are reported here (a full report appears in Petitto, Baker, Baird,
Kovelman, & Norton 2004; Petitto, Baker, Kovelman, & Shalinsky, in
preparation).

For NIRS recording, we used the standard brain imaging system
presently available and used by others: the Hitachi ETG-100 NIRS
device that records simultaneously from 24 channels on the cortex.
Channels mostly record and measure vascular changes from the cortex
that is 2–3 cm below the scalp. The ETG-100 emits infrared light at two
wavelengths, 780 and 830 nm, through the fibers (inter-optode distance
2 cm). Two different wavelengths are used because of the differential
characteristic absorption patterns of oxyhemoglobin (HbO) and deoxy-
hemoglobin (Hb) (Villringer & Chance, 1997). The non-absorbed light is
sampled once every 100 ms. The incoming signal at a given detector is

composed of both source wavelengths, which is separated by synchronous (lock-in) detection using the two source signals as a reference. These two components are low-pass filtered at 20 Hz to remove autonomic signals (e.g., heart beat and respiration), and digitized by a computer. A computer converts the changes in oxygen absorption at each wavelength into relative concentration changes in cerebral chromophores HbO and Hb. The sum of changes in HbO and Hb enables the calculation of the changes in total hemoglobin (THb) in response to task, control, and baseline conditions.

Two types of NIRS probe set placements were used, Temporal and Occipital. To ensure neuroanatomical accuracy in the placement of probe sets, they were placed on the skull using the following highly systematic method. The first position, *Temporal Probes*, utilizes two probe sets, each containing nine optical fibers of 1 mm in diameter. One set was placed over the left hemisphere (LH) and the other was placed over the right hemisphere (RH). Probes were positioned so as to maximize the likelihood of monitoring the frontal and temporal areas, specifically Broca's Area and the Superior Temporal Gyrus. Of the nine fibers per probe, five were emitters and four were detectors. Fibers were placed 2 cm apart, providing twelve recording sites per hemisphere (channels = 24). Each channel corresponds to the central zone of the light path between each adjacent emitter-detector fiber pair. As in the published study with NIRS and infants (Peña *et al.*, 2003), we placed the probe sets using the skull landmark system that is standardly used in Event Related Potential (ERP) brain recording research, called the 10–20 system (see Photos 13 A–B): the vertex was determined as the site where the midpoint of a line going from the nasion to the inion intersects the midpoint of another line going from the left to right prearicular lobule. The second position, the *Occipital Probes*, is where one probe set was placed over the occipital lobe, containing fifteen fibers of 1 mm in diameter (three rows with five probes each, see Photo 13B). Probes were positioned so as to maximize the likelihood of monitoring the visual areas. Of the fifteen fibers in the probe set, eight were emitters and seven were detectors (see Figure 13.1). Fibers were placed 2 cm apart, providing collection for 22 channels. As in the 10–20 system, the probes were positioned such that the bottom row was aligned with the inion.

Six full-term, healthy monolingual English infants (mean age 3 months 29 days) completed three tasks that included exposure to (i) Non-native phonetic units (i.e., real phonetic units, but those that were not present in the child's native language), (ii) English "infant-directed speech" (i.e., the exaggerated sing-song speech in simple but grammatically-correct sentences that adults typically use with young babies and children, e.g.,

(b)

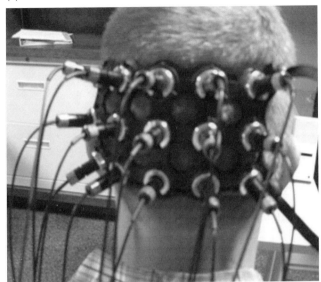

Photo 13B Typical occipital placement (Adult).

Fernald *et al.*, 1989), and (iii) visual checkerboards (i.e., a flashing black and white checkerboard image; for a full report see Petitto, Baker, Baird, Kovelman, & Norton, 2004; Petitto, Baker, Kovelman, & Shalinsky, in preparation).

We found activation within the classic language areas (Broca's Area and Superior Temporal Gyrus-STG) for tasks (i-ii), which were linguistic stimuli, but not for (iii), which was (nonlinguistic) visual stimuli. Taken together, all three sets of data (see Figures 13.2–13.4) imply that the infants' brain honors a distinction between linguistic versus general visual processing areas depending on the specific nature of the stimuli at hand.

This pattern of activation in the infants was exciting both because the infants were so young and because it was the same neural areas observed for language processing as has been observed in the classic studies in adults. Moreover, the activation in the infants was significantly greater in their Left STG and Left Broca's Area as compared to right hemisphere activation in these areas. Thus, the infants' pattern of results, albeit preliminary, suggests that the processing of linguistic information in very young infants is indeed utilizing classic language tissue as it has been known to be used in adults. It also suggests that our language processing areas may be "on-line" and functioning from an early age

Temporal probe holders

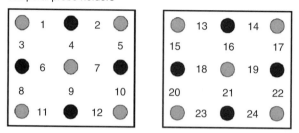

Left probe holder   Right probe holder

Occipital and frontal probe holders

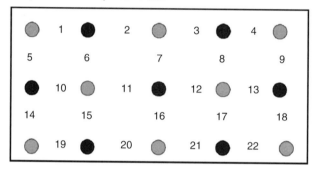

Figure 13.1 Schematic diagram of probes. Schematic diagram of the configuration of the source and detector pairs in the probe holders that were placed on the participant's scalp, as well as the corresponding channels that were used in the analyses. The top two boxes show the temporal probe holders (left probe holder was placed over the participant's left hemisphere temporal lobe; right probe holder was placed over the participant's right hemisphere temporal lobe). The bottom box shows the configuration of the occipital/frontal probe holders that were placed either on the participant's frontal lobe, or on their occipital lobe.

and that these areas may constitute endowed neural sites for language processing in humans; of course, this latter point is a preliminary hypothesis to be tested further in many future studies. To be clear, for the linguistic stimuli, we found only linguistic tissue being engaged, not tissue that would be commensurate with general perceptual processing.

Significance: For decades, scientists and educators alike have been fascinated with the question of how young infants discover the elementary building blocks of language – their phonetic inventory – from the

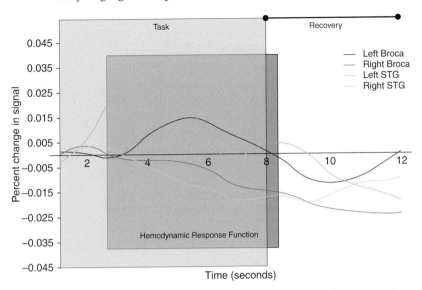

Figure 13.2 Non-Native Phonetic Units: The figure shows that when the linguistic/phonetic stimuli were presented to the infants their brain's classic linguistic Broca's Area and Superior Temporal Gyrus area (STG) in their left hemispheres became activated. Note that activation was not seen in the corresponding tissue in their right hemisphere regarding those areas corresponding to Broca and STG; this can be seen by observing that both lines fall under the horizontal line. (Increases in the signal relative to baseline were found in both left Broca's Area and left STG, r =.25, r =.38 respectively).

steady stream of sounds and sights around them. Indeed, the infant's capacity to segment the linguistic stream (to discover its native set of small meaningless phonetic units and to categorize them) is central to her ability to discover the "word" (and its boundaries), learn word meanings, and to discover the patterned ways that strings of words are arranged in phrases, clauses, and sentences. In essence, the early infant capacity to discover and categorize phonetic units is a central component of the human language acquisition process, with phonological processing resting at the heart of a child's capacity to learn words, language and, ultimately, to be a successful reader! It is little wonder therefore that there have been many years of hot pursuit into the question of how infants do this: what is at the basis of the infant's extraordinary capacity to discover and categorize phonetic units?

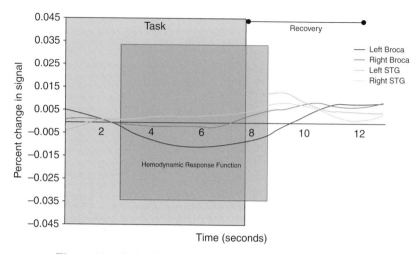

Figure 13.3 Infant Directed Speech: The figure shows that when infant directed speech (sing-song sentences) was presented to the infants their brain's classic linguistic Superior Temporal Gyrus (STG) area in the left hemisphere became robustly activated, and this left hemisphere activation was more robust than that of their right hemisphere's STG activation. As predicted for this type of linguistic task, neither the left hemisphere Broca's Area nor the corresponding area in the right hemisphere showed robust activation; this can be seen by observing that both lines fall under the horizontal line. Interestingly, that the STG activation was greater in the left hemisphere as compared to the right hemisphere suggests that the infants were processing this linguistic information as linguistic and not as general (auditory) perceptual stimuli. If the infants were using general auditory perceptual processing, then we should have seen greater and more comparable bilateral STG activation, which we did not. (An increase in signal relative to baseline was found in left STG, $r = .16$).

Although *behavioral* studies from my own laboratory and others have provided important support for the hypothesis that specialized linguistic mechanisms must be at work in young infants' acquisition of phonology and language (Holowka, Brosseau-Lapré, & Petitto, 2002; Petitto, 2000, 2005; Petitto & Holowka, 2002; Petitto & Marentette, 1991; Petitto, Holowka, Sergio, Levy, & Ostry, 2004; Petitto, Holowka, Sergio, & Ostry, 2001; Petitto, Katerelos, Levy, Gauna, Tétrault, & Ferraro, 2001), key evidence about the infant's *brain* was largely absent.

The present finding provides a new look at an old question. As history taught us, the question of whether young infants are processing linguistic

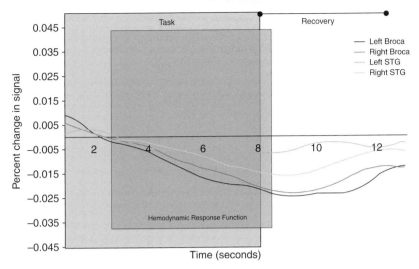

Figure 13.4 Visual Checkerboard Task: The figure shows that when the infants were processing the black and white flashing checkerboard image, no significant activation was observed in classic linguistic processing areas in either hemisphere. This can be seen by observing that all four lines (left Broca, right Broca, left STG, right STG) fall under the horizontal line. Specifically, there were no significant changes in activation observed in linguistic left Broca's area (or corresponding right Broca's) during this visual perception task. Additionally, there were no significant changes in activation observed in linguistic left STG (or corresponding right STG, which would be predicted if processing stimuli as general auditory perceptual information) during this task. Overall, there were no significant differences between right and left hemisphere regions. Recall that the probes were over the left and right temporal lobes and thus these findings were predicted (because of our *a priori* knowledge that the stimuli were perceptual in nature) and are thus encouraging results regarding the efficacy of using NIRS with infants. This suggests that the infants were not processing the visual perceptual stimuli with classic linguistic areas of the brain. Crucially, the results provide exciting confirmation that the identical brain tissue is responding differentially to different input stimuli.

(phonetic) stimuli through linguistic versus general perceptual means was impossible to resolve through the exclusive use of behavioral methods.

From the outside looking in, the infant's behavioral performance did not permit us to adjudicate which types of mental processing were being employed as they engaged in a task. This is the first experiment to demonstrate that we can obtain *within-hemisphere* focal neuroanatomical activation for highly specific tasks in awake, behaving infants as young as 3 months old. To be sure, many more studies will follow to determine the finding's generalizability. Nonetheless, this preliminary evidence suggests that the brains of young infants may be using specific linguistic mechanisms when processing phonetic information rather than general perceptual mechanisms. These results suggest a resolution to a forty-year-old debate in child language.

Educational Neuroscience: From the laboratory to education

We conducted a study that uses innovative NIRS technology, which, for the first time, permitted us to evaluate highly specific neuroanatomical hypotheses about the brain tissue that participates in infant language processing in a manner hitherto not possible in behavioral studies. By doing so, this research helps adjudicate a classic scientific debate about whether language-specific versus perception-general mechanisms initiate and govern early language learning. Research of this sort can provide important answers to scientific questions about (a) the *multiple factors* that underlie early language acquisition and the specific type of processing tissue that underlie them, (b) the *developmental trajectories* of linguistic processing tissue, and (c) the *peaked sensitivity* that linguistic processing tissue has to certain kinds of linguistic input over other input in early development.

Beyond clear advances to our scientific understanding of brain processes in early life, such studies also have important applications to education. Following more experimental replication and standardization studies with NIRS and young babies, we plan to establish and offer the field guidelines for the principled use of NIRS with children that could have important diagnostic, remediation, and teaching utilities in the following way: our earlier studies had established that the Superior Temporal Gyrus (STG), particularly the Planum Temporale (PT), is dedicated to processing specific rhythmically-alternating patterns at the core of phonology (e.g., Penhune, Cismaru, Dorsaint-Pierre, Petitto, & Zatorre, 2003; Petitto *et al.*, 1998, 2000). We also have evidence that this is true in infants from as early as 4–5 months old (Holowka & Petitto, 2002; Norton, Baker, & Petitto, 2003). Our present studies will evaluate whether this is true in much younger infants (from 2 days old). The scientific establishment of the neural tissue that underlies early phonetic segmentation, categorization, and processing – as well as its typical onset age in development – can ultimately be used (in combination with standardized NIRS data from typically developing babies) as one component in the toolkit of diagnostic measures to *identify and predict* babies at risk for language and phonological sequencing disorders (e.g., dyslexia) in very early life even *before* they babble or utter first words. By doing so, we will also provide a new way to distinguish between *deviance* and *delay* in children's phonological processing. *Note that this outcome would not have been possible through behavioral studies alone as children's language and reading problems reveal themselves behaviorally over many years.*

These findings about children's phonological capacity will thus provide scientific "evidence-based" information vital to word segmentation at the core of successful language learning and successful reading (Goswami, this volume). The studies will thus impact US educational policy by providing a tool for the early identification of a core component underlying reading (phonological processing) that will enable more appropriate language remediation programs and methods of classroom teaching. For example, cognitive neuroscience research from our lab and other labs has already provided insights to educational policy and practice regarding when in the curricula to introduce foreign languages, whether phonetic versus whole-word reading instruction methods are most optimal, how teaching phonological awareness can improve both good and atypical (e.g., dyslexic) readers, and the developmental sequence underlying the learning of language (Goswami and Wolf, this volume). All of this research has already begun to impact educational curricula in the United States. To be sure, the coming century of Educational Neuroscience research has the potential to continue to make such advances to educational practice and policy worldwide.

Acknowledgments

It was indeed my distinct honor and privilege to have been invited to speak before The 400th Anniversary of the Foundation of the Pontifical Academy of Sciences in Vatican City, Italy (November 7–11, 2003), and to have had the great honor to meet personally Pope John Paul II. I shall be forever grateful to Professors Kurt Fischer and Antonio Battro for giving me the amazing opportunity to do so. I thank the parents of the babies who participated in this study (as well as the babies!). I thank Elizabeth Norton and Rachael Degenshein for their brilliant assistance on aspects of manuscript preparation and I also thank Elizabeth Norton, as well as this study's other collaborators, Abigail Baird, Stephanie Baker, and Ioulia Kovelman for pioneering together this challenging new NIRS technology. Finally I thank those who funded this research: The Spencer Foundation and Dartmouth College, the Dana Foundation for the Arts, and I am especially grateful for the generous support of the National Institutes of Health (Grant Nos. R01-HD045822–03, R21-HD050558–02).

For reprints and more information, see Petitto's Research web site: www.utsc.utoronto.ca/~petitto/.

Please address correspondence to Laura-Ann.Petitto@utsc.utoronto.ca.

References

Aslin, R. N. (1987). Visual and auditory development in infancy. In J. D. Osofsky (ed.), *Handbook of Infant Development* (2nd edn., pp. 5–97). Oxford, UK: John Wiley.

Baird, A. A., Kagan, J., Gaudette, T., Walz, K., Hershlag, N., and Boas, D. (2002). Frontal lobe activation during object permanence: Data from near infrared spectroscopy. *NeuroImage*, 16, 1120–1126.

Baker, S. A., Golinkoff, R., and Petitto, L. A. (in press). New insights into old puzzles from infants' categorical discrimination of soundless phonetic units." *Learning Languages and Development*.

Baker, S. A., Groh, J. M., Cohen, Y. E., and Petitto, L. A. (submitted). The perception of soundless phonetic units in rhesus macaques. Manuscript submitted for publication.

Baker, S. A., Idsardi, W. J., Golinkoff, R., and Petitto, L. A. (2005). The perception of handshapes in American Sign Language. *Memory & Cognition*, 33 (5), 887–904.

Baker, S., Sootsman, J., Golinkoff, R., and Petitto, L. A. (2003, April). *Hearing four-month-olds' perception of handshapes in American Sign Language: No experience required*. Proceedings of the Society for Research in Child Development 2003 Biennial Meeting, Tampa, FL.

Byrnes, J. P. and Fox, N. A. (1998). The educational relevance of research in cognitive neuroscience. *Educational Psychology Review*, 10(3), 297–342.

Eimas, P. D. (1975). Auditory and phonetic coding of the cues for speech: Discrimination of the (r-l) distinction by young infants. *Perception & Psychophysics*, 18(5), 341–347.

Eimas, P. D., Siqueland, E. R., Jusczyk, P., and Vigorito, J. (1971). Speech perception in infants. *Science*, 171, 303–306.

Fernald, A., Taeschner, T., Dunn, J., Papousek, M., Boysson-Bardies, B., and Fukui, I. (1989). A cross-language study of prosodic modifications in mothers' and fathers' speech to preverbal infants. *Journal of Child Language*, 16, 477–501.

Geake, J. G. (2003). Adapting middle level educational practices to current research on brain functioning. *Journal of the New England League of Middle Schools*, 15, 6–12.

—— (2004). Cognitive neuroscience and education: two-way traffic or one-way street? *Westminster Studies in Education*, 27(1), 87–98.

Geake, J. G. and Cooper, P. W. (2003). Implications of cognitive neuroscience for education. *Westminster Studies in Education*, 26(10), 7–20.

Goswami, U. (2004). Neuroscience and education. *British Journal of Educational Psychology*, 74(1), 1–14.

Hauser, M. D., Newport, E. L., and Aslin, R. N. (2001). Segmentation of the speech stream in a nonhuman primate: Statistical learning in cotton top tamarins. *Cognition*, 78, B53–B64.

Holowka, S., Brosseau-Lapré, F., and Petitto, L. A. (2002). Semantic and conceptual knowledge underlying bilingual babies' first signs and words. *Language Learning*, 52(2), 205–262.

Holowka, S. and Petitto, L. A. (2002). Left hemisphere cerebral specialization for babies while babbling. *Science*, 297, 1515.

Jusczyk, P. W. (1985). On characterizing the development of speech perception. In J. Mehler and R. Fox (eds.), *Neonate Cognition: Beyond the Blooming, Buzzing Confusion* (pp. 199–229). Hillsdale, NJ: Erlbaum.

(1997). *The Discovery of Spoken Language*. Cambridge, MA: MIT Press.

Jusczyk, P. W., Rosner, B. S., Cutting, J. E., Foard, C. F., and Smith, L. B. (1977). Categorical perception of non-speech sounds by 2-month-old infants. *Perceptual Psychophysics*, 21, 50–54.

Kluender, K. R., Diehl, R. L., and Kileen, P. R. (1987). Japanese-quail can learn phonetic categories. *Science*, 237, 1195–1197.

Kuhl, P. K. (1979). Speech perception in early infancy: Perceptual constancy for spectrally dissimilar vowel categories. *Journal of the Acoustical Society of America*, 66, 1669–1679.

(1981). Discrimination of speech by nonhuman animals: Basic auditory sensitivities conductive to the perception of speech-sound categories. *Journal of the Acoustical Society of America*, 70, 340–349.

Kuhl, P. K. and Miller, J. D. (1975). Speech perception by the chinchilla: Voiced-voiceless distinction in alveolar plosive consonants. *Science*, 190, 69–72.

(1978). Speech-perception by chinchilla: Identification functions for synthetic VOT stimuli. *Journal of the Acoustical Society of America*, 63, 905–917.

Kuhl, P. K. and Padden, D. M. (1982). Enhanced discriminability at the phonetic boundaries for the voicing feature in macaques. *Perceptual Psychophysics*, 32, 542–550.

Kuhl, P. K. and Padden, D. M. (1983). Enhanced discriminability at the phonetic boundaries for the place feature in macaques. *Journal of the Acoustical Society of America*, 73, 1003–1010.

Morse, P. A. and Snowdon, C. T. (1975). An investigation of categorical speech discrimination by rhesus monkeys. *Perception & Psychophysics*, 17(1), 9–16.

Norton, E. S., Baker, S. and Petitto, L. A. (2003, June). *Bilingual infants' categorical perception of phonetic handshapes in American Sign Language*. Poster presented at the University of Pennsylvania Institute for Research in Cognitive Science Summer Workshop, Philadelphia.

O'Boyle, M. W. and Gill, H. S. (1998). On the relevance of research findings in cognitive neuroscience to educational practice. *Educational Psychology Review*, 10, 397–400.

Peña, M., Maki, A., Kovacic, D., Dehaene-Lambertz, G., Koizumi, H., Bouquet, F., and Mehler, J. (2003). Sounds and silence: An optical topography study of language recognition at birth. *Proceedings of the National Academy of Sciences*, 100(20), 11702–11705.

Penhune, V., Cismaru, R., Dorsaint-Pierre, R., Petitto, L. A., and Zatorre, R. (2003). The morphometry of auditory cortex in the congenitally deaf measured using MRI. *NeuroImage*, 20, 1215–1225.

Petitto, L. A. (2005). How the brain begets language: On the neural tissue under-lying human language acquisition. Chapter in J. McGilvray (ed.), *The Cambridge Companion to Chomsky*. (pp. 84–101) Cambridge: Cambridge University Press.

——— (2000). On the biological foundations of human language. In H. Lane and K. Emmorey (eds.) *The Signs of Language Revisited* (pp. 447–471). Mahwah, NJ: Erlbaum.

Petitto, L. A., Baker, S., Baird, A., Kovelman, I., and Norton, E. (2004, February). Near-infrared spectroscopy studies of children and adults during language processing. Presentation at the International Workshop on Near-Infrared Spectroscopy, Cambridge, MA.

Petitto, L. A., Baker, S., Kovelman, I., and Shalinsky, M. (in preparation). Near-Infrared Spectroscopy studies of children and adults during language pro-cessing. Manuscript in preparation.

Petitto, L. A. and Dunbar, K. (in press). New findings from Educational Neuroscience on bilingual brains, scientific brains, and the educated mind. In K. Fischer and T. Katzir (eds.) *Building Usable Knowledge in Mind, Brain, & Education*.

Petitto, L. A. and Holowka, S. (2002). Evaluating attributions of delay and confusion in young bilinguals, *Sign Language Studies*, 3(1), 4–33.

Petitto, L. A., Holowka, S., Sergio, L., and Ostry, D. (2001). Language rhythms in babies' hand movements. *Nature*, 413, 35–36.

Petitto, L. A., Holowka, S., Sergio, L., Levy, B., and Ostry, D. (2004). Baby hands that move to the rhythm of language: Hearing babies acquiring sign languages babble silently on the hands. *Cognition*, 9, 43–73.

Petitto, L. A., Katerelos, M., Levy, B., Gauna, K., Tétrault, K., and Ferraro, V. (2001). Bilingual signed and spoken language acquisition from birth: Implications for mechanisms underlying bilingual language acquisition. *Journal of Child Language*, 28(2), 1–44.

Petitto, L. A. and Marentette, P. (1991). Babbling in the manual mode: Evidence for the ontogeny of language. *Science*, 251, 1493–1496.

Petitto, L. A., Zatorre, R., Gauna, K., Nikelski, E. J., Dostie, D., and Evans, A. (2000). Speech-like cerebral activity in profoundly deaf people while processing signed languages: Implications for the neural basis of human language. *Proceedings of the National Academy of Sciences*, 97(25), 13961–13966.

Petitto, L. A., Zatorre, R. J., Nikelski, E. J., Gauna, K., Dostie, D., and Evans, A. C. (1998). By hand or by tongue: Common cerebral blood flow activation during language processing in signed and spoken languages. *NeuroImage*, 7(4), 193.

Polka, L. and Werker, J. F. (1994). Developmental changes in perception of nonnative vowel contrasts. *Journal of Experimental Psychology: Human Perception and Performance*, 20, 421–435.

Ramus, F., Hauser, M. D., Miller, C., Morris, D., and Mehler, J. (2000). Language discrimination by human newborns and cotton-top tamarin mon-keys. *Science*, 288, 349–351.

Saffran, J. R., Aslin, R. N., and Newport, E. L. (1996). Statistical learning by 8-month-old infants. *Science*, 274, 1926–1928.

Sakatani, K., Chen, S., Lichty, W., Zuo, H., and Wang, Y. P. (1999). Cerebral blood oxygenation changes induced by auditory stimulation in newborn infants measured by near infrared spectroscopy. *Early Human Development,* 55(3), 229–236.

Shaywitz, S., Shaywitz, B., Pugh, K., Fulbright, R., Constable, R., Mencl, W., Shankweiler, D., *et al.* (1998). Functional disruption in the organization of the brain for reading in dyslexia. *Proceedings of the National Academy of Sciences,* 95, 2636–2641.

Stager, C. L. and Werker, J. F. (1997). Infants listen for more phonetic detail in speech perception than in word learning tasks. *Nature,* 388, 381–382.

Villringer, A. and Chance, B. (1997). Non-invasive optical spectroscopy and imaging of human brain function. *Trends in Neuroscience,* 20(10), 435–442.

Waters, R. S. and Wilson, J. R. (1976). Speech perception by rhesus monkeys: The voicing distinction in synthesized labial and velar stop consonants. *Perception and Psychophysics,* 19(4), 285–289.

Werker, J. F., Cohen, L. B., Lloyd, V. L., Casasola, M., and Stager, C. L. (1998). Acquisition of word-object associations by 14-month-old infants. *Developmental Psychology,* 34, 1289–1309.

Werker, J. F. and Lalonde, C. E. (1988). Cross-language speech perception: Initial capabilities and developmental change. *Developmental Psychology,* 24(4) 672–683.

Werker, J. F. and Stager, C. L. (2000). Developmental changes in infant speech perception and early word learning: Is there a link? In J. Pierrehumbert and M. Broe (eds.), *Papers in Laboratory Phonology 5,* (pp. 181–193). Cambridge: Cambridge University Press.

Werker, J. F. and Tees, R. C. (1983). Developmental changes across childhood in the perception of non-native speech sounds. *Canadian Journal of Psychology,* 37(2) 278–286.

(1999). Experiential influences on infant speech processing: Toward a new synthesis. In J. T. Spence (ed.), *Annual Review of Psychology, Vol. 50* (pp. 509–535). Palo Alto, CA: Annual Reviews.

Zaramella, P., Freato, F., Amigoni, A., Salvadori, S., Marangoni, P., Suppjei, A., *et al.* (2001). Brain auditory activation measured by near-infrared spectroscopy (NIRS) in neonates. *Pediatric Research,* 49(2), 213–219.

14   Cerebral constraints in reading and arithmetic: Education as a "neuronal recycling" process

Stanislas Dehaene

Overview

Cognitive neuroscience points the way beyond disputes pitting biological causes for behavior against cultural, experiential ones. Dehaene argues compellingly that the cultural tools of reading and arithmetic build directly on fundamental brain processes that are present in infants and other mammals. Common ideas in debates about learning and education seem old-fashioned and outmoded from this viewpoint – ideas such as that the mind/brain is a blank slate at birth, that there are innate, fixed mental organs, and that the brain is a learning machine capable of learning almost anything. The evidence is particularly clear regarding elementary numbers in arithmetic and the forms of letters in the alphabet. Specific, small cortical areas in the parietal lobe in primates and human infants are essential components for automatically detecting numerosity, even though has been no experience with the Arabic symbols for numbers. Indeed, there are even specific neurons tuned to different quantities from 1 to 5. Lesions in these areas produce acalculia (a number deficit). For reading, some restricted visual areas are dedicated to object recognition and to minute details of forms in space, invariant to size, position, or symmetry. These networks seem to form the foundation for building letter shapes, thus setting up the potential for children to learn the alphabet. Lesions in these areas produce alexia or dyslexia. For both mathematics and literacy, cultural objects (numbers and letters) make use of pre-existing brain architectures. In this way education can be understood as a "neuronal recycling process" that builds on cortical structures.

The Editors

Why should brain research be relevant to education? Many parents and educators consider that it is not. No one denies, of course, that the brain is, in the final analysis, the biological organ that supports the child's learning and memory processes. However, this biological fact seems quite remote from the day-to-day events that are occurring in schools. Biology is usually not thought to place much constraint, if any, on education.

Beneath this judgment, I have often observed that educators hold onto an implicit model of brain as a *tabula rasa* or "blank slate" (Pinker, 2002), ready to be filled through education and classroom practice. In this view, the capacity of the human brain to be educated, unique in the animal kingdom, relies upon an extended range of cortical plasticity unique to humans. The human brain would be special in its capacity to accommodate an almost infinite range of new functions through learning. In this view, then, knowledge of the brain is of no help in designing educational policies.

Although admittedly presented here in somewhat caricatured form, this view is not so distant from some modern connectionist or neo-constructivist statements (e.g. Quartz & Sejnowski, 1997). It is also supported by an apparent infallible logical reasoning. Much of current classroom content, so the reasoning goes, consists in recent cultural inventions, such as the symbols that we use in writing or mathematics. Those cultural tools are far too recent to have exerted any evolutionary pressure on brain evolution. Reading, for instance, was invented only 5400 years ago, and symbolic arithmetic is even more recent: the Arabic notation and most of its associated algorithms were not available even a thousand year ago (see Wolf, this volume). Thus, it is logically impossible that there exist dedicated brain mechanisms evolved for reading or symbolic arithmetic. They have to be learned, just like myriads of other facts and skills in geography, history, grammar, philosophy ... The fact that our children can learn those materials implies that the brain is nothing but a powerful universal learning machine.

While such a learning-based theory might explain the vast range of human cultural abilities, it also implies that the brain implementation of those abilities should be highly variable across individuals. Depending on an individual's learning history, the same brain region might become involved in various functions. During learning, random symmetry breaking might ultimately lead to the assignment of dedicated territories to different competences, but this assignment should be randomly determined for different individuals. Thus, one would not expect to find reproducible cerebral substrates for recent cultural activities such as reading and arithmetic.

This prediction, however, is precisely where the paradox lies. As I will show in the remnant of this chapter, a wealth of recent neuroimaging and neuropsychological findings shed light on the ability of the human brain to acquire novel cultural objects such as reading and arithmetic. Those data go against the hypothesis of an unbiased *tabula rasa*. Converging psychological, neuropsychological and brain-imaging evidence demonstrates that the adult human brain houses dedicated mechanisms for reading and arithmetic. Small cortical regions, which occupy reproducible locations in different individuals, are recruited by these tasks. They accomplish their function automatically and often without awareness. Furthermore, the lesion of those regions can lead to specific reading or calculation impairments. In brief, the evidence seems to support the existence of distinct, reproducible and rather specific brain bases for reading and arithmetic (see Wolf, Petitto & Goswami, this volume).

Close examination of the function of those brain areas in evolution suggests a possible resolution of this paradox. It is not the case that those areas acquire an entirely distinct, culturally arbitrary new function. Rather, they appear to possess, in other primates, a prior function closely related to the one that they will eventually have in humans. Furthermore, many of the functional features that make them highly efficient in processing human cultural tools are already present. Relatively small changes may suffice to adapt them to their new cultural domain. I am therefore led, in the conclusion, to tentatively proposing a "neuronal recycling" hypothesis, according to which the human capacity for cultural learning relies on a process of pre-empting or recycling pre-existing brain circuitry. In my opinion, this view implies that an understanding of the child's brain organization is essential to education.

1.   *Cerebral bases of arithmetic*

Many neuroimaging studies, throughout the world, have examined brain activity while adults engage in simple arithmetic tasks. The technology of functional magnetic resonance imaging (fMRI) currently allows us to capture a series of whole-brain images of blood oxygenation, tightly coupled to neuronal activity, with a time resolution of a few seconds. This methodology is sufficient to examine what brain areas are activated when subjects compute a simple subtraction (e.g. 7–2), compared to a control situation in which subjects simply name the digits without calculating (for instance). A remarkable outcome of such studies has been the discovery of a highly reproducible substrate for mental arithmetic (as reviewed in Dehaene, Piazza, Pinel, & Cohen, 2003). A reproducible set of areas is systematically activated during arithmetic, amongst which the left and right intraparietal sulci and the left and right precentral sulci figure prominently (Figure 14.1). Only a few minutes of testing are now needed to isolate this network in every individual tested, with a variability of only about a centimeter in standardized brain coordinates.

The parieto-precentral network for arithmetic has been observed in many different laboratories, with adults from many different countries and with strikingly different languages and educational systems (e.g.

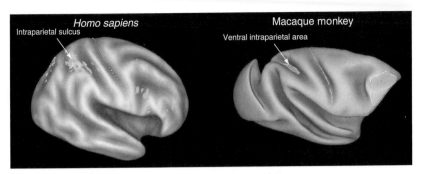

Figure 14.1 Areas activated by various arithmetic tasks in humans (left, redrawn after Dehaene *et al.*, 2003), and areas where neurons coding for numbers have been recorded in the macaque monkey (right, redrawn from Nieder and Miller, in press), There is plausible homology between the parietal areas engaged in number processing in both species.

China, Japan, France, United States). The parietal component of this network also appears to be common to essentially all arithmetic tasks. Its activation is strongest during calculation (e.g. subtraction, addition, multiplication) or approximation of a calculation (e.g. is $21 + 15$ closer to 40 or to 90?) (Dehaene, Spelke, Pinel, Stanescu, & Tsivkin, 1999). However, parietal number-related activity can also be elicited in a completely automatic manner when subjects merely have to detect a digit in a visual or auditory stream (Eger, Sterzer, Russ, Giraud, & Kleinschmidt, 2003). Indeed, the mere subliminal presentation of an Arabic digit for a very brief duration is sufficient to elicit it (Naccache & Dehaene, 2001). Those results present a deep paradox: why is the same brain area systematically assigned to processing Arabic digits, in a highly automated way, while letters, which are an equally arbitrary cultural construction, lead to no activation in this area?

A simple but fruitful hypothesis has been proposed which might begin to resolve this paradox (Dehaene, 1992, 1997; Gallistel & Gelman, 1992). It postulates that, although Arabic digits and verbal numerals are culturally arbitrary and specific to humans, the sense of numerical quantity is not. This "number sense" is present in very young infants and in animals. We learn to give meaning to our symbols and calculation by connecting them to this pre-existing quantity representation.

In support of this view, many experiments have shown that animal and human infants possess a rudimentary and non-verbal sense of number. Pigeons, rats, dolphins, monkeys, and apes can perceive the "numerosity" of a set of visual or auditory objects, even up to forty or fifty. Similarly, six-month-old human infants can perceive the difference, say, between eight and sixteen dots on a computer screen (Lipton & Spelke, 2003). Naturally, this ability is not as precise as ours, and thus cannot support complex digital calculations. Animals and infants cannot discriminate two neighboring numbers such as 36 and 37, but only have an approximate feeling of numerosity which gets progressively coarser as the numbers get larger (Weber's law).

The same approximate representation continues to be evidenced in human adults, not only when we perceive sets of objects, but even when we process symbolic digits. A telling sign of our reliance on this "number sense" is the distance effect in number comparison. When deciding which of two Arabic numerals is the larger, we are considerably faster when the numbers are distant (e.g. 1 and 9, or 31 and 65) than when they are close (e.g. 8 and 9, or 51 and 65). Such a variable performance would not be expected from a digital comparison algorithm, as present for instance in a modern computer. It suggests that, even when confronted with symbolic inputs, our brain quickly converts the numerals into an internal approximate quantity code – an internal "number line" in which similar quantities are coded by similar distributions of activations.

In the last few years, we have learned a lot about how this quantity code is implemented at the neural level. Andreas Nieder and Earl Miller (Nieder, Freedman, & Miller, 2002; Nieder & Miller, 2003, in press) recorded from single neurons in awake monkeys trained to perform a visual number match-to-sample task. Many neurons were tuned to a preferred numerosity: some neurons responded preferentially to sets of one object, others to two objects, and so on up to five objects. The tuning was coarse, and became increasingly imprecise as numerosity increased. The characteristics of this neural code were exactly as expected from a neural network model which had been proposed to account for the distance effect and other characteristics of numerical processing in adults and infants (Dehaene & Changeux, 1993). Most important is the location where the number neurons were recorded. Initially, a large proportion were observed in dorsolateral prefrontal cortex, but more recently another population of neurons with a shorter latency has been observed in the parietal lobe (Nieder & Miller, 2005; see also Sawamura, Shima, & Tanji, 2002). These neurons are located in area VIP, in the depth of the intraparietal sulcus, a location which is a plausible homolog of the human area active during many number tasks.

One may thus propose a simple scenario for the acquisition of arithmetic in humans. Evolution had endowed the primate parietal lobe with a coarse representation of numerosity, which was presumably useful in many situations in which a set of objects or congeners had to be tracked through time. This primitive number representation is also present in humans. It is present early on in human infancy, although its precision is initially quite mediocre and develops continuously during the first year of life (Lipton & Spelke, 2003). It provides children with a minimal foundation on which to build arithmetic: the ability to track small sets of objects, and to monitor increases or decreases in numerosity. In the first year, this knowledge is entirely non-verbal, but around 3 years of life, it becomes connected with symbols, first with the counting words of spoken language (and their surrogate the fingers), then with the written symbols of the Arabic notation.

It is thus not surprising that Arabic digits and their computations become ultimately tied to a restricted brain area located reproducibly in all individuals. Indeed, this area does not emerge through "training" in arithmetic. Rather, it is present from the start and is progressively modified as it gets connected to symbol systems in other brain areas, thus giving numbers their meaning.

While this scenario describes normal number development, it also predicts the existence of specific impairments in arithmetic. In adults, some brain lesions are known to cause acalculia, a selective impairment in arithmetic (Dehaene, Dehaene-Lambertz, & Cohen, 1998). Lesions of the intraparietal sulcus, in particular, may cause severe impairments in addition and subtraction, but also in basic number understanding such as approximation, numerosity estimation and comparison (Lemer, Dehaene, Spelke, & Cohen, 2003). Crucially, a similar syndrome exists in children, where it is called developmental dyscalculia (Shalev, Auerbach, Manor, & Gross-Tsur, 2000). Some children, from birth on, experience severe difficulties in learning arithmetic. Nevertheless, they may be of normal intelligence and from a normal social background, and need not suffer from associated deficits in reading or attention. In some of them, the deficit may even impact on very basic tasks. Even the ability to decide whether a set comprises two or three objects, or which of 5 or 6 is the larger number, may be compromised (Butterworth, 1999). A natural hypothesis, thus, is that the quantity representation may be affected, either by a genetic disease or by an early brain insult.

This hypothesis was recently vindicated by two cognitive neuroscience studies of dyscalculia. In one (Isaacs, Edmonds, Lucas, & Gadian, 2001), young adolescents born premature were sorted in two groups, those that suffered from dyscalculia during their childhood and those who did not. Magnetic resonance imaging was used to estimate the density of gray matter throughout the cortex. Dyscalculics suffered from a selective reduction in gray matter density in the left intraparietal sulcus, at the precise coordinates where activations are observed in normal adults during mental arithmetic. In the second study (Molko *et al.*, 2003), young adult women with a genetic disease, Turner's syndrome, were compared to controls on an anatomical and functional magnetic resonance test. Cortical anomalies were observed in the right intraparietal sulcus, which was also abnormally activated during the computation of additions with large numbers.

It is currently not known why dyscalculia sometimes affects the left or the right parietal lobe – nor which proportion of children with dyscalculia actually have identifiable brain insults. Nevertheless, the very existence of a category of children with normal intelligence and schooling, and yet with a disproportionate deficit in arithmetic, invalidates the view that arithmetic education rests on domain-general learning mechanisms. Rather, a narrow, dedicated pre-representation of numerosity, with a specific brain substrate, acts as a pre-requisite to learning in arithmetic. All humans have the capability of growing mathematics – but only if they start from the right seed.

2.   Cerebral bases of reading

Numbers are a basic parameter of our environment, so it should perhaps not be so surprising that our brains come prepared by evolution to represent it. More paradoxically, similar discoveries have been made in the domain of reading. Reading was invented at most 5400 years ago, and until very recently it concerned only a very small proportion of humanity. Thus, there has been no time or pressure to evolve brain circuits for reading. Indeed, the principles of reading are a mixed bag of tricks, highly variable from culture to culture, combining the rebus principle with the possibility of depicting sound elements ranging from whole words to syllables, rhymes or phonemes using various visual shapes. While it is likely that *Homo sapiens* has evolved dedicated cortical mechanisms for speech processing, which is a defining feature of our species, on the visual side it seems impossible that the brain comes prepared for the arbitrary features of the reading system.

In spite of this seemingly logical arguments, brain imaging studies have identified a strikingly reproducible brain system for the visual stage of reading, which is termed the "visual word form" system. Whenever a good reader is presented with a written word, activation can be observed in an area of the left ventral visual region, located in the occipito-temporal sulcus (for review, see Cohen & Dehaene, 2004). The variability in this activation from person to person is only a few millimeters (Figure 14.2). Furthermore, it is present at the same location in readers of all cultures, including the Hebrew right-to-left script as well as non-alphabetic Chinese and Japanese reading systems (see Paulesu *et al.*, 2001).

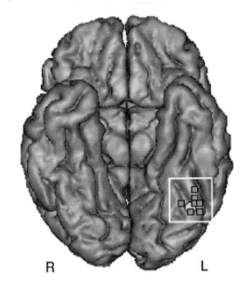

x = −42 y = −57 z= −15

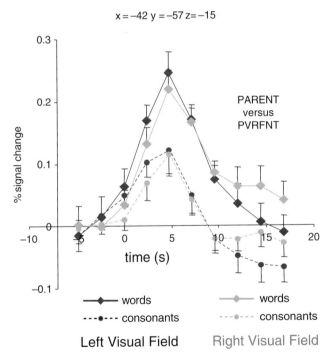

Figure 14.2 Localization and properties of the "visual word form area" in humans (adapted from Cohen *et al.*, 2002). The top figure shows the

The region also presents specificity for reading. For instance, it is distinct from a more mesial activation observed when viewing faces. It also responds more to strings of real letters than to pseudo-letters with a similar shape; or to real words than to strings of consonants that could not possibly form a pronounceable word (Cohen et al., 2002; see Figure 14.2). Rare cases in whom intracranial recordings are available support the existence of micro-territories of visual cortex that respond preferentially or sometimes exclusively to words (Allison, Puce, Spencer, & McCarthy, 1999).

There is also evidence for functional specificity. Several of the computational problems posed by reading appear to be solved by exquisitely adapted mechanisms in the occipito-temporal cortex. One such problem is location invariance: words must be recognized regardless of their location on the retina. The visual word form area achieves location invariance by collecting activation from the left and right hemispheres, in a few tens of milliseconds, throughout appropriate intracortical and callosal fibers (Molko et al., 2002; see Figure 14.2). Another problem is posed by variations in font and case. The same word can have a strikingly different visual form in upper and lower case, for instance RAGE and rage. The mapping between upper and lower case is a matter of cultural convention and must be learned. Nevertheless, brain imaging has revealed that a case-invariant representation is achieved early on in the reading process (Dehaene et al., 2004), through a bank of dedicated letter-detector neurons, each assigned to a different location of the fovea and working in parallel. Visual word recognition is so efficient that the visual word form area can be activated in a subliminal manner by words presented for only 29 milliseconds (Dehaene et al., 2001).

Finally, just like for arithmetic, there is evidence that brain lesions can selectively disrupt the visual stage of reading. Déjerine (1892) reported the first case of "pure alexia," a selective disruption of reading with no concurrent impairment in speech production, speech comprehension, or even of writing. Many cases have been observed since then. Pure alexia

---

Figure 14.2 (continued)
location of activation to visual words in the left occipito-temporal sulcus (each dot represents a different person). The bottom graph shows the profile of fMRI activation in this region. There is a stronger response to words than to strings of consonants, indicating tuning of this area to the cultural constraints of the script that the participants could read. The identical response to words presented in the left and right visual fields suggests that spatial invariance is achieved in this region.

arises from left ventral occipito-temporal lesions that affect the region of visual cortex where activations are observed in normal subjects during reading (Cohen *et al.*, 2003). Outside of reading, vision may be highly preserved, including face and object recognition. Although the patients may remain able to identify single letters, one at a time, they have lost the ability to recognize a whole word at once, by processing the letters in parallel. Furthermore, they are often unable to regain fluent reading, even years after the lesion. The contrast between preserved visual object recognition and impaired reading indicates that a specialized system has been lost – a fast, dedicated and reproducible "mental organ" for visual word recognition, even though the existence of such a system seems impossible on logical grounds.

As in the case of numeracy, resolution of this paradox requires consideration of what could be the prior function of the visual word form system in non-human primates. Many of the properties of the invariant word recognition system are already present in primates – only they are used to recognize objects and faces, not words. The primate occipito-temporal pathway as a whole is concerned with visual recognition. It has evolved as a "what" system capable of invariant identification of faces and objects, and opposed to a dorsal "where" system responsible for the localization of objects and their use in motor acts. Much is known about the neuronal organization of the ventral visual pathway in the macaque monkey, where a hierarchy of neurons with increasingly abstract and invariant properties has been observed. Some neurons respond only to parts of objects, with a relatively narrow receptive field – they might for instance be sensitive to the shape of an eye at a specific place on the retina. Others respond to a larger configuration, for instance the profile of a face or the shape of a fire extinguisher. Finally, some respond to a given person, whether it is presented as a face or as a profile. These computations unfold in an effortless and non-conscious manner, and can be observed even in the anesthetized monkey.

Tanaka and his colleagues (Tanaka, 1996) have studied the minimal features of objects that make monkey occipito-temporal neurons discharge. To this end, they have used a procedure of progressive simplification. First, a large set of objects is presented until one is found that reliable causes a given neuron to discharge. Then, the shape of the object is simplified while trying to maintain an optimal neuronal response. When the shape cannot be simplified further without losing the neuronal discharge, it is thought that one has discovered the simplest feature to which the neuron responds. Remarkably, many of those shapes resemble our letters: some neurons respond to two bars shaped in a T, others to a circle or to two superimposed circles forming a figure 8, etc. Obviously, those shapes have not been learned as letters. Rather, they have emerged, in the course of ontogeny and/or phylogeny, as a simple repertoire of shapes which can collectively be used to represent a great variety of natural forms and objects.

Another essential property of inferotemporal neurons is their plasticity. Training studies with arbitrary shapes such as fractals (Miyashita, 1988) or randomly folded paper clips (Logothetis, Pauls, & Poggio, 1995) have indicated that entire populations of cells eventually become highly responsive to these shapes, and then transfer to these shapes their properties of location, size, and viewpoint invariance. In some cases, cells can become responsive to two arbitrary views that are paired during training. This pairing capacity provides a potential substrate for learning to recognize A and a as the same letter, or the sound /house/ and the word HOUSE as referring to the same word.

Finally, why is there a reproducible localization for the visual word form area amongst the vast cortical territory dedicated to visual recognition? Recent neuroimaging studies by Hasson, Malach and collaborators (Hasson, Levy, Behrmann, Hendler, & Malach, 2002; Malach, Levy, & Hasson, 2002) may begin to explain this surprising finding. This group has described large-scale gradients or biases that cut across the entire set of visual areas and may be laid down very early on in development, perhaps through diffuse morphogens (Turing's model). One such bias is for retinal eccentricity: some cortical territories respond preferentially to the fovea, others to the periphery of the retina. Remarkably, the visual word form area, like the face area, systematically occupies the fovea-sensitive peak of this biased gradient. This makes sense inasmuch as both word and face recognition capitalize on fine-grained details of foveal stimuli. The recognition of places and houses, on the other hand, requires integration of information across a larger extent of the visual field and activates the peripheral peak of the gradient. It thus seems that each category of objects is preferentially acquired by whichever neurons have the relevant pre-learning biases – and that such biases can explain the tight and reproducible localization of the visual word form system without having to assume an innate "mental organ" for reading.

In summary, reading, just like arithmetic, does not rely only on domain-general mechanisms of learning. Rather, learning to read is possible because our visual system already possesses exquisite mechanisms for invariant shape recognition, as well as the appropriate connections to link those recognized shapes to other areas involved in auditory and abstract semantic representations of objects. Learning is also possible because evolution has endowed this system with a high degree of plasticity. Although we are not born with letter detectors, letters are sufficiently close to the normal repertoire of shapes in the inferotemporal regions to be easily acquired and mapped onto sounds. We pre-empt part of this system when learning to read, rather than creating a "reading area" *de novo*.

Indeed, it can be argued that, although the human brain did not evolve for reading, the converse might have occurred: the cultural evolution of writing systems has been shaped, at least in part, by the facility and speed with which the systems could be learned by the brain. This seems to have resulted, over the course of centuries, in the selection of a small repertoire of letter shapes that nicely matches the set of shapes that are spontaneously used in our visual system to encode objects.

Conclusion: Education as a "neuronal recycling" process

The domains of arithmetic and reading, on which this chapter is focused, exhibit significant commonalities but also important differences. In both cases, humans learn to attribute meaning to conventional shapes (Arabic digits or the alphabet), and they eventually do so in a highly efficient manner, even subliminally. Furthermore, the brain activations associated with these cultural activities are highly reproducible. Finally, the brain areas involved turn out to have a significantly related function in primate evolution. There is however an important difference between arithmetic and reading. On the one hand, there is a genuine precursor of arithmetic in primate evolution. Intraparietal cortex already seems to be involved in number representation in primates, and the cultural mapping of number symbols onto this representation significantly enhances, but does not radically modify its computational capacity. On the other hand, the evolutionary precursor of the visual word form area is initially unrelated to reading. It evolved for object recognition, a function significantly different from the mapping of written language onto sound and meaning.

As a generalization of those two examples, I tentatively propose that the human ability to acquire new cultural objects relies on a neuronal "reconversion" or "recycling" process whereby those novel objects invade cortical territories initially devoted to similar or sufficiently close functions. According to this view, our evolutionary history, and therefore our genetic organization, specifies a cerebral architecture that is both constrained and partially plastic and that delimits a space of learnable objects. New cultural acquisitions are possible only inasmuch as they are able to fit within the pre-existing constraints of our brain architecture.

It is useful to contrast this "neuronal recycling" model with the opposite, if somewhat caricatural "blank slate" model of the brain. According to the latter, education can be compared to the filling-in of an empty brain space, capable of absorbing any type of instruction. Yet educators know that this is not what is occurring in the classroom (see Bruer, this volume). The real child is both much more gifted and, occasionally, much more resistant to change than the blank slate model would predict. Under the "neuronal recycling" model, both children's intuitions and their occasional stubbornness can be understood as effects of prior brain structure. In many cases, the cerebral representations that we inherit from our primate evolution facilitate school-based learning. Mathematical education, in particular, should capitalize on such early intuitions, which probably extend beyond the numerosity dimension to many other domains of science and mathematics including space, time, movement, force, and so on . . .

In a few cases, however, education must go beyond the child's intuitive understanding of a domain, or even fight actively against an existing bias. For instance, in arithmetic, it seems that the brain's spontaneous approximate representation of numerosity is initially unable to represent zero, negative numbers, or fractions. Children's intuition must therefore be extended to those cases, a difficult enterprise which was also a major hurdle in the history of mathematics – but one which can probably be helped by teaching appropriate metaphors such as the notion that negative numbers correspond to an extension of the number line towards the left side.

Similarly in reading, a possible source of difficulty for the child lies in having to unlearn one type of invariance which is spontaneously provided by our visual system: invariance for left-right symmetry. There is evidence that the primate visual system, once it has learned to recognize a shape, spontaneously generalizes to the corresponding symmetrical shape (Baylis & Driver, 2001; Noble, 1968; Rollenhagen & Olson, 2000). However, this capacity is actually counterproductive when having to learn that p and q, or b and d, are unrelated letters. In agreement with the neuronal recycling model, many if not all children appear to pass through a stage where they spontaneously make left-right reversal errors, and only slowly learn that this generalization is inappropriate in reading (McMonnies, 1992).

Another, perhaps more central limitation in reading is that alphabetic systems map letter shapes onto elements of sound, phonemes, that are not initially made explicit by our auditory processing system. Understanding what a phoneme is, and connecting phonemic representations to abstract letter shapes, appears as a major hurdle for many children (see Usha Goswami's chapter in this volume). Indeed, it may be the single most important source of reading difficulties in children with developmental dyslexia.

As shown by these examples, understanding the child's initial representations, and how these representations are modified in the course of learning, is likely to be essential in order to improve basic education in language and mathematics. I have chosen to deal specifically with two domains, arithmetic and reading, but a very similar argument could be developed for second-language learning or for many other aspects of mathematics. In each case, educators will gain much by understanding the initial state, the developmental trajectory, and the end state of the brain changes that they are trying to teach. Finally, teachers must also be aware that a small category of children may have genuine brain impairments that do not affect general intelligence, but have a restricted impact on learning in domain-specific areas of knowledge. In this field too, understanding the cerebral basis of these pathologies is likely to improve our ability to rehabilitate or bypass them.

References

Allison, T., Puce, A., Spencer, D. D., and McCarthy, G. (1999). Electrophysiological studies of human face perception. I: Potentials generated in occipitotemporal cortex by face and non-face stimuli. *Cerebral Cortex*, 9(5), 415–430.

Baylis, G. C. and Driver, J. (2001). Shape-coding in IT cells generalizes over contrast and mirror reversal, but not figure-ground reversal. *Nat Neurosci*, 4(9), 937–942.

Butterworth, B. (1999). *The Mathematical Brain*. London: Macmillan.

Cohen, L. and Dehaene, S. (2004). Specialization within the ventral stream: The case for the Visual Word Form Area. *NeuroImage*, in press.

Cohen, L., Lehericy, S., Chochon, F., Lemer, C., Rivaud, S., and Dehaene, S. (2002). Language-specific tuning of visual cortex? Functional properties of the Visual Word Form Area. *Brain*, 125(Pt 5), 1054–1069.

Cohen, L., Martinaud, O., Lemer, C., Lehéricy, S., Samson, Y., Obadia, M., et al. (2003). Visual word recognition in the left and right hemispheres: Anatomical and functional correlates of peripheral alexias. *Cerebral Cortex*, 13, 1313–1333.

Dehaene, S. (1992). Varieties of numerical abilities. *Cognition*, 44, 1–42.

(1997). *The Number Sense*. New York: Oxford University Press.

Dehaene, S. and Changeux, J. P. (1993). Development of elementary numerical abilities: A neuronal model. *Journal of Cognitive Neuroscience*, 5, 390–407.

Dehaene, S., Dehaene-Lambertz, G., and Cohen, L. (1998). Abstract representations of numbers in the animal and human brain. *Trends in Neuroscience*, 21, 355–361.

Dehaene, S., Jobert, A., Naccache, L., Ciuciu, P., Poline, J. B., Le Bihan, D., et al. (2004). Letter binding and invariant recognition of masked words: Behavioral and neuroimaging evidence. *Psychological Science*, in press.

Dehaene, S., Naccache, L., Cohen, L., Bihan, D. L., Mangin, J. F., Poline, J. B., *et al.* (2001). Cerebral mechanisms of word masking and unconscious repetition priming. *Nat Neurosci*, 4(7), 752–758.

Dehaene, S., Piazza, M., Pinel, P., and Cohen, L. (2003). Three parietal circuits for number processing. *Cognitive Neuropsychology*, 20, 487–506.

Dehaene, S., Spelke, E., Pinel, P., Stanescu, R., and Tsivkin, S. (1999). Sources of mathematical thinking: behavioral and brain-imaging evidence. *Science*, 284(5416), 970–974.

Déjerine, J. (1892). Contribution à l'étude anatomo-pathologique et clinique des différentes variétés de cécité verbale. *Mémoires de la Société de Biologie*, 4, 61–90.

Eger, E., Sterzer, P., Russ, M. O., Giraud, A. L., and Kleinschmidt, A. (2003). A supramodal number representation in human intraparietal cortex. *Neuron*, 37(4), 719–725.

Gallistel, C. R. and Gelman, R. (1992). Preverbal and verbal counting and computation. *Cognition*, 44, 43–74.

Hasson, U., Levy, I., Behrmann, M., Hendler, T., and Malach, R. (2002). Eccentricity bias as an organizing principle for human high-order object areas. *Neuron*, 34(3), 479–490.

Isaacs, E. B., Edmonds, C. J., Lucas, A., and Gadian, D. G. (2001). Calculation difficulties in children of very low birthweight: A neural correlate. *Brain*, 124(Pt 9), 1701–1707.

Lemer, C., Dehaene, S., Spelke, E., and Cohen, L. (2003). Approximate quantities and exact number words: Dissociable systems. *Neuropsychologia*, 41, 1942–1958.

Lipton, J. and Spelke, E. (2003). Origins of number sense: Large number discrimination in human infants. *Psychological Science*, 14, 396–401.

Logothetis, N. K., Pauls, J., and Poggio, T. (1995). Shape representation in the inferior temporal cortex of monkeys. *Curr. Biol.*, 5(5), 552–563.

Malach, R., Levy, I., and Hasson, U. (2002). The topography of high-order human object areas. *Trends Cogn. Sci.*, 6(4), 176–184.

McMonnies, C. W. (1992). Visuo-spatial discrimination and mirror image letter reversals in reading. *J. Am Optom Assoc.*, 63(10), 698–704.

Miyashita, Y. (1988). Neuronal correlate of visual associative long-term memory in the primate temporal cortex. *Nature*, 335(6193), 817–820.

Molko, N., Cachia, A., Riviere, D., Mangin, J. F., Bruandet, M., Le Bihan, D., *et al.* (2003). Functional and structural alterations of the intraparietal sulcus in a developmental dyscalculia of genetic origin. *Neuron*, 40(4), 847–858.

Molko, N., Cohen, L., Mangin, J. F., Chochon, F., Lehéricy, S., Le Bihan, D., *et al.* (2002). Visualizing the neural bases of a disconnection syndrome with diffusion tensor imaging. *Journal of Cognitive Neuroscience*, 14, 629–636.

Naccache, L. and Dehaene, S. (2001). The priming method: imaging unconscious repetition priming reveals an abstract representation of number in the parietal lobes. *Cerebral Cortex*, 11(10), 966–974.

Nieder, A., Freedman, D. J., and Miller, E. K. (2002). Representation of the quantity of visual items in the primate prefrontal cortex. *Science*, 297(5587), 1708–1711.

Nieder, A. and Miller, E. K. (2003). Coding of cognitive magnitude. Compressed scaling of numerical information in the primate prefrontal cortex. *Neuron*, 37(1), 149–157.

Nieder, A. and Miller, E. K. (2005). Neural correlates of numerical cognition in the neocortex of non-human primates. In S. Dehaene, J. R. Duhamel, M. Hauser and G. Rizzolatti (eds.), *From Monkey Brain to Human Brain*. Cambridge: MIT Press.

Noble, J. (1968). Paradoxical interocular transfer of mirror-image discriminations in the optic chiasm sectioned monkey. *Brain Res*, 10(2), 127–151.

Paulesu, E., Demonet, J. F., Fazio, F., McCrory, E., Chanoine, V., Brunswick, N., *et al.* (2001). Dyslexia: cultural diversity and biological unity. *Science*, 291(5511), 2165–2167.

Pinker, S. (2002). *The Blank Slate: The Modern Denial of Human Nature*. London: Penguin Books.

Quartz, S. R. and Sejnowski, T. J. (1997). The neural basis of cognitive development: a constructivist manifesto. *Behav. Brain Sci.*, 20(4), 537–556; discussion 556–596.

Rollenhagen, J. E. and Olson, C. R. (2000). Mirror-image confusion in single neurons of the macaque inferotemporal cortex. *Science*, 287(5457), 1506–1508.

Sawamura, H., Shima, K., and Tanji, J. (2002). Numerical representation for action in the parietal cortex of the monkey. *Nature*, 415(6874), 918–922.

Shalev, R. S., Auerbach, J., Manor, O., and Gross-Tsur, V. (2000). Developmental dyscalculia: prevalence and prognosis. *Eur. Child Adolesc. Psychiatry*, 9(Suppl 2), II, 58–64.

Tanaka, K. (1996). Inferotemporal cortex and object vision. *Annual Review of Neuroscience*, 19, 109–139.

Index